P9-CFV-517

ALSO BY RICK ATKINSON

The Long Gray Line
Crusade
An Army at Dawn

IN THE COMPANY OF
SOLDIERS

IN THE COMPANY OF
SOLDIERS

A Chronicle of Combat

RICK
ATKINSON

HENRY HOLT AND COMPANY

NEW YORK

Henry Holt and Company, LLC
Publishers since 1866
115 West 18th Street
New York, New York 10011

Henry Holt® is a registered trademark of Henry Holt and Company, LLC.

Copyright © 2004 by Rick Atkinson
All rights reserved.
Distributed in Canada by H. B. Fenn and Company Ltd.

Library of Congress Cataloging-in-Publication Data
Atkinson, Rick.
    In the company of soldiers : a chronicle of combat / Rick Atkinson.
        p. cm.
    ISBN 0-8050-7561-5
    1. United States. Army. Airborne Division, 101st—History—21st
century.   2. Iraq War, 2003—Campaigns—United States.   I. Title.
DS79.764.U6A85   2004
956.7044'3—dc22   2003067607

Henry Holt books are available for special promotions and premiums.
For details contact: Director, Special Markets.

First Edition 2004

Designed by Fritz Metsch
Maps by Gene Thorp

Printed in the United States of America
1   3   5   7   9   10   8   6   4   2

FOR
MARGARET HOWE ATKINSON
January 3, 1929–November 11, 2003
WITH LOVE

What history, I say, can ever give—for who can
know—the mad determin'd tussle of the armies . . .
the devils fully rous'ed in human hearts,—the
strong shout, *Charge, men, charge*—the flash of
naked sword, and rolling flame and smoke?

WALT WHITMAN

CONTENTS

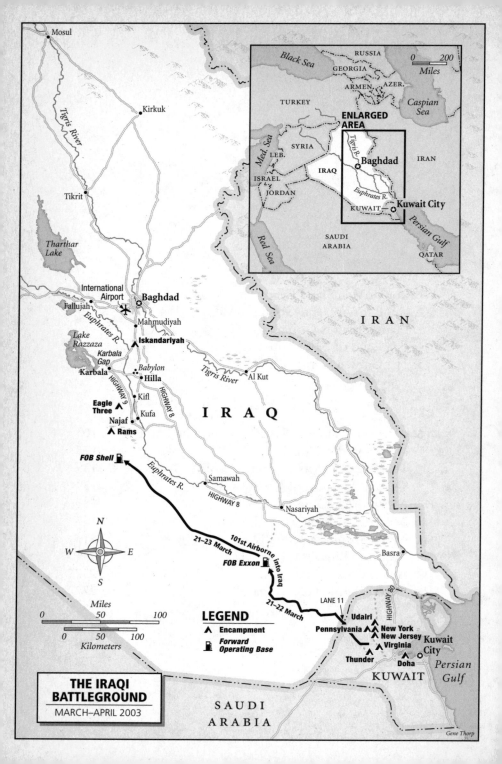

THE IRAQI
BATTLEGROUND

MARCH–APRIL 2003

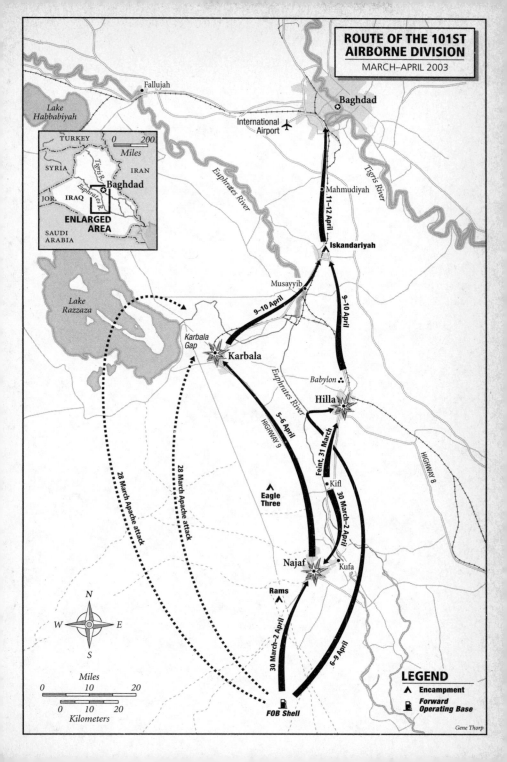

CHAIN OF COMMAND

101st AIRBORNE DIVISION IN IRAQ, MARCH 2003

LT. GEN. WILLIAM S. WALLACE
Commander, V Corps

MAJ. GEN. DAVID H. PETRAEUS
Commander, 101st Airborne Division

BRIG. GEN. BENJAMIN C. FREAKLEY
Asst. Division Commander,
Operations

BRIG. GEN. EDWARD J. SINCLAIR
Asst. Division Commander,
Support

COL. BEN HODGES, 1st Brigade
COL. JOSEPH ANDERSON, 2nd Brigade
COL. MICHAEL S. LINNINGTON, 3rd Brigade
COL. GREGORY P. GASS, 101st Aviation Brigade
COL. WILLIAM H. FORRESTER, 159th Aviation Brigade
COL. WILLIAM L. GREER, 101st Division Artillery
COL. JAMES E. ROGERS, 101st Division Support
COL. GERALD A. DOLINISH, 101st Corps Support Group

PROLOGUE

They found the sergeant's body at midmorning on Saturday, April 12, 2003, just where an Iraqi boy had said it would be: in a shallow grave in south Baghdad, near the Highway 8 cloverleaf known to the U.S. Army as Objective Curley. His interment was imperfect: an elbow and a knee protruded from the covering rubble. He had been stripped of boots and combat gear but not of his uniform, and his rank stripes and the name tape sewn over his right breast pocket made identification easy: Sergeant First Class John W. Marshall, who had been missing since Iraqi forces ambushed his convoy below Curley on April 8. A rocket-propelled grenade had ruined Sergeant Marshall's back and arm; four days in the ground had spoiled the rest of him. Soldiers from the 101st Airborne Division recorded the point on the map grid that identified his makeshift burial plot, MB 4496275295, and a chaplain read from Psalms. By the time I arrived, the remains had been lifted into a body bag, draped with an American flag, and carried—headfirst, as prescribed by Army custom—to a Humvee. A Graves Registration team took the body for eventual burial in Arlington National Cemetery.

I learned more about Sergeant Marshall in the coming weeks. He was fifty years old, making him the senior American soldier killed in the war. He had served in the 3rd Battalion of the 15th Infantry Regiment, a legendary unit in the 3rd Infantry Division, and he died while firing an Mk-19 automatic grenade launcher at marauding Iraqi soldiers and their Syrian allies. The fatal RPG round had blown him from his Humvee turret, and in the chaos of combat his corpse had been left behind. Born in Los Angeles, Marshall had joined the Army at eighteen. His father, Joseph, was an Army quartermaster during World War II; his mother, Odessa, had been a medical technician in the Women's Army Auxiliary Corps, an unusual distinction for a black woman in those days. Odessa Marshall would wear her uniform to her son's funeral.

Sergeant Marshall had left the Army for four years in the 1980s in a successful fight against Hodgkin's lymphoma. With the cancer in remission, he rejoined the service. The war in Iraq was his first combat tour, and he was nearing retirement. He was killed after volunteering to lead a resupply convoy to soldiers besieged on Highway 8. His survivors included a widow, Denise, and six children, ages nine to seventeen. They collected his posthumous Bronze Star and Purple Heart.

In a political democracy, every soldier's death is a public event. Every soldier's death ought to provoke the hard question: Why did he die? Even without having met Sergeant Marshall, I could surmise that he would have had his own answers. His rank indicated enough time in service to have sorted out such existential issues. Later, I would learn that in his last dispatch home he had said he saw little merit in debating the mission in Iraq. "It's really not an issue with me," he wrote. "I am not a politician or a policy maker, just an old soldier. Any doubts on my part could get someone killed."

But private rationales, however valid and honorable, rarely satisfy public inquiries. Why did Sergeant Marshall die? The question seemed particularly poignant that Saturday afternoon because the war appeared to be over. Saddam Hussein's regime had collapsed—the twenty-fourth overthrow of an Iraqi government since 1920, by one tally—and the shooting had virtually stopped. Thousands of Iraqi looters swarmed through the streets, trundling off with their booty while waving white surrender flags fashioned from rice bags or undershirts; we had made the world safe for kleptocracy. Soon we would see that April 12 was as good as it got, the high-water mark of the invasion, and a brief lull between war and an equally dangerous not-war. Certainly the soldiers sensed, as perhaps Sergeant Marshall had, that Iraq was only one campaign in a perpetual war, waged at varying degrees of intensity since the Cold War ended fourteen years earlier. They knew, even if their political leaders declined to tell them, that victory in a global war against terrorism meant, at best, containing rather than vanquishing the enemy, that there would be no more palmy days of conventional peace. Soldiers in the 101st Airborne Division joked darkly about permanent postings in Iraq, at Fort Baghdad or Camp Basra, or they joked about returning home to Fort Campbell, Kentucky, only after an extended anabasis through Iran, or North Korea, or perhaps Afghanistan again, where many had already served.

As a correspondent for *The Washington Post* and as a military historian, I had accompanied the 101st from Kentucky with ambitions of observing the U.S. Army from the inside. For nearly two months, during the deployment and staging in Kuwait, and the subsequent up-country march to Baghdad through Najaf and Karbala and Hilla, I had watched how war is waged in an age when wars are small, sequential, expeditionary, and bottomless. I had seen soldiers become invested in the cause, stirred by jubilant throngs yearning to breathe free. Liberation is an intoxicant for the liberator as much as the liberated, and U.S. troops became compulsive wavers, as if willing these people to like them. (Had other armies invading Mesopotamia also been wavers—the Persians, the Greeks, the British in 1916?) Like most Americans, I had been swept up in the adventure without ever quite shucking my unease at what we were doing here.

Combat in Iraq had given the lie to certain canards about

American soldiers, including the supposition that they were reluctant to close with the enemy, particularly in urban firefights. Troops could be crude and they could be cynical; ample mistakes had been committed, including friendly-fire episodes and wrong turns and sufficient miscalculations to reaffirm the old military bromide that no plan survives contact with the enemy. But overwhelmingly the soldiers kept their humor, their dignity, their honor, and their humanity, in circumstances that strained humanity. The U.S. military had again demonstrated that it was peerless among world powers.

A country the size of California, with 24 million people, had been conquered in three weeks, at a cost of fewer than 125 American lives. The task had been accomplished with admirable economy. In the Persian Gulf War of 1991, the attacking force included seven Army divisions and a pair of armored cavalry regiments, two Marine divisions, a French division, a British division, and tens of thousands of Arab and allied troops, all mustered to liberate Kuwait, a country with the landmass of New Jersey. This time, a much bigger military challenge had been surmounted with three Army divisions, a Marine division, and a British division. American combat power had included a stunning array of weapons and technological innovations, many of them new to the arsenal, but also leadership, will, and exceptionally well-trained soldiers at all ranks. The invaders had attacked simultaneously from the south, west, and north, demonstrating prowess at both joint warfare (the integration of the Army, Navy, Air Force, Marines, and Special Operations) and combined arms warfare (the integration of air power, infantry, artillery, and other combat arms). The war had been both a culmination of American military developments since the Vietnam War and a preview of wars to come.

True, Iraqi resistance was brittle and deeply inept ("Iraqi generals," one U.S. Marine Corps commander observed, "couldn't carry a bucket of rocks"). Yet the melting away of entire divisions left tens of thousands of armed men capable of waging guerrilla war in a country with five thousand years' experience at resisting invaders. The victor of 1991, General H. Norman Schwarzkopf, once said of his own, limited invasion, "I am certain that had we taken all of Iraq, we would have been like the dinosaur in the tar pit—we would still be there." Indeed, by early summer 2003, more than half of the United States Army's ten active-duty divisions would be mired in Iraq as an occupation force, along with a substantial slice of the National Guard and Reserves; those ten divisions were barely half of the eighteen that had existed at the end of the Cold War, when a new epoch of international comity was supposed to allow a sizable portion of the U.S. military to stand down. No historian could study the chronicles of Mesopotamia without disquiet at the succession of often violent regime changes—Sumerian, Akkadian, Babylonian, Hittite, Hurrian, Kassite, Elamite, Assyrian, Arab, Persian, Ottoman, British, and now Anglo-American. As the historian George Roux wrote, a generation ago, about Mesopotamian civilization: "A country like Iraq required, to be viable, two conditions: perfect cooperation between the various ethnic and socio-political units within the country itself, and a friendly or at least neutral attitude from its neighbors. Unfortunately, neither one nor the other lasted for any length of time."

If joining the 101st Airborne allowed close observation of American soldiers at war, it also disclosed much about the art of generalship. I had witnessed a great deal through the forbearance of the division commander, Major General David Howell Petraeus, and his superior, the V Corps commander, Lieutenant General William Scott Wallace. I had long believed that the extravagant stress of combat is a great revealer of character, disclosing a man's elemental traits the way a prism refracts light to reveal the inner spectrum. Petraeus kept me at his elbow in Iraq virtually all day, every day, allowing me to feel the anxieties and the perturbations, the small satisfactions and the large joys of commanding seventeen thousand soldiers under fire. I had watched him and his subordinates come of age as they wrestled with a thousand tactical conundrums, from landing helicopters in a dust bowl to taking down a large Shiite city. I also watched them wrestle with the strategic implications of the twenty-first-century military they now commanded, an expeditionary force that darted from one brushfire war to another, safeguarding the perimeters of the American empire. The task seemed both monumental and perpetual. During the past month, Petraeus several times had posed a rhetorical question, which became a private joke between us: "Tell me how this ends."

An hour after Sergeant Marshall's body was removed, I drove with Petraeus in his Humvee toward the Al Qadisiyah State Establishment, a vast Iraqi weapons factory, where the 101st intended to move its division headquarters. Looters waved; we waved back. A young Iraqi man sat in a wheelchair along Highway 8, a bloody bandage wrapped around the stump where there had once been a left leg; he did not wave. U.S. troops protected the Iraqi Oil Ministry and virtually nothing else. Mobs were ransacking seventeen of twenty-three government ministries, along with museums, libraries, factories, office buildings, military compounds, and villas of the ruling Baath Party elite. At Objective Curley, several charred Army vehicles and a pair of large palm trees with splintered trunks bespoke the intensity of the combat. Spent shell casings carpeted the ground, glittering in the sunlight. Three Iraqis in *dishdasha* robes exhumed a body with a shovel and a blanket. Graffiti on a wall west of the highway read: "No Love U.S.A." Someone had crossed out "no" and scratched "yes."

In the weapons complex, where hundreds of workers had once assembled mortars and AK-47s, soldiers bustled about organizing the bivouac: stringing wire, sweeping up debris, aiming satellite dishes. Passages from the Koran adorned the front gate, where a large tile portrait of Saddam Hussein—in uniform, with a red sash and a sword—had been riddled with bullets. Unopened mail on the gatehouse counter included correspondence from Al-Breamq Commercial Agencies, Ltd., and various bills that would never be paid. On the façade of a seven-story office building that soldiers had dubbed the Hotel the hands of a large clock were frozen at twenty-five minutes past seven. "Still some fighting and killing left, but I think the war is ending," Petraeus said as we explored the factory. "Now comes the hard part."

The warm air bore a scent of eucalyptus from gum trees lining the street. Next to the gatehouse, the division band rested in the shade before moving to sentry posts around the compound; when not playing their instruments, bandsmen often pulled security for a headquarters. At the sight of their commanding general, the musicians jumped to their feet and braced at attention. Petraeus pulled his shoulders back, pressed his heels together, and in his rumbling baritone led them in a chorus of the division song:

> *We have a rendezvous with destiny.*
> *Our strength and courage strike the spark*
> *That will always make men free.*
> *Assault, right down through the skies of blue,*
> *Keep your eyes on the job to be done!*
> *We're the soldiers of the 101st,*
> *We'll fight till the battle's won!*

I thought of Sergeant Marshall, a single soldier lost in a small war. His battle was over. He had begun his long journey to Arlington. Every soldier's death is a public event.

PART I

PEACE

1

ROUGH MEN STAND READY

The road to Baghdad began in the Shoney's restaurant parking lot at the Hopkinsville, Kentucky, mall at 8 A.M. on Wednesday, February 26, 2003. Snowflakes the size of chicken feathers tumbled from the low clouds. *How to Lose a Guy in Ten Days* and *The Recruit* took top billing on the marquee of the Martin Five Theaters. Sixty journalists, their hair whitened and wet with snow, straggled onto two buses chartered by the Army to haul us to nearby Fort Campbell, home of the 101st Airborne Division. "I just spilled my fuckin' coffee," a reporter announced to general indifference. A young woman holding a small mirror limned her eyes with mascara; her hand trembled slightly. An impatient Army officer called roll from a clipboard, then nodded to the civilian driver, who zipped up his Tennessee Titans windbreaker and shut the door. "Let's go," the officer told the driver. "Man, this is like herding cats."

As the bus eased through a military police checkpoint at the back gate, I scanned a seven-page document sent by e-mail two days earlier. "This is a formal invitation for you to embed with elements of the 101st Airborne during our deployment," it began. "The agenda calls for travel via military contract transportation from Fort Campbell to the U.S. Central Command (CENTCOM) Area of Responsibility." Some 777 reporters and photographers were to join various Army, Navy, Air Force, and Marine Corps units under a Defense Department plan for covering a war with Iraq that now seemed inevitable and imminent. A twelfth of those journalists would be sprinkled throughout the 101st Airborne, in various battalions, brigades, and support units.

The document included rules and suggestions. For "messing and billeting purposes," reporters were "considered the rank of 'major' equivalents," a putative commission that overpromoted most of us by at least four grades. Reporters could not carry weapons and should not bring "colorful news jackets." A dozen recommended inoculations included anthrax, smallpox, and yellow fever. Each journalist was to bring a sleeping bag, "two months' worth of personal hygiene items," dog tags—"helicopter crashes tend to mess up the bodies," an officer had told me with a wink— and fieldcraft articles ranging from a pocket knife and flashlight to goggles and baby wipes. "Items to avoid" included curling irons, hair dryers, pornography, and alcohol.

"The current conditions in the area of operations are being described as 'austere.' You should not anticipate having laundry facilities available. Hand washing in a bucket is the norm. The Army will provide you with MREs (Meals Ready to Eat). We look forward to working with you on our next Rendezvous With Destiny!"

The snow tapered off as the small convoy rolled across Fort Campbell. A billboard declared: "Screaming Eagle Country. Salute With Pride." The 105,000-acre post straddles the Kentucky-Tennessee border and is populous enough to require multiple zip codes. Many wood-frame World War II buildings remain in use, such as the division headquarters. An electronic sign near a traffic intersection flashed advertisements, including notices for "Bingo Bingo Bingo Bingo World" and "Air Assault Towing and Storage." A new black stone memorial across the street commemorated the division's classic battles and featured an engraved quotation from Major General William C. Lee, a World War II commander who is considered the founding father of U.S. Army airborne operations: "We shall habitually go into action when the need is immediate and extreme."

Waiting outside a small Army conference center was Major Hugh Cate III, the division public-affairs officer, whom I had already met during a reporting trip to Fort Campbell in early January. An affable former West Point rugby player from Alabama, Cate—known to his friends and family as Trey—shook hands and squeezed elbows as the reporters trooped from the buses. Pulling me aside, he asked, "You ready to go? We have forty-nine aircraft leaving in the next seventy-two hours. General Petraeus and most of the command staff are already in Kuwait. You and I are leaving tomorrow night."

Inside, a large U-shaped table dominated the room. Immense historical photographs covered the walls, depicting the division in France, Holland, Vietnam, and, during the 1991 Persian Gulf War, southern Iraq. One photo famously captured General Dwight D. Eisenhower in earnest conversation on the eve of D-Day with young paratroopers about to board their aircraft for the jump into Normandy. Created in August 1942, the 101st Airborne had been featured in the Stephen Ambrose best-seller *Band of Brothers,* which subsequently became a popular ten-part television series.

Cate got everyone seated, then dimmed the lights and cued a five-minute indoctrination video. While an unseen chorus sang a treacly anthem—"When we were needed / We were there"— images flashed by of Bastogne, Tet, and Desert Storm, and of coffins from Gander, Newfoundland, where a battalion returning from peacekeeping duty in the Sinai peninsula had been obliterated in a plane crash in December 1985. A wall poster on the second floor of the conference center quoted George Orwell: "People sleep peaceably in their beds at night only because rough men stand ready to do violence on their behalf."

Not since 1974 had the 101st Airborne been a parachute unit, which made the nomenclature inconvenient if not annoying. Rather, the division had been converted into an "air assault" force, exploiting the "vertical envelopment" tactics first tried by U.S. Marines in the Korean War. Equipped with 256 helicopters, the 101st could mount deep attacks behind enemy lines with six dozen Apache gunships—far more than any of the Army's nine other divisions—while simultaneously shuttling up to four thousand soldiers at least a hundred miles in six hours with Blackhawk and Chinook transport helicopters. "Powerful, Flexible, Agile, Lethal," a division briefing paper asserted. "Trained and ready to fight and win." Collectively and formally, the seventeen thousand soldiers were now the 101st Airborne Division (Air Assault). Informally, and with considerable pride, they called themselves the Screaming Eagles, and greeted one another with the snappy salutation "Air assault!"

All this became clear over the next few hours in a series of briefings. A grizzled civilian public-affairs officer named George Heath leaned over the podium and said, "If you prefer vegetable MREs to regular MREs, if you have a particular brand of cappuccino you prefer, if you'd rather have a room with a morning view rather than an evening view, just let us know and we'll see if we can accommodate you." Momentary confusion rippled through the journalists, a blend of hope and skepticism, until Heath's flinty squint revealed his facetiousness.

The Fort Campbell hospital commander displayed slides of four horribly disfigured smallpox victims, their faces blistered beyond even a mother's love. An autopsy slide of a Russian victim of inhalation anthrax showed a human brain transformed by the bacteria into a black, greasy lump. "A sequence of three vaccination shots has proved 92.5 percent effective in protecting rhesus monkeys from anthrax," the commander said. "In rabbits, it's 97 percent." Journalists who wanted smallpox or anthrax immunizations filled out several government forms—joking nervously about whether to check "monkey" or "rabbit"—and then marched to a nearby clinic where Army doctors waited to prick them.

Those who still had an appetite were bused to the Fort Campbell food court for lunch at Anthony's Pizza or Frank's Franks. Vendors in the atrium peddled T-shirts demanding "No slack for Iraq!" as well as 101st Airborne Division baseball caps and cheap lithographs of raptors in various spread-eagle attitudes.

Back at the conference center, the briefings continued all afternoon. A sergeant with expertise in nuclear, biological, and chemical matters, known simply as NBC, demonstrated how to don an M-40 protective mask. "Most of the Iranians who died from chemical weapons in the Iran-Iraq war were wearing beards, and their pro masks didn't seal properly," the sergeant said. "If you have a beard, I recommend you lose it."

Among those most discomfited by this advice was Jim Dwyer, a wry, gifted reporter for *The New York Times* who would become my closest comrade for the next seven weeks. The son of Irish immigrants and winner of a Pulitzer Prize in 1995 for his lyrical columns about New York City, Dwyer was an eleventh-hour draftee into the ranks of *Times* war correspondents. "If you're having a midlife crisis," his doctor had asked him before the deployment, "why don't you get a girlfriend like other men your age?" At forty-six, he was the proud owner of a thirteen-year-old beard. Dwyer asked the NBC sergeant several questions of a rear-guard sort, then surrendered. The next morning he would appear with his plump, clean-shaven Irish face aflame with razor burn but ready for masking.

As masks were issued, reporters debated the probability that Saddam Hussein would attack with sarin gas, botulinum toxin, or mustard gas. Like most reporter conclaves, this discussion was long on opinion and short on hard intelligence; a narrow majority held that "getting slimed," as the Army called a chemical attack, was probable.

"The signal for a gas attack is three honks of a horn or someone yelling, 'Gas! Gas! Gas!'" the sergeant continued. "How do you know when there's a gas attack? When you see someone else putting on their mask." I thought of Wilfred Owen and his poem "Dulce et Decorum Est": "Gas! Gas! Quick, boys!—An ecstasy of fumbling." The standard for donning the mask was nine seconds. I was not sure I could even extract it from the case in nine seconds, much less get it seated and strapped on.

Next the sergeant produced a canvas bag containing the Joint Service Lightweight Integrated Suit Technology, a cumbersome name for a cumbersome garment more commonly known as a JLIST, pronounced "jay-list," and made of charcoal-impregnated polyurethane foam. "The standard for going from MOPP zero— that's Mission-Oriented Protective Posture—where you only have your mask in the case, to MOPP four, which includes putting on the full suit, vinyl boots, mask, and gloves, is eight minutes." Piece by piece the sergeant pulled on his gear, periodically advising us to secure this or that with "the hook-and-pile fastener tape." It took several references before I realized that he was talking about Velcro. The expert needed more than eight minutes to get outfitted and accessorized. When he peeled off the mask after just thirty seconds, he was sweating like a dray horse.

"It's been pretty lighthearted so far," said Major Cate, moving to the podium. "But I just want you to know that this is serious stuff." Anthrax, smallpox, sarin, botulinum, mustard: in truth, the day had not seemed excessively frivolous. Cate reviewed some of the ground rules for covering combat operations. No journalist could be excluded from the front line because of gender; if a female reporter wanted to live with a rifle company, so be it, even though by law female soldiers could not serve in such units. "Our attitude is that information should be released and that there should be a good reason for not releasing it rather than that it should be suppressed until someone finds a good reason for letting it out," Cate added. This statement provoked mild skepticism, both as a statement of policy and as a syntactical construct.

Safety was paramount, he continued. "Dead press is bad press." Not a soul in the room disagreed. "There's gonna be bad news. There's gonna be tension between people. Take a big bite of that patience cheeseburger."

A civil affairs expert then delivered the same lecture on Iraqi culture that thousands of soldiers were hearing. "Never use the A-okay or thumbs-up hand gestures," he advised. "They are obscene in the Arab culture. I believe the A-okay sign, with thumb and forefinger, has to do with camel procreation." (I would recall this assertion a month later when thousands of jubilant, liberated Iraqis flashed thumbs-up at passing American soldiers.) Another expert gave a twenty-minute summary of Iraqi history and geography. Three quarters of Iraq's 24 million people lived in cities. Twelve percent of the country was arable. Baghdad's population exceeded 5.5 million. The average high temperature in Baghdad in May topped 100 degrees Fahrenheit. The oil-for-food program, organized under United Nations' sanctions, allowed Saddam to export about 75 percent as much oil as he had sold before the 1991 war; smuggling earned him another $3 billion annually. The briefing ended with another cultural warning: "Never point, or show the bottoms of your feet, to Arabs."

The final lecture in a long day came from Captain Nick Lancaster, who identified himself as the division's chief of justice. Wars had rules, Captain Lancaster began. Internationally recognized combat regulations were "intended to prevent suffering for the sake of suffering. Basically we want to be the good guys. We want everybody to know that we are the good guys and that we play by the rules." A rule of thumb for combatants held that "suffering must not be *excessive*. There is a Department of Defense lawyer in Washington whose job is to review all weapons under consideration for purchase to determine if they comply with the laws of war and will not inflict unnecessary suffering." Once a soldier was wounded, he could no longer be considered a combatant. Lancaster acknowledged that the rules of war had many finely parsed legal distinctions. A parachutist, for example, is a pilot descending by chute; a paratrooper—a different species altogether, in the eyes of the law—is a combatant deliberately attacking by airborne means.

He raced through other legal nuances. The basic rule for treating captured Iraqis would be "humane treatment, which means food, water, medical treatment. If they are formally given the status of EPWs—enemy prisoners of war—they get other rights, including access to tobacco and musical instruments."

Finally, the captain warned, General Order No. 1 would be enforced during the deployment. Usually known as the "no alcohol" edict, the order in fact contained numerous clauses, some of which Lancaster said had been violated the previous year in Afghanistan by soldiers from the 3rd Brigade of the 101st. Among the prohibitions: No privately owned weapons in a combat zone. No entry into religious sites for reasons other than military necessity. "We don't want to assault their sensibilities by having a bunch of soldiers trooping through a mosque," Lancaster explained. No religious proselytizing. No looting of archaeological sites. No black marketeering. No pets.

A reporter asked whether General Order No. 1 applied to embedded journalists. Lancaster paused judiciously. Prosecutions were unlikely, he admitted, then added, "My advice would be that you comply."

Any U.S. military campaign in Iraq would seek to minimize damage to the country, the captain concluded. The reason, however, was less an issue of jurisprudence than of enlightened self-interest. "The more infrastructure that's still there after the war, the less that we will have to rebuild," he said. "And the quicker we can leave."

As we filed from the conference room for a final night in our Clarksville hotels, it occurred to me that Captain Lancaster had articulated what American soldiers have fought for in every conflict since the Mexican War: the right to go home quickly.

We were on our way—slowly, the Army way.

By late afternoon on Thursday, February 27, in a journalistic diaspora, the reporters had been farmed out to their assigned units. The 101st comprised seven brigades, each commanded by a colonel who was like a duke in the larger kingdom. Each of the three infantry brigades, for example, had roughly 3,500 soldiers and typically was expanded into a "combat team" with its three infantry battalions augmented by an artillery battalion, a couple of aviation battalions, and company-sized units of engineers, communications experts, intelligence analysts, and air defense troops. Most of the division's equipment, from helicopters to howitzers, had already been shipped by rail to Jacksonville, Florida, and was now aboard five huge ships steaming to Kuwait. The soldiers, however, would fly on chartered airliners, carrying their personal baggage, individual weapons, gas masks, night-vision goggles, and the harness of buckles and shoulder straps known as an LBE, for load-bearing equipment.

I was assigned to division headquarters, where I was the only reporter shadowing the commander, Dave Petraeus. I had known Petraeus casually since he was a major working for the Army chief of staff in the early 1990s. My premise in requesting this assignment was that a division command post in combat afforded a good vantage point for looking down, into the operations of its subordinate brigades and battalions, as well as for looking up, into corps operations. I also knew that Petraeus was a compelling figure: smart, articulate, and driven. "Probably the most talented person I have ever met in the Army," General Barry R. McCaffrey, a retired four-star, had recently said of Petraeus. "This guy has sparks jumping off of him."

As the son of an infantry officer, I had been around the Army all my life, including extended stints as a correspondent in Somalia, Bosnia, and the Persian Gulf in 1990–1991. I had also written books about the Army in Vietnam, in the Gulf War, and, most recently, in North Africa during World War II; for four years I had been on extended leave from the *Post,* and I was engrossed in researching a narrative history of the campaigns in Sicily and Italy in 1943–1944 when the newspaper solicited my temporary return to journalism. This view of the Army, I believed, would be uniquely intimate.

That it would be a view of an army at war seemed probable. A confrontation over Iraqi disarmament had persisted between Washington and Baghdad virtually since the end of the Gulf War in March 1991. Iraq without doubt had violated various United Nations Security Council resolutions; renewed American resolve had goaded the Security Council, in November 2002, to unanimously approve a tougher resolution demanding the return of UN weapons inspectors to Iraq after a four-year absence, and the inspectors' unrestricted access to facilities throughout the country. Grudging, obnoxious, and ever recalcitrant, Saddam Hussein nevertheless over the winter readmitted the inspectors, and he destroyed dozens of missiles deemed in violation of UN range limitations.

Yet President George W. Bush and his senior advisers insisted that Iraq prove that it had dismantled programs to make nuclear, biological, and chemical weapons. "You do know they have weapons of mass destruction, don't you?" Paul Wolfowitz, the deputy defense secretary, told the chief UN weapons inspector. Bush also asserted that "confronting the threat posed by Iraq is crucial to winning the war on terror," although he presented no evidence linking Baghdad to the Al-Qaeda killers responsible for the atrocities of September 11, 2001.

The administration's cocksure bellicosity alienated many allies, particularly in light of Bush's repudiation of various international agreements—from the Kyoto Protocol on the environment, to the 1972 Anti-Ballistic Missile Treaty, to the Comprehensive Test Ban Treaty—as well as a new U.S. national security doctrine, published in September 2002, that endorsed preemptive attacks against perceived threats. Millions of antiwar demonstrators had marched in 350 cities around the world on February 15. Another resolution, authorizing force against Iraq and introduced at the Security Council the day before my arrival in Kentucky, had little hope of attracting even a simple majority. Opinion surveys showed that a thin majority of Americans supported military action against Iraq, even without explicit UN appoval. "At some point," Bush declared, "we may be the only ones left. That's okay with me. We are America." If the dispatch of U.S. forces to Southwest Asia, which had begun in earnest the previous summer, initially helped stiffen international resolve toward Iraq, now the floodtide of troops appeared to be driving the United States inexorably toward war. The 101st Airborne Division's was the most conspicuous deployment to date, an unambiguous and perhaps irreversible signal of deadly intent.

The Personnel Marshaling Area at Fort Campbell was a dim, drafty warehouse with a concrete floor. Two hundred and ninety-four passengers, designated collectively as Chalk 19, included staff officers, the division band, the 101st headquarters company, a signal unit, MPs, Trey Cate's public-affairs warriors, Jim Dwyer of the *Times,* who was assigned to the division's assault command post, and me. The soldiers wore desert camouflage uniforms and suede desert boots. Smokers huddled outside on a loading dock. A voice carried above the hubbub: "Hey, DeSouza. Just because you're smoking a fucking cigarette is no reason somebody else should hold your fucking weapon." Another voice sang out, "I need a hug. I need a hug."

At 4 P.M., after two hours of general milling, we hauled our bags into a parking lot, where "Chalk 19" was scrawled on a pair of immense twenty-four-wheel flatbed trucks. In a lifetime of travel I have never learned to pack concisely, and my High Sierra rucksack—Chinese red in a sea of Army green—bulged with reporter notepads, clothing for hot weather, clothing for cold weather, extra batteries (sizes AA, AAA, and C), extra computer and satellite-phone cables, a sleeping bag and foam mat, a power strip, two flashlights with red lenses, a Gerber folding knife with enough attachments to build a house or perform a heart-lung transplant, a tape recorder, spare tapes, extra reading glasses, a flak vest, a helmet, a shaving kit with two months' worth of toiletries, and too many books I had never read and would never read. With a heavy grunt I managed to heave the thing onto the flatbed, certain and perhaps a bit glad that I would never see it again.

In two shoulder bags I still had the gas mask and JLIST, a laptop, two satellite phones, a digital camera, a thick sheaf of unintelligible instructions on how to operate these things, pens, pencils, more notebooks, another flashlight, and various items I could only think of collectively as *stuff*. Whatever happened, I wondered, to the doughty war correpondent with a pencil, a pad, and a battered Underwood? A modern hack's greatest fear, besides running out of gin, was having no means to write or to transmit written copy to the home office; for the sake of redundancy, given the harsh conditions that awaited us, within two weeks I was to accumulate three satellite phones; three digital cameras; a loopy assortment of cables, cords, wires, and adapters; and two laptops, including one variant encased in a metal box that supposedly could withstand being run over by a Humvee. There was irony here: I have never been comfortable in a world fraught with electrons. A week earlier, upon arriving for laptop and satellite-phone instruction at *The Washington Post,* I overheard one technician tell another, "The guy coming in this morning is a real technology moron." I could only concur.

From the parking lot we were herded to another holding tank in a large cafeteria. A television near the front door was tuned to CNN; the crawl across the bottom of the screen noted that the national threat level had been lowered from orange to yellow. "Pass the word," a soldier in front said. "No weapons or LBEs on the new furniture in the mess hall. Pass it on." Inside, a soldier reading the *Odyssey* laid his head on a table and dozed off, no doubt dreaming of lotus-eaters and men turned to swine.

At 5:45 P.M. we were rousted and sent back outside. Fog and dusk had settled over Fort Campbell. "Let's go, let's go. Chalk nineteen over here," called Sergeant First Class Henry DeGrace, a senior noncommissioned officer for the headquarters company. "Give me a formation. Troop, Ten-*hut*! Who does *not* have a mask?" Silence. "*Who* is missing their protective mask?" Silence. DeGrace held up a canvas sack and read the stenciled number. "Mask 104." A miscreant private skulked forward to claim it.

A squadron of buses pulled up. DeGrace stood in the door of the first bus and looked each boarding soldier in the eye. "Got all your sensitive items?" "Yes, sergeant," they answered. "Yes, sergeant." The driver, a civilian with brilliantined hair and thick glasses who referred to his vehicle as Big Boy, stood to the side. "There's fifty-five seats, if that helps," he said as the NCOs repeatedly counted noses. "You need to lose them soft caps," DeGrace barked. "Only Kevlars from here on." He pronounced the term as a single word: *softcaps*. With a hiss of air brakes the convoy rolled toward the airfield, led by a police cruiser with flashing blue lights. "I feel important," DeGrace said, with just the right sardonic pitch.

I noticed a 10th Mountain Division combat patch on his right sleeve and asked DeGrace if he had been in Somalia when the unit deployed to Mogadishu in the mid-1990s. He had indeed, and he had also served in Haiti, in Bosnia, and on various other deployments. "I've been married seventeen years and my wife has been through every one of them." He removed his helmet and showed me a yellowing snapshot, tucked in the webbing, of his four children. "The oldest one turned sixteen this month," he said. "This is the same photo of them I had in Somalia, and I kept it in the same place. I told my kids we'll be home when the job is done. I hope this is the last time I have to do this."

DeGrace was lean and quick-spoken, with a handsome hussar's mustache. A native of New Bedford, Massachusetts, he'd joined the Army in 1985. He told me that his father, also named Henry, had enlisted at sixteen, deceiving the authorities with the birth certificate of an older brother who had died in infancy. Eventually promoted to sergeant, Henry Senior had surrendered three stripes in order to join the newly created 101st Airborne Division, and had fought with G Company of the 506th Parachute Infantry Regiment from Operation MARKET GARDEN, in Holland, until the end of the war. Henry Senior was eighty-two years old and had worked in the post office for forty-five years after the war; Henry Junior had a Screaming Eagle tattooed on his calf. It was that kind of unit, a confederacy not only of foxhole brothers but also of fathers and sons.

The buses pulled up to an empty hangar and Chalk 19 trooped inside. Metal bleachers lined two walls and the troops settled in with a clatter of rifles. A chaplain at a table draped with a desert camouflage dropcloth handed out vest-pocket New Testaments and a devotional volume titled *The Power of Crying Out.* "It's really good," he told me pleasantly. "Would you like one?" I turned to the first page, and a verse from Psalm 86: "In the day of my trouble I will call upon You, for You will answer me." Various chapters included advice on "release from demons" and "self-control."

The atmosphere in the hangar was neither jovial nor somber. For most troops, the day of trouble was not here yet, only the day of leaving. Soldiers who still required inoculations peeled off their uniform blouses and lined up to be pricked against smallpox or hepatitis or influenza. Sergeants circulated through the hangar, herding female soldiers toward a restroom for a final pregnancy test; expectant mothers could not deploy to a combat zone. A young specialist groaned and tossed her rucksack on the floor. "Watch my shit, will you?" she asked a male corporal before joining the long line.

Snatches of conversation drifted from the bleachers. A few

soldiers made final, teary calls on their cell phones. Some Chinook helicopter pilots, I knew, had been home from Afghanistan for only three weeks before shipping out for Kuwait. "I wonder if I'll ever get one consecutive year at home," a sergeant first class told another soldier. "This is my fourth year in a row to deploy. I'd like to spend just one year at home. Maybe when I retire." He sounded more weary than angry. "I took a job in the headquarters company because I didn't think we'd go anywhere unless the whole division went. So guess what? The whole division is going."

Much palaver was devoted to whether Chalk 19 would land in Kuwait City before midnight on February 28, which would earn each soldier an income tax exemption for the entire month of February. Few soldiers considered themselves mercenaries, but most were keenly aware of the deployment pay entitlements. "Desert Dollars," as the Fort Campbell newspaper called the benefits, included a $3.50 per diem, $100 per month in separation pay, $150 per month in hostile-fire pay, a $241-per-month basic subsistence allowance, and up to $5,533 in monthly salary tax-free under the "combat zone exclusion." A sergeant with two young children told me he was already borrowing against the extra income; at Fort Campbell, he was so strapped for cash by the end of each month that he rarely ate lunch. "It's an extra six or seven hundred bucks a month I can really use," he said.

There was a commotion in the middle of the hangar and I spied an officer I had known since the Gulf War, when he was a major. Now Benjamin C. Freakley was a brigadier general and the assistant division commander for operations, often referred to simply as the O. Freakley was a force of nature, an old-fashioned warfighter with a big heart and five sons. Another West Point rugby player, he was a devout Methodist, a collector of antiques, a natural pedagogue, and a talented drummer whose solo rendition of "Wipeout" at the division Christmas party was still much discussed. Freakley had been delegated by Petraeus to oversee the deployment; he was unhappy both at being left behind for two weeks and at various bureaucratic malfeasances, which he was now trying to correct.

He halted his finger-jabbing long enough to let me introduce him to Dwyer, who would eventually join the assault command post, typically the O's domain in combat. "The plan is changing quickly," Freakley told us. The Turkish government appeared disinclined to let the 4th Infantry Division attack through eastern Turkey into northern Iraq. "If the planners want to protect the oil fields in the north, the 101st would be a good candidate for that job." Asked how long he anticipated the campaign would last, he mulled the question for a moment. "Two weeks if it goes well, two months if it doesn't. If it gets into Baghdad, or the other cities, the plan is to use precision strikes by identifying points of resistance and hitting quick and hard, then getting out. There will be no kicking-in of doors."

Freakley strode off to resume his scourging. At 10 P.M., Chalk 19 was ordered outside yet again, this time to a small hangar on the edge of the runway. Each soldier carried twenty rounds of ammunition in the unlikely event the 101st would have to come off the plane shooting. I pulled my wheeled backpack behind me, feeling like a tourist. An assistant chaplain, Major Len Kircher, ruminated on the flurry of marriages that had preceded the deployment. One accommodating local magistrate had even been dubbed the Love Judge. Kircher disapproved. "I don't do spur-of-the-moment jobs," he said. "I won't marry teenagers and I won't marry privates. The failure rate is too high."

Several hundred heavily armed soldiers listened impassively as an MP read a required government warning: "It is a federal crime," she said with no trace of irony, "to carry concealed weapons aboard an aircraft." Then, as directed, the troops shouldered their rifles and grenade launchers and shambled onto the runway.

Four big charter jets waited in the fog, including a Northwest Airlines Boeing 747 and an airliner whose fuselage advertised Hawaiian vacations. The runway lights were orange and weird, casting long shadows. Chalk 19 tramped in a column along the tarmac to World Airways Flight 6208. As the soldiers climbed the boarding ramp and stowed their weapons beneath the seats, butts toward the aisles, a flight attendant apologized over the public-address system: because of a broken valve, the aircraft had no running water. Each passenger was handed a liter of bottled water, "for flushing."

At 12:30 A.M. on Friday, February 28, the plane lifted into the night. Spiderman leaped around the cabin during the in-flight movie. At 3 P.M. German time, we descended over the golden Hessian landscape to refuel in Frankfurt. Three-bladed windmills slowly turned in the afternoon sun. Old Europe looked tranquil, far from war and rumors of war, and ready for happy hour to begin the *Wochenende*. The plane taxied past the Luftbrücke memorial, commemorating the Berlin airlift organized by the U.S. Army in 1947. The ironies, I thought, were beginning to pile up. For an hour, soldiers wandered through a gift shop, studying the Hummel figurines and beer steins and T-shirts boasting, "I Drove the Autobahn."

The second leg began with a flight steward reminding passengers that "this is a nonsmoking flight, and that includes smokeless tobacco." Soldiers dutifully put away their tins of Copenhagen. Across the Alps and down the boot of Italy we flew through the night. Below the glitter of Naples, I picked out the dark curve of Salerno, where so many boys had died sixty years before. Most of Chalk 19 was watching *Harry Potter and the Chamber of Secrets*. A soldier across the aisle was engrossed in Field Manual 3-19-4, "Military Police Officer Leader's Handbook." If we seemed more like a tour group flying off on holiday than an army marching to war, the very familiarity of our conveyance seemed to accent the anxious sense of uncertainty.

Across the Mediterranean, the plane flew up the Nile, then banked east at the Valley of the Kings to cross the Red Sea and Saudi Arabia. As we descended on the final approach, the pilot ordered all window shades lowered and cabin lights extinguished to make the plane less conspicuous to anyone below armed with a shoulder-fired missile and bad intent. "We really do appreciate everything you are doing for us and our nation," a flight attendant added. "Godspeed."

Seventeen hours after leaving Fort Campbell, the plane touched down in Kuwait City at 1:50 A.M. local time on Saturday, March 1, too late to qualify for a tax-exempt February. The first three soldiers down the ramp were eighteen, nineteen, and twenty-three years old. They did not mention the money.

2

GOOD FOR YOU AND
GOOD FOR ME

It took Chalk 19 almost as long to travel the ten miles from Kuwait International to Camp Doha as it had to cover the 8,851 miles from Fort Campbell. Gray with fatigue, we were bused from the plane at 3 A.M. to an immense green tent in a corner of the airport. We sat on benches precisely arranged on the plywood floor. Fluorescent lights hummed overhead as a young sergeant delivered a welcome-to-Kuwait speech in the same bored monotone undoubtedly used to welcome American troops to France in 1917, to Britain in 1942, and to Vietnam in 1968. A column of newly arrived British riflemen lumbered past outside the tent; the sight of allies seemed oddly reassuring at a time when the Bush administration had embraced preemptive unilateralism. The U.S. government had compiled a list of coalition confederates supposedly recruited in the campaign against Iraq, beginning with Afghanistan, Albania, Azerbaijan, and Bulgaria, continuing through the Marshall Islands and Micronesia, and concluding with the Solomon Islands and Uzbekistan. I had my eyes peeled for that Micronesian army.

Dawn had broken by the time we boarded a dozen leased city buses, outfitted with passenger straps and McDonald's ads touting a confection called the McArabia, "dressed in Arabic flatbread." Glassy-eyed soldiers played with the stop-call buttons or stared at colorful maps of Kuwait City commuter routes. Two punchy lieutenants who served as protocol officers discussed the memorabilia to be presented to the dignitaries from Washington who inevitably would come inspirit the troops once victory was secured. One officer suggested a boxed set of the little Tabasco bottles included in every MRE pouch, which he proposed emptying of hot sauce and refilling with "Genuine Sand from Kuwait."

A few of us were bound for Camp Doha, the sprawling base near Kuwait City where the 101st Airborne headquarters was temporarily bivouacked until the division's equipment arrived by ship. But most of our fellow travelers were moving directly to Camp New Jersey, a desert staging area in north-central Kuwait, and it was decided to deliver these passengers first. Our convoy skirted Kuwait Bay and angled north up the six-lane Route 80. This was the infamous Highway of Death, where Iraqi troops fleeing Kuwait City in February 1991 had been trapped and butchered by American warplanes. I had last seen the highway twelve years before, when a charred procession of stolen vehicles and scattered loot stretched to the horizon. After more than a decade of weathering, the pavement seemed bleached and antiseptic.

Beyond the rocky escarpment known as Mutlaa Ridge, the buses turned west into the desert and crawled for two hours across a wretched rumor of a road. Except for a solitary scraggly tree, so singular as to seem a hallucination, the landscape was utterly barren until the sand berm and watchtowers of Camp New Jersey hove into view. "What a beautiful country," said Sergeant DeGrace with profound sarcasm. "I can see why we're here."

For nearly an hour we waited outside the camp gate in another of those inexplicable frictions that bind any Army movement. I was reminded of the postulate that the U.S. Army performs so well in the chaos of war because it practices chaos every day. Soldiers tromped off the bus to relieve themselves along the outer berm; when a few men dawdled, a female corporal hollered, "Hey, hurry up. It's our turn." At last a sentry waved us through the checkpoint and into the compound.

Camp New Jersey had been named by someone with a corrupt sense of humor: the Garden State it was not. Three square miles of flat, seared nothing was disrupted only by a few clusters of tents. The 3rd Infantry Division had recently been evicted to make room for the 101st. Before moving to an even ruder desert encampment to the east, the 3rd had stripped New Jersey of amenities, including most of the outhouse toilet seats. Across this wasteland an Italian named Pietro della Valle had traveled for more than a decade in the seventeenth century, lugging the embalmed body of his dead wife in his baggage train. It was that kind of place.

The baggage for Chalk 19 was dumped in a large pile for three hundred passengers to paw through. A southerly wind abruptly picked up, and within thirty minutes every soldier and rucksack was coated with fine brown dust. As we pulled on our goggles, Jim Dwyer knotted an undershirt across his mouth and nose; he resembled a cross between a Berber shepherd and Jesse James. Dwyer patted his hair, now stiff with grit, and observed, "After a while the dust acts as a kind of gel." Two soldiers sang as they blinked dirt from their eyes and manhandled their barracks bags—*Take this job and shove it / I ain't workin' here no more.* A veteran with a combat patch from Afghanistan wailed, "I miss Kandahar!" Those of us bound for Camp Doha hauled our encrusted bags onto the bus and settled in for the three-hour ride. Camp New Jersey receded behind us, a pestilential brown outpost to which we would return soon enough.

Just before 6 P.M. on Sunday, March 2, I stood waiting for General Petraeus outside the Doha mess hall. A division staff officer had informed me that we were to have supper together. The evening was cool and breezy. I zipped up my old field jacket.

In the middle distance, two pairs of power-plant smokestacks framed the camp. Soldiers called them Scud goalposts. A squad doing p.t.—physical training—jogged past. The troops in unison answered a sergeant's jody call:

> Momma and me lyin' in bed,
> Momma turns to me and Momma says,
> Gimme gimme p.t.
> Good for you and good for me.

Camp Doha had been here since the end of the Gulf War, growing from a spare industrial park to a bustling encampment with eight thousand residents and a $100 million annual budget, part of the half-billion dollars invested by the U.S. Army in Kuwaiti infrastructure. It reminded me of Long Binh during the Vietnam War, a vast rear-area compound whose denizens were dubbed "Dial Soapers" by their unwashed comrades in the field—or, less generously, REMFs, an acronym for "rear-echelon motherfuckers."

After my brief view of New Jersey, I was pleased to be a REMF while it lasted. Across from the mess hall, just past the video-rental drop box, Frosty's Recreation Center featured spades, dominoes, and table-tennis tournaments. Signs hung in the front windows of the camp barbershop ("military haircut—$5.25") and the camp dry cleaner ("DCUs laundered—$3.50"). In the recreation center down the street, soldiers romped on the indoor volleyball and basketball courts, or busied themselves with yoga classes and dozens of aerobic machines. Over-achievers could also qualify for the Camp Doha Physical Fitness Award by jogging 270 miles, rowing 180 kilometers, and completing 9,000 sit-ups and 9,700 push-ups. An indoor mall next to the post exchange included the Pamas Souvenir Shop, with carved wooden camels and T-shirts picturing a mushroom cloud captioned, "Weather Forecast: Baghdad 32,000 Degrees and Partly Cloudy." Other shops peddled Iranian carpets, custom-engraved wedding bands, and Harley-Davidson Sportster 1200s. Soldiers browsed in the PX, which sold everything from Sony boom boxes and Halston cologne to barbecue tongs and Jay-Z CDs. President Bush had asserted that we were fighting for a way of life, and here it was.

As I leaned against a traffic barrier, Avenue D resembled the bar scene in *Star Wars*. Tough-guy soldiers from half a dozen countries sauntered past. Each army had its own variant of desert fatigues, so that everyone was mottled in distinctive national patterns. Gurkhas and Kiwis, Czechs and Yanks brushed sleeves with potbellied contractors, Pakistani cooks, and Red Cross volunteers. Kuwaits, Saudis, and all others with vaguely Semitic features were known collectively as hajjis, which could also be used adjectivally, as in "This hajji satellite dish isn't worth a damn." British paratroopers cooed in admiration at a pair of passing female helicopter pilots in U.S. Army flight suits. "Hallo. Hallo, there." Combat troops sported berets and boonie hats, go-to-hell caps and Kevlar helmets; many carried the obligatory Big Knife. The only thing they all had in common, besides a swagger, was the gas mask carried on the hip in a canvas creel.

I patted my hip. Once again I had left my M-40 in the warehouse where I was living in an open bay with two hundred soldiers. At that moment Petraeus appeared. He immediately noticed the missing mask. "Cheating death, I see," he said.

I shrugged. "Every coal mine needs a canary."

He smiled and led the way into the mess hall with short, quick steps, returning salutes with a snappy, "Air assault!" Petraeus's upper torso was stiff and slightly canted, as if he were breasting a headwind. Three years earlier, he had survived the abrupt collapse of a parachute sixty feet up while skydiving; his shattered pelvis had been reassembled with a plate and long screws. At five foot nine and 155 pounds, he reminded me of George Bernard Shaw's description of Field Marshal Bernard L. Montgomery: "an intensely compacted hank of wire."

Pakistani kitchen workers scooped fried chicken, mashed potatoes, and canned corn onto our plates in the cafeteria line. Hundreds of soldiers tucked into their food while Fox TV and CNN blared from nine television sets. I followed Petraeus through the salad bar. In a back corner, Kayani's Ice Cream Corner offered French vanilla, banana, and other flavors, hand dipped, while Jungle Juice Junction provided mango, orange, and kiwi concoctions.

We found two empty chairs and Petraeus wasted no time describing the issues that had bedeviled him for the past month. Since taking command of the 101st the previous summer, he had been preoccupied with 1003 Victor, code name for the U.S. military's secret plan for conquering Iraq. But because of the political and diplomatic byplay in Washington over the winter, the 101st had not received a formal deployment order until February 6; Petraeus's immediate challenge was not the conquest of Baghdad, but rather how to get 5,000 vehicles, 1,500 shipping containers, 17,000 soldiers, and a couple hundred helicopters to Kuwait by mid-March, in time for any attack on Iraq. Deployment occurred in three immensely complex phases: from Fort Campbell to Jacksonville, Jacksonville to Kuwait City, Kuwait City to a battle assembly area. Army logisticians called the phases fort to port, then port to port, then port to foxhole.

He speared a forkful of salad and rattled through the events of the past few weeks. To haul equipment from Fort Campbell to Jacksonville required 1,400 rail cars. The CSX rail-freight company had promised four thirty-car trains each day, but as the deployment began only three a day, on average, had arrived. "I had a conference call with the president of CSX at eleven one night," Petraeus said. "He was on the phone with some of his executives and I was trying to explain to him why it was absolutely critical that we get to the port as quickly as possible. The ships were going to be there on certain dates. There was no margin for error. As I was telling him this, he interrupted me, twice."

"Did you lose your temper?" I asked.

"No, but I told him he was contributing to the diminished combat effectiveness of my division. There was a long silence on the other end. He fixed it."

One challenge led to others. Several hundred stevedores hired in Jacksonville insisted on two-hour lunch breaks and hourly pauses. The military, never tolerant of goldbricking, fired them and used soldiers and nonunion supervisors to load the ships; the assistant division commander for support, Brigadier General Edward J. Sinclair, had personally guided vehicles into the hold at 3 A.M. When Washington delayed the deployment order, which among other things provided the legal authorization needed to pay for moving the division, Petraeus concocted an elaborate training exercise that happened to take 112 helicopters to Jacksonville; mechanics there removed the rotor blades and shrink-wrapped the fuselages in protective plastic for eventual loading onto the ships. When quartermasters balked at issuing desert camouflage uniforms to the 101st—although forty thousand extra sets were in storage at Fort Campbell—Petraeus appealed to the Army's vice chief of staff, who ordered the uniforms released so the troops would not go to the desert in the forest-green pattern designed for war in northern Europe.

Petraeus spoke with an intriguing blend of urgency and irony. Clearly he was entranced by the problem-solving nature of high command. "The devil is in the details," he said, a phrase he would often repeat. Some senior Army officers, I knew, found him too intense, too competitive, too *different*. His father, Sixtus Petraeus, a Dutch sea captain, had taken refuge in New York when World War II began, than married a Brooklyn woman whom he met at the Seamen's Church Institute. After commanding a Liberty ship through the war, the elder Petraeus eventually gave up sea duty to work for a New York power company. He settled in Cornwall, a few miles north of the U.S. Military Academy at West Point. His son would arrive at the academy as a new cadet in July 1970, at the bottom of the war in Vietnam, when a military career and the five-year service obligation required of academy graduates appealed to few seventeen-year-old American boys.

Dave Petraeus, whose cadet nickname was Peaches, finished near the top of the class of 1974. "A striver to the max, Dave was always 'going for it' in sports, academics, leadership, and even his social life," the academy yearbook observed. A month after graduation, he married Holly Knowlton, daughter of Lieutenant General William A. Knowlton, the academy's superintendent. Petraeus had kept their engagement secret until cadet captains had been selected before his senior year. "I had worked my ass off and I didn't want anybody saying that I was a cadet captain because I was going to marry the supe's daughter."

As an infantry lieutenant assigned to an airborne unit in Italy, Petraeus was "very, very focused," recalled an officer who served in the same unit. "It was unusual to find an officer that young who was so directed." Even when he was merely a captain, his confidence and expanding résumé led one officer to dub him Superman. Over the next twenty-five years, he alternated command and staff assignments—including peacekeeping tours in Haiti and Bosnia—with duty as an aide to several of the Army's most prominent four-star generals: John R. Galvin, Carl E. Vuono, and Henry H. Shelton when they were, respectively, NATO supreme commander, Army chief of staff, and chairman of the Joint Chiefs of Staff. (One skeptical and perhaps envious peer called Petraeus "a professional son.") Along the way he earned a doctorate in international relations from Princeton University. His dissertation, "The American Military and the Lessons of Vietnam," examined the caution that seized the high command after that catastrophe, a caution that Petraeus shared by disposition.

In the mid-1970s he went to Ranger School, perhaps the Army's toughest physical and psychological challenge. Three prizes were awarded to signify the honor graduates in each class; Petraeus won all three. During one grueling exercise, he tied a rope around another Ranger candidate and virtually dragged him through the course. A soccer player and expert skier at West Point, Petraeus at fifty remained obsessive about what he called the p.t. culture. When he was a brigade commander in the 82nd Airborne Division, according to a former superior, his competitive ardor sometimes caused him "to drive young officers half his age into the ground like tent pegs." Recently he had run an Army ten-mile race in under sixty-four minutes. At Fort Campbell, a staff officer told me, "If anyone beats him in the shorter runs, four miles or so, he takes them out for ten miles and smokes them."

In 1991, shortly after taking command of a battalion in the 101st, Petraeus was watching an infantry squad practice assaulting a bunker with live grenades and ammunition. Forty yards away, a rifleman tripped and fell, hard. Petraeus never saw the muzzle flash. The M-16 round struck just above the "A" in his uniform name tag on the right side of his chest, and blew through his back. Had it hit above the "A" in "U.S. Army," on the left side over his heart, he would have been dead before he hit the ground.

He staggered back and collapsed. Standing next to him was Brigadier General Jack Keane, the assistant division commander, who by 2003 would be the Army's four-star vice chief of staff. "Dave, you've been shot," Keane told him. "I want you to keep talking. You know what's going on here, David. I don't want you to go into shock."

Keane later described the day for me. "He was getting weaker, you could see that. He said, 'I'm gonna be okay. I'll stay with it.' We got him to the hospital at Campbell and they jammed a chest tube in. It's excruciating. Normally a guy screams and his body comes right off the table. All Petraeus did was grunt a little bit. His body didn't even move. The surgeon told me, 'That's the toughest guy I ever had my hands on.' "

A medevac helicopter flew Petraeus, with Keane at his side, to Vanderbilt University Medical Center in Nashville, sixty miles away. "It was a Saturday and I was afraid the top guys wouldn't be on duty. I had them call ahead to make sure their best thoracic surgeon was available. We got off the helicopter and there's this guy they'd called off the links, still in his golf outfit, pastel colors and everything." It was Dr. Bill Frist, who a decade later would become majority leader of the U.S. Senate. More than five hours of surgery followed. "Petraeus recuperated at the Fort Campbell hospital and he was driving the hospital commander crazy, trying to convince the doctors to discharge him. He said, 'I am not the norm. I'm ready to get out of here and I'm ready to prove it to you.' He had them pull the tubes out of his arm. Then he hopped out of bed and did fifty push-ups. They let him go home."

For all his experience and accomplishments, Petraeus had not yet been to war. In an army full of veterans, whose fighting experience in the turbulent epoch following the Cold War ranged from Panama to Afghanistan, the absence of a combat patch on his right sleeve was conspicuous. I suspected that he was keen to earn the credential of the blooded vet.

We had finished eating but lingered over our trays. Soldiers on either side sawed at their chicken legs with flimsy plastic cutlery or stared at the television newscast, ignoring the two-star general next to them. "It's very important that our helicopter pilots have time to get accustomed to flying conditions here, which are a lot different than they are back home," Petraeus said. Four Blackhawk crewmen from another unit had been killed the previous week in a dust storm. A preliminary investigation indicated that the helicopter had slammed into the ground at more than 100 knots, with the nose inclined eighteen degrees and the fuselage canted twenty-seven degrees to the right—symptoms of severe pilot disorientation. Extra fuel tanks on the Blackhawk had made the crash particularly fiery.

Petraeus was determined to minimize the chance of further disasters by providing his eight hundred aviators at least four days and nights of acclimation flying before he certified that they were ready to fly in combat. Within a week or so, 150 Apaches would be based at Udairi airfield in northern Kuwait, fully seven of the Army's fifteen Apache battalions. "I wish Saddam Hussein could just see that, see them lined up out there, all that killing power. I have to believe that it would bring him to his senses."

I asked how the United States would respond if Saddam employed chemical weapons.

"No one knows what will happen if the Iraqis use chemicals," Petraeus said. "It's not at all clear that he has the capacity to use them effectively. It's not that simple, and the intel on where they are seems a little shaky. I don't believe that the national command authority will decide on a course until they're forced to make that decision."

The mess hall had nearly emptied by the time we dropped our trays at the wash rack and stepped out onto Avenue D. Red warning lights blinked atop the Scud goalposts. If war with Iraq was to come, the U.S. Army would be led by division and brigade commanders who, like Petraeus, had joined the service in the wake of the Vietnam War, had endured that battered and disheartened postwar military, and now had inherited leadership of the service. After a quarter century of keeping faith and learning the art of command, their hour had come round.

Politically liberal sensibilities are rare in the Army's senior officer ranks. But I knew that Petraeus, by virtue of his intellect and long experience at the elbow of senior generals, was a nuanced thinker. "A certain degree of intellectual humility is a good thing," he said before we went our separate ways. "There aren't always a helluva lot of absolutely right answers out there."

What had struck me more forcefully than Petraeus's subtle mind, however, was his description of a recent electronic exercise in which an exceptionally robust "enemy" had inflicted substantial casualties on U.S. forces. "Yet at the end of the day the board is swept clean. You start over and send the electrons into battle again," Petraeus said. "In this"—he gestured at the little world around us at Camp Doha—"it's real, and real people will die."

On Tuesday morning, March 4, Trey Cate took Dwyer and me into Kuwait City to get our official press passes from the Combined Forces Land Component Command, which controlled all Army and Marine forces gathering in Kuwait. The CFLCC media center was now ensconced at the Hilton Hotel, and we drove down the boulevard that paralleled the handsome corniche. The city looked rich and manicured. A dozen years earlier, after the Iraqi occupation, it had lacked electricity and running water, and greasy smoke from a thousand sabotaged oil wells blanketed the entire country. We passed the Al-Corniche Health Club, Fuddrucker's, Applebee's, and billboards extolling the Five-Star Burger at Hardee's. An innocent-abroad soldier next to me asked, "Can they read English here, or do they just write it on the signs for us?"

The Hilton made Camp Doha seem like the trench line at Verdun. Piped-in baroque airs played while gardeners tended the pansy beds at the base of perfectly pruned palms. Kuwaiti men in elegant white robes and onyx cuff links talked on their cell phones and worked their worry beads, starched head scarves held in place with a double coil of black braid around the skull. Contractors whacked tennis balls on the nearby courts or lounged on the sand beneath beach umbrellas. Around the turquoise pool, a few American officers sipped fruit drinks garnished with little paper parasols; their identity was betrayed by their crew cuts and farmer tans, and by the gas masks worn on the hip of their swimsuits. Reporters could be found in the Star-bucks, in the omelette and waffle bar, and in the lounge, which served Budweiser products, all scrupulously nonalcoholic.

"I would say," the combat photographer Robert Capa once wrote, "that the war correspondent gets more drinks, more girls, better pay, and greater freedom than the soldier." At the Hilton, the amenitites appeared evenly divided. Capa had landed with his Burberry raincoat in the first wave at Omaha Beach and had ended the war in Paris, having a torrid affair with Ingrid Bergman. There were no Ingrids evident in the lobby here, but Capa aspirants lurked everywhere.

Almost no one had been satisfied with news coverage of the Persian Gulf War, where most reporters had been kept at arm's length from the action. "Embedding" was a fair effort by the Pentagon to allow greater transparency of military operations. Contrary to conventional wisdom, it was not a new concept; I had been embedded with the Marines in Somalia and with the 1st Armored Division in Bosnia. Nor was the battalion of nearly 800 embeds unprecedented in size—557 accredited print and radio correspondents covered the Normandy landings with Capa, filing 700,000 words on the first day, and at least 500 reporters had covered the Union Army's actions during the Civil War. In this war, 527 journalists would actually cross into Iraq, and coverage would intensify to the point that some 6,000 stories a week were being filed.

Yet this deployment was hardly business as usual, given the animosity that had persisted between the military and the media for a generation. One in five embeds worked for a foreign news organization, including several from countries hostile to the U.S. government. There also seemed to be a good-faith effort to integrate journalists into most military operations, from company to corps level, although they were conspicuously absent from among the thousands of Special Operations troops in the region. Unit commanders had received "formal media guidance" in the form of a twenty-seven-page order that essentially insisted they cooperate. A booklet prepared by the 101st Airborne, "A Soldier's Guide to the Republic of Iraq," contained a four-page section called "Dealing with the Media." The advice included "eight steps to successful interviews." ("Step 4—answer the question.") The next chapter, "Dangerous Animals," warned that "there are 46 species of poisonous snakes in the region."

As for the reporters, it was hard not to recall the fate of Mark Kellogg, a newspaperman who had persuaded the 7th Cavalry to take him along on an expedition to the High Plains in 1876. "I go with Custer, and will be at the death," Kellogg wrote, all too presciently. I would be in a division headquarters, where the risks were reasonable; but many of my colleagues lived at the point of the spear, in battalions and companies. If some saw themselves as swashbuckling heirs to Hemingway and Kipling, John Reed and Richard Harding Davis, so be it. No one could know that sixteen journalists soon would be dead in Iraq, according to a tally later published in the *Columbia Journalism Review,* or that it would be more dangerous to be a reporter in the coming war than to fly combat sorties.

I wolfed down a Hilton club sandwich, then signed a CFLCC document in which I pledged not to divulge certain types of information, such as troop movements. The ground rules resembled those imposed on reporters in Vietnam.

A public-affairs captain gave me my new laminated badge. It warned that the "bearer must be escorted at all times," a requirement that was immediately and universally ignored. I was no longer just another hack with too much baggage. I was, according to the credential now hanging from a lanyard around my neck, "Embedded Journalist 03-063-018."

3

"THIS THING IS GOING TO GO"

Most of the enlisted troops and officers from the 101st who were billeted temporarily at Camp Doha had been wedged into Bay 7 of Warehouse 6. A note from the headquarters commandant taped to the metal door advised, "Hotel 6 is coming under new management. The bay will be straightened up and dressed right. We need to squeeze in more cots." As additional chalks arrived from Fort Campbell, more collapsible cots were indeed squeezed in, until 210 soldiers lived in an area half the size of a football field, giving the warehouse the rude ambience of Calcutta. Major Brian Coppersmith, a division staff officer who occupied a cot down the row from Dwyer and me, likened it to "a Greyhound bus. The more people you cram aboard, the less they talk to one another."

Crowding made for aggressive claim-staking. Notices on the blue portable toilets outside Warehouse 6 displayed the silhouette of a kangaroo and a warning: "These dunnies are for the use of Australian Task Force personnel. Cheers, mate." But crowding also allowed close study of the U.S. Army in microcosm. If Bay 7 represented a very tiny fraction of the nearly half million soldiers in the service, it still looked roughly typical of the larger Army racially: 59 percent white, 25 percent black, 10 percent Hispanic, and 7 percent classified as "other." Our little world also reflected the reality that America in the twenty-first century could not wage war without women. Fifteen percent of the Army was now female—including ten thousand of sixty-seven thousand officers—and more than one soldier in every ten was married to another soldier; several husband-and-wife teams occupied Bay 7 and the neighboring hostels, swapping sad stories of young children abruptly left in the care of grandparents or other surrogates.

Bay 7 also reflected the Army's youth. The up-or-out promotion system, under which those who did not continue to rise through the ranks were forced to leave, meant that even career officers retired, on average, as lieutenant colonels at age forty-three, after twenty-two years' service.

Occasional expressions of truculence could be heard at Doha, a "bring-me-Saddam's-head-on-a-spit" pugnacity. One linguist wore a T-shirt that said, "I Learned Arabic So You Don't Have To." But most soldiers evinced a cool detachment toward their potential Iraqi adversaries. Certainly no hate lodged in their bones. Many had an inchoate conviction that this deployment was somehow linked to the terror attacks of September 11, 2001, a delusion encouraged by the nation's political leadership. Long before 9/11, however, the Army had become an expeditionary force that careered among global hot spots. If they were modern legionnaires, these soldiers nevertheless thought of themselves as defenders of a secular faith embracing sundry liberties and entitlements, including many that were noble, and others—such as the daily consumption of more than 25 percent of the world's oil supply by only 5 percent of the world's population—that were less so.

Outside Bay 7, shortly after my initial dinner with Petraeus, I overheard the following conversation between two privates:

SOLDIER 1: "This guy who represents Iraq at the UN keeps saying that we want to take over all the oil in the region. C'mon! Get over yourself."

SOLDIER 2: "I don't think we even *want* the Arab region."
SOLDIER 1: "We don't. Too much of a hassle."

One advantage to cheek-by-jowl living was the opportunity for expedited friendships. Among my favorite officers in the 101st was Lieutenant Colonel Jim Larsen, the deputy G-3, or division operations officer, who had been so violently sick in Afghanistan the previous year that in ten days he dropped twenty pounds. Larsen had spent a decade in the Special Forces, and in December 1989 he parachuted with Army Rangers into Rio Hato during the invasion of Panama. After the fighting died down, the men were given time to clean up, rest, and read mail from home.

"There were boxes and boxes of Christmas cards addressed 'to any soldier' from well-wishers in the States," Larsen told me. "Guys just sat there weeping openly as we read through these cards. There had been such a buildup of emotional tension that all it took was a Christmas card from a stranger to release it.

"I've wondered," he added, "whether there's a similar tension building here, without the soldiers even realizing it."

Another neighbor, who lived five cots over, was the division's senior lawyer, Colonel Richard Hatch. One morning I sidled over to chat about the many legal issues that seemed to infest modern warfare. I knew from Petraeus that the list of potential Iraqi targets also included an appendix of some ten thousand protected sites—mosques, schools, archaeological digs, hospitals. The appendix changed daily and even hourly as intelligence was refined. Certain target categories, known as the Big Seven, also mutated. Number four among the Big Seven, for example, had been Al-Qaeda, the organization responsible for the September 11 attacks; but that was amended in early March to a more generic "terrorist groups," which included fourteen organizations. Some protected sites would lose that status if they were occupied by Iraqi military forces. Other targets required approval by Central Command in Qatar, or even by the secretary of defense, before they could be attacked; among these were places whose attack was likely to incur "thirty or more estimated non-combatant casualties."

Hatch was straightening his sleeping bag. He was tall and bony, with a prominent Adam's apple and an expression of wry preoccupation. A copy of the *Book of Mormon* lay in his kit.

"There are seventeen attorneys, plus two defense lawyers, deployed in the division," he told me. "Each brigade has a BOLT, a brigade operational law team. In Afghanistan, every battalion that deployed wanted a lawyer. Things have certainly become more legalistic. I came into the Army in 1982. The invasion of Grenada occurred a year later, and shortly after that the Ranger battalions began deploying with lawyers whenever they went anywhere. When we began to get into a lot of these operations-other-than-war, like peace enforcement, where soldiers spent a lot of time talking to local mayors and that sort of thing, all of a sudden everybody said, 'Oh, that sounds like something a lawyer would do.' "

Some of the legal work was prosaic—including reviewing the many contracts signed by the Army with local vendors, for instance. "The Kuwaitis are taking full advantage of this opportunity," Hatch said with a faint smile. "They are making some money." The lease on a four-wheel-drive vehicle that recently had been available for $1,500 a month now cost $3,000. But for the Army at this point, money seemed inconsequential.

Hatch talked about the rules of engagement intended to regulate how force was applied. The 101st had distributed orange-and-yellow ROE cards, which included ten brief scenarios intended to provide soldiers with practical guidance. Number 7, for instance, advised:

> Your unit comes under fire, and you notice a young civilian woman who appears to be pointing to the location where friendly

troops are concealed. Based on her actions, those locations are then targeted. Response: Shoot to eliminate the threat. The woman has become a combatant.

But the CFLCC had just printed 150,000 ROE cards of its own for distribution to the troops. They were similar to but not identical with the division's cards, and I asked Hatch if all this legal advice might befuddle a nineteen-year-old private. He gave a slight shrug.

"Our thought process goes: Can we, and then, should we? If we're taking fire from a mosque, can we return fire? Absolutely. Should we? Well, that's another question. Maybe it will be possible to go around it rather than risk being on the front page of every newspaper in the country, and being live on CNN."

Can we, and then, should we? That seemed like a fair Socratic interrogatory, not only for a rifleman deciding whether to shoot up a minaret, but also for the strategic conduct of the world's sole remaining superpower.

If Camp Doha had some undeniably penal characteristics— because of terror threats, no one could leave without signed permission from a colonel or general—it also was fabulously odd. A yellow Swedish street sweeper—a Brodd-son 2500 Scandia— rolled through the streets with the Sisyphean task of cleaning the dust from this dust bowl. On the north end of the base, soldiers ordered latte and fresh croissants in a little trailer called the Green Beans Café. An Abrams tank occasionally rumbled past with a sign banging against the fender: "Road Test."

Down the street from Warehouse 6, a German chemical detection platoon had built a *Biergarten* behind razor wire, with festive lanterns and high round tables of the sort seen in Berlin pubs. On 15th Street, Company A of the 152nd Infantry, an

Army Reserve unit from Vincennes, Indiana, often fired up a Weber grill for a Hoosier barbecue. In front of an adjacent warehouse, I watched two Czech soldiers flip back the tarpaulin from a truck bed and unload fifty cases of Radegast *pivo*; General Order No. 1 evidently did not apply to foreign troops. As Dwyer and I walked to another stupendous mess-hall breakfast— French toast, oatmeal, bacon, sausage, eggs—we passed 101st soldiers who barked, "Morning, sir. Air assault!" Dwyer answered with the *Times*'s slogan: "Morning, sir. All the news that's fit to print!"

My favorite place to eavesdrop was the checkout line at the PX. Power-shopping soldiers bound for the desert stood with their wire baskets full of baby wipes and sunblock, thumbing through the *National Enquirer* ("Streisand AIDS Tragedy") and the *Star* ("Brad: I'm in Big Trouble"). What kind of trouble, I wondered, could Brad be in?

"She has a great body," a soldier standing next to me one morning told another. "You just didn't see her from behind." A sergeant just ahead sighed heavily. "Why are you asking 'Why?' " he asked another NCO. "I argued when I got here that it made no sense, and they shot me in both feet. Bullshit moving at the speed of light is still bullshit." A private first class holding two cartons of Marlboro Lights said, "There's this sweet gun called a Spider. It can fire three hundred and ninety rounds a minute." He gave a maniacal chuckle.

Late on Wednesday afternoon, March 5, I walked over to the garrison commander's headquarters to see the man in charge of Camp Doha, Colonel Ulysses Brown, Jr. I found him in a spacious office with four leather armchairs and a leather couch arranged on a blue rug. A replica of the Statue of Liberty crowned a filing cabinet; behind Brown's desk stood American, Kuwaiti, U.S. Army, and Third Army flags on varnished staffs. The colonel seemed stern and rather humorless. "Everyone in this headquarters lives in terror of him," a staff officer had told me in a whisper. "I've never received an ass-chewing like the one I got from him on my first day on the job."

"It's grown from about eight hundred people living on Doha to the current seventy-eight hundred," Brown said. "The base was initially established after the Gulf War to support a brigade set of equipment. Now it is supporting more than two divisions." Civilian contractors, who these days accompany every U.S. military deployment, provided water, food, Porta-Johns, and "access control"—another forty security guards had just been hired. At Doha the biggest contractor was a consortium named Combat Support Associates, Ltd. "The CSA contract has grown extensively since the buildup began," Brown said. "They were authorized twenty-two hundred people last summer, and now it's up to twenty-eight hundred and still growing. Fourteen hundred of those are TCNs"—third-country nationals.

Outside Doha, nine camps had been built in the Kuwaiti outback. A tenth was on the drawing board. Brown rattled off their names: Virginia, Pennsylvania, New York, New Jersey, Victory, Commando, and so forth. (Several were named for states hit hardest by September 11.) When I asked how much they cost to operate collectively, he shrugged. "I have no idea."

As I stood to leave, Brown offered a last observation. "People ought to realize," he said, "that this thing is going to go."

I hesitated a moment. "What thing?"

"War," he said. "It's going to go."

At eight the next morning, March 6, I climbed into a sport-utility vehicle with E. J. Sinclair, the S, or assistant division commander for support. An Apache pilot who had recently commanded a brigade in Korea, Sinclair was large and cheerful, with a broad, open face, the sort of man whom other men instantly like. In the 1920s, his father had moved from Pennsylvania to Montana, where he became a rancher and ran a construction company.

Sinclair played basketball at West Point, including a year for legendary coach Mike Krzyzewski. Now, as a brigadier general, the S was the division's chief logistician.

We drove first to the Kuwait City port, threading a maze of oil-storage tanks, cranes, and security checkpoints manned by Kuwaiti guards who had posted a sign: "Solgers, this lane." The air smelled of brine and petroleum. We parked near the water and I followed Sinclair up six flights of stairs to the roof of the harbor administration building, which afforded a panoramic view of the piers. The first ship from Jacksonville, the USNS *Larry G. Dahl*, carried seventy-two helicopters and nearly two thousand vehicles for the 101st; she was scheduled to arrive at midnight. Three others now crossing the Mediterranean or the Red Sea were due within a week.

Sinclair pointed to a large concrete expanse extending from the nearest berth. "That parking lot—it's thirty-three acres—is what we'll use for rebuilding the aircraft. There are three hundred and fifty mechanics waiting for the first ship. We think we can assemble an Apache battalion in a day, a Blackhawk battalion in two days. With the Kiowas, you basically turn the key and fly off."

Four hundred shipping containers, twenty- or forty-footers, would be trucked directly to the various camps, including New Jersey, where the division main headquarters, or D-Main, would be. Each container was tagged with a bar-coded sticker that, in theory, allowed an electronic reader to determine what was inside and which unit owned it. But the division's hasty deployment had already caused difficulties. "You've probably heard," Sinclair said, "that the D-Main computer server is on ship three, and won't get here until March fourteenth or fifteenth. Somebody forgot to check to make sure that it was on the first ship." I hadn't heard.

Before we turned to head downstairs, Sinclair nodded toward the small courtyard below. "That's where the Iraqis executed the

Kuwaiti port commander when they rolled through here in August 1990," he said.

We got back into the SUV and headed north to Udairi airfield, a two-hour drive. I asked Sinclair what issues most preoccupied the S these days. He answered instantly: "Fuel." Engineers had built a pipeline from the port to Udairi, where more than a million gallons of JP-8 jet fuel were already stockpiled; the supply would grow to 7 million gallons in the next two weeks. (In a sensible move some years before, the Army had converted nearly all tactical vehicles to JP-8, from Humvees and trucks to tanks and helicopters.)

But hauling fuel hundreds of miles into Iraq was more complicated. Army planners calculated that the 10,000-vehicle cavalcade sweeping into Iraq needed to refuel about every one hundred kilometers, or five times between Kuwait and Baghdad. A single armored division could burn a half million gallons in a day. The 3rd Infantry Division, heavily mechanized with hundreds of tanks and personnel carriers, had 170 tanker trucks, most of them carrying 5,000 gallons. But JP-8 used in helicopters had to be filtered and tested to guarantee purity, so it required specially outfitted 2,500-gallon tankers. A pair of Apache battalions could drink more than 60,000 gallons in a single night's attack. For the 101st, with 256 helicopters, fuel choreography involved proper nozzles, hoses, truck maintenance, security, supply, positioning, and a hundred other variables. The Army calculated that it alone would burn 40 million gallons in three weeks of combat in Iraq, an amount equivalent to the gasoline consumed by all Allied armies combined during the four years of World War I.

I asked whether the Army, for reasons of cost, had rejected any of the division's requests.

"No," Sinclair replied.

"What are the chances of finding chemical or biological weapons in Iraq?"

He again answered instantly. "One hundred percent."

Sinclair had served as the S for nearly two months under the previous 101st commander, Major General Richard Cody, another Apache pilot who a dozen years earlier had been credited with firing the first shots of the Gulf War in an attack on an Iraqi radar site. I asked whether much had changed with Petraeus's arrival.

"Cody's style was to run through walls, and the men would run through those walls with him. He just had that effect on soldiers," Sinclair said. "General Petraeus is more cerebral, less emotional. I've asked him what the point is of running junior officers into the ground. What's that prove? So a guy isn't a great runner. Does that mean he isn't necessarily a great officer? Ben Freakley and I won't run with him. I've told him that I'll be happy to meet him on the basketball court anytime."

Beyond Mutlaa Ridge we turned onto a dusty trail and headed west. Udairi loomed into view, Oz-like. Half a dozen hangars and a row of prefabricated buildings lined the airfield. A scorched patch of sand marked the spot where an electrical fire had recently incinerated the camp's five mess tents within three minutes.

It was a windy day with poor visibility, but ghostly ranks of helicopters from the 11th Attack Helicopter Regiment and other units could be seen on the runway. The CIA occupied a compound encircled with cyclone fence and barbed wire; several Predators—the agency's unmanned aerial vehicles—were housed in the far hangar.

Among other duties, the S had responsibility for all Army aviation in the theater. "When I got here in mid-February there was really nobody in charge," Sinclair said. "Helicopters were flying around without much control over them. Now we're running the airfield almost like an aircraft carrier. The helicopters are parked according to what their mission is and when they're going out, which is how you do it on a carrier.

"There will be about two hundred and seventy helicopters here, plus twenty UAVs, and about eleven thousand people. It will be the largest gathering of attack helicopters in the history of the U.S. Army. That also makes it a prime target. Scares the hell out of me. If Saddam was ever able to get a Scud into the middle of this, it would be devastating."

Sinclair's small office was outfitted with cheap carpet, a desk, and a single chair. A brown band stained the floor beneath each wall where dust had sifted through the siding seams. He moved into an adjacent conference room and plopped into a folding chair. Soon he was joined by five of the Army's most senior aviators, who collectively had amassed tens of thousands of flying hours, in Apaches, Blackhawks, Chinooks, or Kiowas.

There was work to do, serious work, and one seemingly trivial item on Sinclair's agenda was in fact vital: Should helicopter blades be taped or painted? Apache and Blackhawk rotors revolve at such high speeds—1,456 feet per second at the tips—that blowing grit could bore through the titanium spar on the leading edge of each blade. Wormlike, a sand grain would then eat out the honeycombed material inside the blade, which might unbalance the helicopter aerodynamically and cause a crash. Traditionally, the blade edges were protected with strips of black tape, which had to be reapplied after every mission or two. But taping was time-consuming, difficult in the desert, and required an adhesive that wore badly in hot weather. Some aviation experts insisted that a thick coat of black paint, reapplied to the edges after every flight, was an effective substitute for tape.

Rotor blades were in short supply—the 101st had only five spare Blackhawk blades, which cost $80,000 each. More to the point, each Apache cost $20 million, and each Blackhawk carried the souls of four crewmen and as many as sixteen passengers. The tape-versus-paint conundrum neatly illuminated the thousand technical challenges facing every commander. You had to sweat the details in the Army or you failed, and failure meant dead soldiers. The issue had been hotly debated by Army aviators for months—"I'll go to my grave before I put tape on," one helicopter battalion commander had told me. "Go with the paint." While some other units still opted for tape, Petraeus had bought thirteen thousand cans of black spray paint for the 101st. But second-guessing persisted outside the division—and inside.

Sinclair opened the discussion with a disclaimer. "I'm not convinced that we need to revisit this issue. We spent a hundred and twenty thousand dollars on spray paint, and I still think that's the right thing to do."

"The downside is that once you get a hole in the blade—well, you know what that means," said Chief Warrant Officer Jack Bartol. A former Apache test pilot, Bartol had been flying for twenty-three years and was the principal aviation adviser in the 101st. "It's a green-tab call. *I* don't care." "Green-tabber" is Army slang for a commander. Bartol flashed a diffident smile that somehow suggested he cared very much.

"Yeah, but half you dicks say yes and the other half say no. You're not just worried about getting paint on your hands, are you?" Sinclair's lips smiled. His eyes did not.

"I would like the airplane I'm flying to be taped," Bartol said. "But if it's painted, that'd be fine, too." He held up his hands, open-palmed.

"Unless somebody convinces me, we're going to paint," Sinclair said. "We're not going to all do our own thing."

Someone mentioned that the Raytheon Corporation had a contractor team at Udairi. Sinclair sent for the team's helicopter maintenance specialist.

"I know from the last time"—the Gulf War in 1991—"that you can land with silver blades, easy," Bartol said. "But you land two, three days with silver blades, you get holes in them."

Lieutenant Colonel Jim Lauer, a Blackhawk pilot and assistant chief of staff, said, "Any kind of protection is better than none."

"If I owned my personal Apache," Bartol repeated, "I would want it taped."

Sinclair gave him a quizzical look, perhaps contemplating the likelihood of a warrant officer owning a $20 million helicopter.

He sighed heavily and shuffled a stack of three-by-five note-cards. The cards slipped through his fingers, scattering across the floor.

"It's a question of how long you're planning on flying them," Bartol said.

"Months. A year."

Bartol nodded. "It's a helluva decision, I know."

"To do it right with paint," Lauer added, "takes a whole can per blade."

Roger Gonzalez, the Raytheon contractor, walked into the room. Chipper and well-groomed, he had the name "Speedy" tattooed on his right bicep. Gonzalez handed Sinclair a rubbery strip of new 3M tape. "If you're going to do a lot of dust land-ings," he said, "that beats 'em up bad."

Sinclair replied with a baleful look. Gonzalez plowed ahead. "Either way, the blades have to be cleaned first. Also, the tape needs to cure twenty-four hours before you fly.

"Give it some cure time or you're going to be shredding," Gonzalez added. Shredded tape could snarl the tail rotor. He mentioned another helicopter unit. "Theirs is a mess. I don't know what they're doing, but those blades look like shredded wheat."

The S exhaled with a theatrical hiss. "Well, that gives me a lot of confidence." Everyone began to talk at once until Sinclair cut them off. "Hey, guys, we're not dicking around. You've got four or five days to get ready, and then we're going to go do some-thing. You guys aren't helping me any." The *something* hung in the air.

Sinclair studied the ceiling. "Maybe we go back and tell him"—there was no need to specify Petraeus—"that we tape only the Apaches. He isn't going to like it."

"I'm going to support you whatever you do," Bartol said. "I'm not trying to piss in your cornflakes."

Gonzalez mentioned that several helicopters were parked in the maintenance hangar next door. He suggested a quick inspection.

As we walked outside, Sinclair extravagantly praised the new Apache Longbow, how it needed only a fraction of a second to "unmask"—pop up from behind a hill—and record more than a thousand potential targets that were then automatically sorted by priority and targeted by up to sixteen Hellfire missiles. From a range of several miles, a Longbow battalion could reduce an enemy armored brigade of more than a hundred tanks and personnel carriers to smoking wreckage in twenty minutes.

Inside the hangar two Blackhawks stood eviscerated, their blades plucked off and hydraulic lines exposed. Sinclair studied a Blackhawk blade that had been laid across several sawhorses. Another warrant officer, Brian Twigg, listened as Sinclair explained his dilemma. "Sir," Twigg said, "you gotta do the tape."

Sinclair grinned, this time with his eyes. "If this gets dicked up, I'm gonna come looking for you." He threw a big arm around Twigg, who was a head shorter.

At 3:20 P.M., as we drove south, Sinclair called Petraeus on his cell phone. "I hear some pluses about the tape," he told him, "but in my gut I remember the problems we've had with it."

Back at Doha, a few phone calls solved Sinclair's dilemma. Hardly a single roll of tape for the 101st could be found in Kuwait. The division's supply had been stored in an East Coast warehouse that had collapsed during a recent blizzard. "All that discussion," Sinclair said with a shake of his head, "and there's no tape."

Thirteen thousand cans of spray paint would not go to waste. Another small crisis had been finessed. That, I realized, was what leaders did: they finessed an endless succession of crises. "I've been in command for six of the last seven years," Colonel William H. Forrester, who commanded the Blackhawks and Chinooks in the 159th Aviation Brigade, had told me. "And no one has ever called me after nine-thirty P.M.—not once—to say, 'Hey, Bill, did you have a nice day?' "

The tape-versus-paint issue seemed prosaic, yet it illuminated certain features of Army culture. Debate was encouraged. Dissent was tolerated, grudgingly. Absolute answers were rare, and comfort with ambiguity was a command virtue. Banter helped bridge the gap between ranks; it also prevented life-and-death decisions from becoming too oppressive. And camaraderie was a rough-hewn communion, a bond of shared circumstances and collective fate for which soldiers would warrant their lives.

Fifty-knot winds and heavy seas delayed the arrival of the first ship, the *Dahl,* much to the irritation of every officer in the 101st. Wind tore sheet metal from the Doha warehouses and filled the bays with murky brown talc that obscured the far wall. We slept in paper respirators and awoke on Friday, March 7, coated in dust. Sergeant Mark Swart, who occupied the cot next to mine, rubbed the grit from his front teeth with a forefinger. "This is *shit,*" he said. "Let's go to war and get it over with."

With Swart at the wheel, Dwyer and I drove thirty miles west to Camp Victory, to visit the Blackhawk and Chinook battalions awaiting the arrival of their helicopters. The wind intensified at noon as we entered the gates, cutting visibility to a few feet beyond the front bumper. Swart stepped outside to ask directions, only to have a gust wrench the SUV door from his hand—springing it badly, with a sound of tearing metal—and snatch his cap, which was last seen tumbling across the desert toward Syria.

In goggles and bandannas, Dwyer and I trudged across the sand for a closer look at a pathetic sight: hundreds of soldiers, whose large tents had blown away during the night, had piled rucksacks, weapons, and MRE cases on their exposed cots to keep the cots from also disappearing. Faces wrapped in balaclavas, the troops huddled in sleeping bags for protection. Many had been up all night, holding on to guy ropes like circus roustabouts. Others, unable to find their boots and goggles in the gale, sheltered in a shower trailer. At least seventeen tents, each capable of sleeping sixty, had collapsed or vanished, including the camp mess tents.

"We're in self-preservation mode right now," Captain Jeff Beirlein, a company commander, told us. When he smiled, his teeth were brown with dust. A twenty-seven-year-old Chinook pilot confided that his second wedding anniversary was approaching; he had spent the first one in Afghanistan. "All I want to do," he said, "is go home and knock up my wife."

The wind died, the skies faired, and just before dawn on Saturday the *Dahl* slipped into port. At sixty-two thousand tons and 956 feet, she required two berths, numbers 18 and 19. The great slab of a stern ramp was lowered and nearly two thousand tons of cargo began pouring from the holds, including kit for three infantry battalions. Two huge yellow gantry cranes lifted ammunition crates onto the dock—everything from Hellfire missiles to rifle rounds—while Humvees, fuel trucks, and hospital generators rolled off the rear.

I found E. J. Sinclair on C Deck, wearing a white construction helmet with a brigadier's single star on it. The roar from the ship's ventilators was deafening, so Sinclair simply smiled and pointed to a dozen soldiers in hard hats who ripped the plastic shrink-wrap off an Apache, then hooked a tow bar to the rear wheel. A John Deere tractor dragged the helicopter down the ramp. A blade container, painted olive drab, bore the admonition "Do Not Push Against Skin with Forklift Prongs." Every square foot of the deck not occupied by helicopters was covered by elliptical fuel tanks and square crates containing fire control radars, neatly stacked despite a warning chalked on each one: "Do Not Stack!"

Lieutenant Colonel Joe Dunaway, commander of the 101st's aviation maintenance battalion, led me up a ladder and onto the weather deck, where soldiers were unchaining a Chinook. The noise outside was slightly less oppressive. Sunshine richocheted off the blue water in silver spears. "The door height on the rear ramp of the *Dahl* is sixteen feet. Two aircraft are lower than that, the Apache and the Kiowa, so they can roll off," Dunaway said. "The Blackhawks and the Chinooks are taller, so they have to be lifted off the ship and lowered by crane. We can do one aircraft about every twelve minutes, from the time we hook them up to the time we set them on the ground. There are seventy-two helicopters on this ship, and ninety-six on the next one, the *Bob Hope*."

Dunaway watched as a newly unloaded Humvee crawled onto the dock, driven by a Pakistani longshoreman. Son of a national rodeo champion from Oklahoma, Dunaway had joined the Army as an armored cavalryman in Germany in 1985; some senior officers considered him the most valuable battalion commander in the division. "If you're living right, it all works," he said. "In the thirteen deployments I've made, this one has been the smoothest."

Before returning to Doha, I joined Sinclair for lunch in a clean, windowless dining room with a faded print of Venice on one wall. Our host was the *Dahl*'s skipper, Bradford Collins, a Maine native with a walrus mustache and blue coveralls with "Captain" stitched on the right breast pocket.

"We own this ship, you and me, the American taxpayer. I'm proud of that," Collins told us over cheeseburgers. "There are seven *Bob Hope*–class ships and eight *Watson*-class, including the *Dahl*." The fleet had been built after the Gulf War to permit quicker dispatch of expeditionary forces. It was not easy moving an army to a place as distant as Kuwait, but it was easier than it used to be. The retooling of the armed services—and particularly the Army—into an effective twenty-first-century force centered largely on a quest for mobility and intelligence. Army firepower was still predicated on five weapons systems originally designed after Vietnam to fight Soviet legions in central Europe: the Abrams tank, the Bradley Fighting Vehicle, the Apache attack helicopter, the Patriot air-defense missile, and the Multiple Launch Rocket System. Quickly hauling this aging "legacy force" to contemporary combat zones was half the battle. (Deploying the 101st alone was like moving a hundred Wal-Mart stores halfway around the world in three weeks, according to an Army analysis.) The Army also had prepositioned equipment sufficent to outfit seven brigades at depots in bad neighborhoods around the world, including Doha.

Collins raked his mustache with two fingers. "*Dahl* is bigger than the *Hope* by six inches," he said.

"I guess size matters," I said, "even when you're a thousand feet long. I know who Bob Hope is, but who was Dahl?"

"Ahh." Collins smiled and led us into the passageway. From a boom box in the galley came the strains of an old Buffalo Springfield song: "There's something happenin' here / What it is ain't exactly clear." A photo on one wall celebrated the "2001 Diego Garcia Volleyball Champions."

On the opposite wall a plaque commemorated Specialist Larry G. Dahl, who, while guarding a truck convoy near An Khe in South Vietnam on February 23, 1971, threw himself on an enemy hand grenade to save his comrades. He was awarded the Medal of Honor, posthumously. Larry Dahl was not yet twenty-two when he died.

4

THE LAND OF NOT QUITE RIGHT

New signs of impending war appeared every day. On March 9, commanders announced that all forces poised to attack Iraq would switch to Zulu time, a synchronization often imposed before combat operations. The adjustment sent the chronologically challenged—including those of us preoccupied with newspaper deadlines in the Eastern time zone—scurrying to the Doha post exchange in search of an extra wristwatch: 6 P.M. in Kuwait, which was 10 A.M. in Washington, would become 3 P.M. Zulu, the same as Greenwich Mean Time.

The Army, of course, used the twenty-four-hour clock, so that 6 P.M. became 1800, or 1000 EST, or 1500Z. Another adjustment would be required in a few weeks with the advent of daylight savings time, which was observed in Iraq and the United States but not in Kuwait or the Zulu world. If all this was a bit confusing, there could be little doubt that regardless of the precise time, the clock surely was ticking.

Antiwar protests continued to flare on six continents. The proposed UN Security Council resolution authorizing force against Iraq had little support beyond the United States and Britain, and seemed likely to fail even without a threatened French veto. On March 1, Turkey's parliament had narrowly voted to prohibit U.S. troops from using Turkish bases, the latest example of botched American diplomacy and another reminder of how Bush had failed to assemble an alliance comparable to the broad international coalition built by his father in 1991. Unless it was reversed, the Turkish decision precluded a second front from the north; three dozen ships, orbiting in the Mediterranean with equipment for the 4th Infantry Division, would now have to divert to the Persian Gulf, while the division's 17,000 soldiers— still waiting in Texas and Colorado—would be funneled through Kuwait City, in all likelihood after the shooting had started. Turkey's stand also emboldened other countries opposed to war.

At Doha, we followed such events with remote curiosity, as if watching from a great distance. Shopping carts at the PX cash registers previewed the dusty desert life to come: Ziploc bags, orange chemical sticks that glowed for twelve hours when snapped, spare bath towels, prickly-heat powder, Vaseline Intensive Care lotion, Chapstick, and CamelBak water pouches, which were worn as backpacks. Soldiers clutched boxes of Q-Tips like family heirlooms.

Subtle psychological changes could be sensed at Doha. Many troops now hoarded toilet paper, and scavenging became epidemic. A length of heavy cord found in the street provoked an internal dialogue: Can I use that? Will it fit in my rucksack? Soldiers spent hours repacking and rearranging. Fussing with your kit, I realized, consumed an enormous amount of time in the Army. Even the meticulously organized seemed to be incessantly rifling through various flaps, pockets, bags, and compartments, zipping and unzipping, snapping and unsnapping. The sound of tearing Velcro—or rather, hook-and-pile fastener tape— was the sound of the modern military.

In the mess hall, soldiers bound for the field gorged themselves on ice cream and doughnuts, not so much for culinary pleasure as to stockpile memories. Customers jammed the barbershops for a final high-and-tight; every extra millimeter of hair in the desert would be a nuisance. I also noticed that graffiti in the latrines dwelt on themes of infidelity and cuckoldry. Betrayal seemed to prey on the minds of young soldiers. Political commentary also grew more acerbic, like the graffito that read, "If you'd voted for Gore, you wouldn't be here."

All troops were ordered to begin carrying not only their gas masks but also their JLIST chemical-protective suits. As instructed, I pulled mine from the vacuum-sealed plastic bag and slipped it on to be sure no components were missing: pantaloon pants, baggy smock with a drawstring hood, gloves, shower cap, disinfectant wipes, atropine injectors, and my size thirteen rubber overshoes, which had been the only pair left when I drew my gear at Fort Campbell. All that was lacking was a clown car to pile into. Each suit was said to cost $221. Stuffing the ensemble into a canvas sack, I tossed it beneath my cot. The coal mine still needed a canary.

Mass at Our Lady of the Desert Parish drew a standing-room-only congregation to hear the Catholic chaplain deliver a rambling homily on "patience and courage" for the first Sunday of Lent, a time for "testing one's mettle, testing one's self." A young soldier in sneakers and jeans, pressed into duty as an altar boy, yawned hugely throughout the service. The sermon was so disjointed that I wondered if the priest was speaking in tongues. Dwyer, the product of a Jesuit education, shrewdly observed that the U.S. Army and the Society of Jesus shared a mutual love of ritual, hierarchy, and private languages.

The headquarters of the 101st tracked the division's progress through the Battle Update Briefing, or BUB, a twice-daily conference that had its own liturgical formality. The BUBs at Doha typically lasted for more than an hour and were held in Petraeus's office, a partitioned corner of a warehouse near the main gate. Three dozen staff officers on folding chairs jammed an eighteen-by-eighteen-foot room. A cheap Persian carpet covered the floor and a Screaming Eagle banner draped one wall. The room grew stifling despite a noisy oscillating fan, and those in the rear rows could barely hear. Exhausted officers with heavy eyelids nodded off, only to regain consciousness with an abrupt jerk, and the room echoed with hacking coughs from the dust-induced respiratory ailment known as Kuwaiti crud.

However inelegant, the BUB provided intimate glimpses of an army preparing for war. A PowerPoint projector balanced on a crate of bottled water flashed slide after slide, all stamped SECRET, while staff officers stood in a precise sequence to describe whatever issues had bedeviled them on that particular day. The minutiae could be fatuous—some mess-tent sergeants, for instance, had discovered they had to double-stack flimsy Kuwaiti chairs because large American butts were ending up on the floor after single chairs collapsed.

But more often the litany was sober if not somber: purchasing agents had combed Kuwait for 3,500 fire extinguishers following the conflagration of tents at Udairi; commanders needed an extra twenty thousand nine-volt batteries because, they had found, the new infrared signal lights designed to identify U.S. vehicles and prevent fratricide burned through a battery every night; the division had stockpiled six thousand tourniquets and more than ten thousand pressure bandages; and forty "negligent discharge" incidents had been logged across Kuwait, including episodes in which trigger-happy GIs shot at Kuwaiti and British vehicles.

The BUB on Tuesday, March 11, at 7:30 P.M. was typical. Petraeus entered two minutes late, carrying his large black notebook and a tan backpack containing his mask and JLIST. " 'Ten-*hut!*" a voice barked. Staff officers scrambled to their feet. "You got the room plenty hot," Petraeus said, and gestured for everyone to sit. An Air Force meteorologist led off with predictions of more foul weather, including a "wind event" that would cut visibility to two hundred meters. Then the division intelligence officer, the G-2, showed a sequence of reconnaissance and satellite photos with intricate details of Iraqi surface-to-air missile deployments southwest of Baghdad.

Virtually all of the 101st had already arrived in Kuwait, nearly sixteen thousand soldiers. But few units had any equipment beyond what they had lugged onto the eighty or so chalks from Fort Campbell. The *Bob Hope* was scheduled to berth that night, soon followed by the *Stockham*.

Since no one knew when the war would start, it remained uncertain whether the 101st would muster sufficient combat power in time to participate in the invasion. The U.S. attack plan had mutated dramatically over the past eighteen months, through roughly a dozen iterations with different names—such as VIGILANT GUARDIAN, Operations Plan BLUE, and IMMINENT BADGER—as well as different ambitions, from securing Iraqi oil fields to "isolating" Baghdad. The latest plan, COBRA II, was based on an attack by two corps—the Army's V Corps and a combined force of U.S. Marines and British troops—in order to extirpate Saddam Hussein's regime. Dramatic amendments were being made even into February, when the Army was told not to count on two tank divisions that had figured in V Corps plans. Moreover, the Army had been ordered to abandon its traditional scheme for moving combat forces overseas, a meticulous matrix known as the TPFDD, an abbreviation, pronounced "Tip-fid," for Timed, Phased Force Deployment Data. The TPFDD listed units scheduled to deploy and their priority sequence in order to guarantee that combat soldiers were properly accompanied by logistics and support units. Instead, in an effort to streamline and expedite the deployment, units were dispatched in ad hoc "force packages."

In consequence, the American assault force had shrunk by roughly half from the more than 200,000 troops initially called for. Speed, mobility, and the quick capture of Baghdad were now paramount. "This is a new paradigm for us," one general had said. "Get off the boat and fight." The sixteen-day air campaign planned to precede the ground invasion had been narrowed to twelve hours—compared with five weeks of preliminary bombing in 1991. Petraeus knew it was possible, even probable, that ground and air attacks would be launched simultaneously.

"The purpose of this division, initially, is to position the Apaches to get into the fight," he had told me over dinner. "Apaches are to be the star of the show." With the Marines and British to the east, the Army V Corps would rely on the 3rd Infantry Division to slash toward Baghdad along the western edge of the Euphrates valley, avoiding the marshy terrain between the Tigris and Euphrates Rivers. That division, fielding roughly twenty thousand soldiers and normally based in Georgia, had been training for months in Kuwait and was among the most lethal in the Army's history; its firepower included some 250 Abrams tanks, 260 Bradley Fighting Vehicles, Apache attack helicopters, and ample artillery. The 101st would follow the 3rd ID in trace, establishing at least two forward air refueling points— FARPs, in the inevitable acronym—deep inside Iraq.

These desert gas stations would allow the three Apache battalions from the 101st to attack Iraqi defenses on the southern and western approaches to Baghdad, helping clear a path for the 3rd ID and then the rest of the 101st. The Medina Division, which was perhaps the best provisioned of the six Republican Guard divisions, and which blocked Highways 1 and 8 into the capital, was to be obliterated.

Ultimately, part of the 101st could end up at Objective Lions, the code name for Saddam Hussein International Airport, although the attack plan at that point remained ambiguous. ("Flexible," one officer told me, "but *never* limp.") The scheme for capturing Baghdad was still a work in progress. The Army intended to establish three operating bases around the capital's western perimeter—code-named Lions, Saints, and Bears, after the professional football teams—while the Marines built a couple more on the east. Brigade combat teams of five thousand or more soldiers would launch raids into the city from these bases, chewing up Iraqi defenses and whittling away the regime. Which Army divisions controlled the respective operating bases would depend on how the up-country march to Baghdad progressed, as well as on technical issues such as communications capabilities. The V Corps commander, Lieutenant General Wallace, later told me he suspected that "as we got to Baghdad we'd reverse roles, with the 101st providing boots on the ground and 3 ID supporting them" in an infantry-intensive urban fight where tanks would be more vulnerable. But first the Army had to fight its way to Baghdad.

"The Medina is the key to this whole thing," Wallace had advised his subordinates in early March. "When the Medina is destroyed, it will send a message to the rest of the Republican Guard units and Saddam." Later, after Baghdad had indeed fallen, Wallace would elaborate: "Since we were coming from the south, we had to get rid of that dude. Our focus was always on the Medina Division, for twelve months. And the son-of-a-bitch never moved. We were tracking him all the time."

Yet if the 101st was tardy gathering itself in Kuwait, the war would start without the division. I knew that more was at stake than simply the glory of one proud unit. For many months the U.S. Army had been feuding with the secretary of defense, Donald Rumsfeld, who made no secret of his conviction that the Army was sluggish and hidebound, an image embodied by the failure in 1999 of a unit named Task Force Hawk to deploy Apaches into muddy Albania with sufficient alacrity during the Kosovo campaign. Numerous skirmishes and a few large battles had been waged over Rumsfeld's efforts to build a more agile force, capable of quick deployment, stealthy maneuver, and overpowering violence effected with precision weapons. Rumsfeld had scotched a new Army artillery system, the Crusader, as an obsolete behemoth, and he had politically castrated the Army chief of staff, General Eric Shinseki, by anointing his successor more than a year before Shinseki's scheduled retirement. There had even been talk of trimming the Army from ten divisions to eight, or perhaps of reorganizing the service to eliminate divisions in favor of supposedly more sprightly brigades.

Many retired and active-duty generals believed that Rumsfeld was politicizing the officer corps and caricaturing the Army. There was some truth in this. The concept, often heard in Washington, of "Clinton generals"—those inherited by the Bush administration, or skeptical of the Rumsfeld vision—was ludicrous and alarming. The Army, led by Shinseki, had begun "transforming" itself into a more supple creature—with an avowed capacity for "forced entry at multiple points"—long before George W. Bush took office.

But there also was some truth in the current stereotype: the Army could be club-footed, a dutiful but homely daughter, particularly when compared with her more nimble and glamorous sister services, whose leaders also had more public relations savvy. Disagreements between the Army and the Pentagon civilian leadership had grown toxic. When Shinseki on February 25 warned Congress that postwar Iraq could require "several hundred thousand" U.S. troops, the deputy defense secretary, Paul Wolfowitz, denounced the estimate as "wildly off the mark." Wolfowitz had testified in late February, "It's hard to conceive that it would take more forces to provide stability in post-Saddam Iraq than it would take to conduct the war itself and secure the surrender of Saddam's security force and his army. Hard to imagine."

So the Army was heading to Iraq with a grudge and with something to prove. A failure by the 101st—one of its most famous divisions, and a unit that often boasted of its murderous agility—to show up for the war would be, at best, dispiriting.

The BUB droned on. Five hundred bags of lime had been requisitioned for camp sanitation, and twenty thousand pairs of Wiley X sunglasses had been shipped. "If we have extra, we'll give them to the 3rd Division," Petraeus said. A voice in the rear quipped, "We'll trade them to get our toilet seats back."

Since December, the 101st's had spent $30 million to buy extra equipment, much of it suggestive of a medieval siege or the urban combat the Army hoped to avoid in Iraq: 162 battering rams, 486 grappling hooks, 81 folding assault ladders, 81 battle axes, 27 .50-caliber sniper rifles, 16,000 sets of reusable plastic hand-cuffs, optics that could see around corners. Another slide showed how much of the division's ammunition had arrived in Kuwait, including various missiles: 169 Hellfires, 216 Stingers, 106 Jave-lins, 96 TOWs.

Several officers rocked rhythmically in their chairs to stay awake. It was a rare major who could snatch more than three or four hours of sleep a night. Additional slides flashed onto the screen. A sequence of color-coded charts indicated the battle readiness of each subordinate unit within the 101st, in categories ranging from "shoot" and "move" to "communicate" and "train-ing." A green box meant the unit was more than 85 percent ready in a particular category. Amber and red indicated lower degrees of readiness, while black, for less than 50 percent readiness, marked a unit as demonstrably unprepared for combat. Because only one ship had berthed, the slides remained heavily peppered with black.

Petraeus's running commentary during the BUB made it clear that he was anxious to leave Doha for Camp New Jersey. But first the D-Main—the division main headquarters—had to be set up. The 101st's tactical operations center, or TOC, would occupy an enormous white tent, which had been custom built to allow more than a hundred staff officers to work in a single large room with all the electronic and communication equipment needed to control a division in combat. I had seen the tent at Fort Campbell—it lacked only a ringmaster and trapeze artists to complete the Ringling effect—and I understood why wags called it the TOC Mahal.

Unfortunately, the tent had gone missing. It was supposed to be aboard the *Dahl,* but could not be located. Quartermasters were poised to sweep through the *Bob Hope* in hopes that the container had been diverted to the second ship, just as the D-Main computer server had been sidetracked to the third.

"Are these folks working twenty-four hours a day? I'll bet they're not," Petraeus said. "Who's going to pull it off the boat? Find it, pull it out, and escort it up to New Jersey. We just have to get after this. I know you're as antsy as I am to get out there."

He stood and faced his staff. "Actually, you're not. No one is as antsy as I am. I'd sure like to be ready a little before the United Nations' deadline. Talk about going down to the wire. Time's a-wastin'. This is what I'm talking about: it's *not* business as usual."

Petraeus studied the ceiling for a moment. Three dozen pairs of eyes were fixed on his face. "I know we've got a roller-coaster existence now," he said. "You just have to bear with my impatience. We're really racing here. At the end of the day, there will be one, or two, or three of us who will have to make the decision about whether the division is ready. I don't have any qualms about saying we can't do it. But I would regret saying we can't do it just because we didn't put enough effort into it."

The room grew silent but for the throbbing fan. "Okay," Petraeus said. "Thank you. Air assault."

I had seen a fair amount of Dave Petraeus since our initial supper in the mess hall. We had met for dinner twice more, including steak and crab legs one Wednesday night during the weekly Camp Doha surf'n'turf special. He also had taken me along on a couple of inspection trips. He patiently endured my incessant questions about preparing both his division and himself for combat.

I did not want to make Petraeus's burden heavier by making him feel that every comment and gesture was under scrutiny. Having a reporter at his elbow, and sixty in the division, made the 101st something of a fishbowl. But I sensed that he liked having someone to talk to outside the chain of command. Even amid seventeen thousand soldiers, a division commander can feel isolated and alone.

I knew him better now. Intense, good-humored, and driven, he was someone who had stopped skiing because "if I couldn't do it at a certain level, I didn't want to do it anymore." At West Point, he had initially considered becoming an Army doctor, not because he was drawn to medicine but because "it was the toughest challenge." He embraced a personal code that required him "to set the bar high and to do it publicly. That's key. Then, when you succeed, it really means something."

He was under great stress but showed it only on occasion. During one BUB, when a staff officer reported persistent communications problems that V Corps seemed unable to fix, Petraeus had snapped, "Call that full colonel at corps and tell him that it's now at my level and he has until sunup. Tell him he's got two divisions in the corps, and one of them doesn't have commo right now. What's wrong with this picture?"

The devil, of course, still remained in the details. Petraeus's ability to spot a small anomaly—in the fuel-consumption rate of a truck company, or in the number of TOW missiles available to 1st Brigade—was impressive given the flood of data that washed over him all day long. "As an infantryman, I used to be no more interested in logistics than what you could stuff in a rucksack," he told me. "Now I know that, although the tactics aren't easy, they're relatively simple when compared to the logistics."

He was a stickler, pure and simple, and subordinates never knew when he would pop up with his stickler's eye. Petraeus had an enduring affection for the 3rd Battalion of the 187th Infantry Regiment, which he had once commanded, but he suspected while the 101st was still at Fort Campbell that during bad weather the unit was cutting corners on its physical training. "I got so I would run past the battalion on rainy mornings just to make sure they were doing p.t.," Petraeus had told me one afternoon at Doha. "They never let me down."

"So you've cut them some slack?" I asked.

He gave a toothy grin. "Went by yesterday."

If war now seemed likely, it still was not certain, and for commanders this ambiguity posed both a psychological challenge and a moral dilemma. Could an officer legitimately feel disappointment if Saddam Hussein capitulated, forcing the Army to stand down? Early Wednesday morning, March 12, Dwyer and I were loitering outside the division offices when Petraeus wandered out to chat. We asked how he would feel if the confrontation with Iraq was resolved without gunfire.

"There would be conflicting emotions," he said. "There would be relief at not putting these wonderful soldiers in harm's way. There might also be a bit of a letdown, and it would only be that: a *bit* of a letdown. This is the biggest prizefight in our careers, and every soldier at every level has been training for this for months, if not years."

He paused to contemplate the metaphor. "If this were resolved without war, it might be like winning the most high-stakes endeavor by having your opponent just throw in the towel. But it's always at the back of your mind that if we go to war there will be some of America's sons and daughters who won't come home, no matter how well it goes."

Petraeus had saved the bloody uniform shirt he had been wearing when he was shot in 1991, and I wondered if it was his own red badge of courage, a keepsake from an awful day that had clearly made him stronger. I asked about commanding in combat for the first time. The question seemed to vex him slightly, and he alluded to a couple of tense episodes in his career, including the apprehension of a particularly notorious war criminal in Bosnia. "That was one of the few occasions in my life— and I believe I can count them on one hand—when I could actually feel my blood pressure spike," he said.

"Have you felt that spike in this operation?" I asked.

He shook his head. "Not yet," he said with a smile, then

changed the subject. "I'm going down to the port and up to V Corps. Do you and Jim want to come?"

We did indeed. Scrambling into the commanding general's Chevy Suburban, we joined two men who would shortly become daily companions. Captain David G. Fivecoat, a thirty-one-year-old West Pointer from Delaware, Ohio, was a smart, curious, sinewy towhead serving his second tour as Petraeus's aide, an experience his peers teasingly suggested he record in a memoir to be titled *Success Through Pain*. Sergeant Jeremy Miller, the driver, was a former Texas high school wrestling champion with a young son, an incandescent smile, and an ambition to fly helicopters.

By noon we found ourselves back at berths 18 and 19. The *Dahl* was gone, replaced by the *Bob Hope*. "Funny, it doesn't look six inches shorter," I said. Then, with a touch of mischief, I told Petraeus, "By the way, E. J. Sinclair says he won't run with you, but he'll be happy to meet on the basketball court, anytime."

"Fine," Petraeus said, climbing from the SUV. "One-on-one, full court. That's the game. Full court." He shut the door and strode toward the ship with his short, quick gait.

"That," Dwyer said, "is one competitive son of a bitch."

Fivecoat climbed from the rear seat and nodded. "He is the most competitive man on the planet."

Petraeus stalked up the ramp, climbed a ladder to the weather deck, then swept back down the ramp. "Okay. Hoo-ah. Air assault," he called, slapping backs and flashing a thumbs-up. "Hoo-ah. Air assault. Keep working this thing. Good work, guys."

On the pier near the stern, he stopped long enough to banter with a private first class named Jonathan Aleshire. One thing led to another, and within thirty seconds the fifty-year-old commanding general had challenged the nineteen-year-old PFC to a push-up contest. They dropped to the concrete as a small circle of soldiers gathered around, like schoolboys ringing a playground fight.

"All right, here's the standard," Petraeus said. "Chest touches the ground, arms out and locked." He smiled. "Just stay with me." Stiff as an ironing board, eyes fixed on Aleshire, Petraeus dipped, rose, dipped, rose. So did Aleshire. Five, six, seven. The watching soldiers counted and shouted encouragement. Eleven, twelve, thirteen. Neck veins bulged. Eighteen, nineteen, twenty.

At twenty-seven, PFC Aleshire gasped and collapsed on the concrete. Petraeus did twenty more, then popped to his feet without breaking a sweat. Rocking up on his toes, thumbs hooked into his flak vest, he told the panting young soldier, "You can write that off on your income tax as part of your education."

As we climbed back into the car, a sergeant who had combed the *Bob Hope* for the missing D-Main tent came up to the passenger window. "Sir, it's not on the ship. I've been through the entire hold."

"Son of a bitch," Petraeus said softly. "Heck of a note."

Rain began to spit as we left the port. "There are times when I think, damn, I hope they know what they are putting us through," Petraeus said. "And the immutable truth is that they never do."

Before returning to Camp Doha, we swung north to Camp Virginia. The speedometer nicked 170 kilometers per hour—105 mph—as we neared Mutlaa Ridge. While Petraeus met privately with Wallace, the V Corps commander, Dwyer and I chatted with the 101st Airborne Division's liaison officer at V Corps, Lieutenant Colonel Rick Carlson. The missing tent was yet another friction to fret over.

"We call this the Land of Not Quite Right," Carlson told us. "Everything is hard out here."

By Thursday, March 13, when it was finally time to leave Doha, nearly all of our fellow squatters had moved to staging encampments in the desert, and Bay 7 was largely vacant. It seemed a bit forlorn, like a ballpark after a doubleheader. Most cots were gone, folded up and silently stolen away. Camp life detritus littered the floor: empty water bottles, discarded smallpox bandages, MRE packets. The sound of Led Zeppelin's "Stairway to Heaven" carried faintly from a soldier's tape player: *And so we ride on down the road.*

More peace protests were expected in Washington, New York, Madrid, and other cities over the weekend, but peace had become a wan hope. President Bush planned to meet in the Azores on Sunday with the British and Spanish prime ministers, his two staunchest partners in the futile campaign to secure a new Security Council resolution authorizing force against Iraq. Bush proposed giving Saddam Hussein four more days, until March 17, to prove that he was disarming. After that, the president appeared determined to attack preemptively, despite overwhelming international opposition.

As for the 101st, the amber, red, and black boxes on unit readiness charts were gradually turning green; it was like viewing, in reverse, a time-lapse sequence of changing autumn foliage. A fourth ship bringing more kit was expected on Friday, and at that point, according to a report sent to V Corps, "the division will have all necessary equipment and munitions to complete preparations for combat. . . . We now have 15,797 Screaming Eagles in theater." Gunnery practice and desert acclimation flying had intensified. Flocks of Apaches, Blackhawks, Chinooks, and Kiowas flew from the port to desert bases every day—about a hundred aircraft belonging to the 101st now sat at Udairi airfield, with another fifty at Camp Thunder, more than half the division total.

I made a last compulsive shopping foray to the PX. A young specialist in line pointed to the AAFES sign at the register and said, "That doesn't mean 'Army Air Force Exchange Service.' It means 'Always And Forever Exploiting Soldiers.' " I emerged with chewing gum, a pair of swimming goggles that could be worn in a sandstorm, and—in a purchase suggesting pathos if not imbalance—a set of blank dogtags. Having neglected to buy dogtags at Fort Campbell, I reasoned that if killed in a helicopter crash I would be identifiable, by process of elimination, as the Man Who Never Was, the only passenger wearing anonymous tags.

Dwyer and I ate a final lunch in the mess hall. A sign at the serving-line entrance notified us that we were packing away 425 calories with the beef teriyaki, 255 more with the fried rice, 125 with the egg noodles, 110 with the green beans, and a final 80 calories with the gravy. The cheesecake was not listed.

Back at Warehouse 6, Trey Cate organized a final scrounging sweep. We collected discarded clothes hangers, a few abandoned cots, and a dozen sheets of cardboard, cramming everything into a pair of Pajero SUVs. Rucksacks, MRE cases, and an enormous satellite dish were lashed to the vehicles. As we drove out the gate at 2:15 P.M., we looked like the Beverly Hillbillies, with assault rifles.

Five of us wedged into the trail vehicle. Phil Collins sang from the radio. My companions held a lively debate about where Osama bin Laden was hiding. Speculation ranged from India to Costa Rica. On the northbound highway, we passed long convoys of trailers hauling British armor. Tommies in truck beds wore balaclavas at their throats and goggles on their helmets. "Is England still supporting us?" one lieutenant asked. "I don't see the news much."

A highway billboard advertised Givenchy products. Turning west into the desert, near Main Supply Route Barbara, we skirted a vast junkyard where Kuwaitis had dragged debris from the 1991 Highway of Death. Acres of tank hulls, charred Mercedes, and bent antiaircraft tubes rusted in the sun.

Shadows had begun to lengthen when we spied the cocked

canisters of a Patriot missile battery, pointing north. Machine-gunners at a guard post hunched over their weapons and squinted into the middle distance. A sentry carefully scrutinized our identification cards, then waved us through a maze of sandbags and coiled concertina wire that marked the main gate of Camp New Jersey, our new home.

5

THE GARDEN STATE

I rose early on Friday, March 14, and hiked with Dwyer to breakfast in the mess tent, nearly a mile away. Camp New Jersey was more crowded than it had been during our brief stop two weeks earlier, but it was no less primitive. We shared a living room–sized tent with fourteen soldiers, male and female; so intense was the coughing at night that one trooper complained, "I feel like I'm in a damned tuberculosis ward." New Jersey's charms did not include running water. Showers were rationed—we got two each week—although a sergeant warned me that the water trucks often failed to arrive. Shaving could be finessed with bottled water and an empty MRE pouch converted into a basin. Thick black smoke coiled from drums of burning human waste, pulled from beneath the plywood latrines—known as burn shitters—and doused with fuel. So much of any military expedition involves prodigious efforts of self-sustainment. At New Jersey, everything, every little thing, took longer, from getting a cup of coffee to standing in line at the "piss tubes"—hollow, groin-high plastic cylinders that were hammered into the ground.

Yet a desolate, edge-of-the-empire beauty obtained. As Dwyer and I walked, dawn spread over the eastern horizon in a molten

brew of orange and indigo, silhouetting the wooden guard towers. Platoons ran wind sprints across the desert or jumped about
in calisthenic exuberance. The cuffs of the troops' desert boots
were indelibly inked with their blood types, a legion of Os and
As and A-positives. A soldier ambled past with a grenade
launcher on his shoulder, singing in a sweet falsetto: "Sha-na-na-
na, goood-bye!" I fancied that in its remote, martial spirit this
encampment was of a piece with Roman outposts, perhaps
ancient Timgad in North Africa, built by the Third Legion in
A.D. 100, where a traveler described the scuffing cadence of Tra-
jan's soldiers helmed in bronze, and "barbarians from the outer
desert in paint and feathers flitting along the narrow byways."

We reached the saffron-colored tent shortly after 7 A.M. to
find the cafeteria line stretching seventy-five yards along a gravel
path lined with sandbags. A frayed American flag hung limply
from a short pole, and a placard advised: "Please clear all weapons and ensure your weapons are on safe before entering tent.
Thanks!"

Behind us, a trio of soldiers from the 3rd Brigade, known as
the Rakkasans, chattered happily.

SOLDIER 1: "I keep me on her mind. The first Monday of every
month she gets a flower arrangement. I arranged for it with a
florist. Put it on my credit card, and it goes automatically from
me to her job."

SOLDIER 2: "You're a smooth criminal."

SOLDIER 3: "You must have read a lot of books, huh, Specialist?"

SOLDIER 1: "The things I know about love, it's scary."

SOLDIER 2: "Send her eleven roses and tell her she makes the
bouquet complete."

SOLDIER 1: "Growing up with four aunts, I have an interesting
perspective on women. It's a miracle I'm not a little light
in my loafers. I'll tell you what, I can find my way around
a mall."

It took just over thirty minutes to reach the kitchen servers ladling out scrambled eggs and fried potatoes. A cooler held stacked cartons of Danish milk and a syrupy concoction labeled "Orange Drink." Fluorescent lights hung from the metal frame of the tent, which was embroidered with a flowered border and filled with ten long rows of flimsy tables of the sort seen at your lesser garden parties. Each table could accommodate twenty-four soldiers. There were women in the ranks, but not many. This was a combat infantry camp, full of lean young men whose faces grew more bronzed with each day in the sun. Some Rakkasans wore T-shirts that read, "Battle hard. Violence of action." Testosterone filled the tent like a gas.

"I was talking to Dickinson," an officer sitting next to us told his friend across the table. "His boys were telling him that I was going soft. I've gotta take it up a notch." Dwyer and I struck up a conversation and learned that the two men were Captain Robert Kuth, commander of Bravo Company, 1st Battalion of the 187th Infantry, and his executive officer, Captain Ben Fielding.

Both had served in Afghanistan with the Rakkasans. Fielding was thirty-three, having left the Army for several years to pursue a professional boxing career. Kuth was twenty-nine. He had 126 men in his company—"not full strength, but close." Since arriving at New Jersey from Fort Campbell, he told us, "most training has focused on battle drills. Clear a building, clear a room, clear a trench. Initial breach through mines and wire obstacles. Creating a safe passage through those obstacles."

A soldier walked past carrying a Mossberg 12-gauge shotgun. "For knocking down doors," Kuth advised. Fielding's wife had given birth to a baby girl two days before. "I'm motivated," he said, "because I want her to grow up in a safe, free nation."

I spent the morning exploring New Jersey. Six thousand soldiers lived here, including the Rakkasans and the division staff. Other components of the 101st had bivouacked at Pennsylvania, Udairi, Thunder, and other bases.

From a boom box in one tent came the exquisite strains of Mozart's Piano Concerto No. 21 in C Major. In an adjacent tent, where Sergeant DeGrace and soldiers from the headquarters company lived, I heard a voice snarl, "I'm gonna kick your ass you do that again." Trey Cate stood over his cot and told no one in particular, "You wake up in the morning, you scream, 'Air assault!' Then you run out the door and everything's uphill all day. But the day has started all right because you're a Screaming Eagle."

Two hundred yards from our tent enclave stood the division artillery encampment. At 11 A.M. I wandered over to see the artillery commander, Colonel William L. Greer, a tall, craggy strawberry blond who had studied agriculture at Kansas State University. A sign in the divarty TOC listed "Possible Threats to Camp New Jersey"; among the hazards cited were "ambush/opportunity attacks on single and stopped vehicles." Like many gunners, Bill Greer had a passion for his art. "It wasn't any damned infantryman who gave the order to hold Bastogne during the Battle of the Bulge," he said. "It was an artilleryman, General Anthony McAuliffe, who told the Germans 'Nuts!' when they wanted him to surrender."

Greer offered a succinct tutorial on gunnery. The 101st carried two types of gun: the 105mm howitzer, with a range of 11 miles, and the 155mm, with a range of 18 miles. The 105 was more mobile—each shell weighed 35 pounds and had a killing radius of 75 meters—while the 155, with 100-pound shells that had a 250-meter killing radius, was more lethal.

"We'll take plenty of illum—white phosphorus illumination rounds—and not so many dud-producing munitions, because if you have light infantrymen working through the area afterwards you prefer to use munitions that have a dud rate that's close to zero. DPICM, for example—dual-purpose improved conventional munition—has lots of little bomblets with a dud rate of two to five percent, depending on the range. The longer the range, the lower the dud rate in general."

I asked how far gunners preferred their own infantrymen to be from an impact area. Greer ticked off the ranges. "Danger-close for a 60mm mortar is 200 meters. It's 300 meters for the 81mm mortar, 500 meters for the 105s, and 600 meters for the 155s.

"We're basically putting together five days' worth of supplies to take with us into Iraq, and then we'll have to be resupplied," he added. "Given the density of vehicles, there will be lots of friction. Vehicles broken down, that sort of thing. That's what leaders get paid to do: make the frictions go away."

Before I left, Greer introduced me to Captain Jim Peay, who commanded a counterbattery radar detachment and whose father, General H. Binford Peay III, I had known when he commanded the 101st during the Gulf War. "I would like to come back to Baghdad ten years from now, to see what it's like," young Peay said. "I'd like to see if it's like France, where there are liberation monuments all over the country."

The missing TOC Mahal remained missing, but a serviceable spare tent had been erected for the division headquarters, and an extra computer server was installed. Technicians were still string-ing wires and adjusting lights for the command post when I walked in. Gas masks, helmets, and rifles were piled along the sides of the tent. Several officers washed down cold MREs with water from their CamelBaks; they pulled on the mouthpieces like hookah pipes. Brian Coppersmith, whose staff duties included moderating the BUBs as a kind of master of ceremonies, strolled past with an enormous mug of coffee.

"You a Pistols fan? 'Road runner, road runner / Fifty thou-sand watts of power!' " With his free hand Coppersmith stroked an air guitar, a Johnny Rotten in desert camouflage. "I figured out what my problem is," he said. "I've been undercaffeinated." He walked away, singing, " 'Road runner, road runner.' "

Petraeus sat at the front table with the chief of staff, Colonel Thomas J. Schoenbeck, on his left, and on his right, the O, Ben Freakley, who finally had been able to join the division in Kuwait. Behind them, thirty-three officers sat at three rows of tables, their staff positions identified by placards fixed to the backs of their raised laptop computer screens. Everyone faced the front of the room, and microphones had been placed on each table so officers could hear one another over the throb of generators outside. At noon even the normal din was briefly overpowered by the wail of the camp's missile-warning siren, known as the Giant Voice, which was being tested.

An enormous map of Kuwait and southern Iraq dominated the front wall, flanked by four video screens. Plotted on the map, roughly parallel to the Euphrates valley, were potential helicopter flight routes with names like Mars and Eclipse; ground supply routes were named for American cities. A digital clock with red numerals showed the time in Kuwait, Kentucky, and Zululand.

Readiness charts indicated the division's steady progression from black to red to amber to green; the greenest units were mostly those given priority because they were going into combat first, notably 3rd Brigade and the Apache units. A large placard displayed six questions in bold type: "What are we doing? What is the enemy doing? Where are we vulnerable? Where is the enemy vulnerable? How is our plan doing? What changes do we need to make to that plan?"

Another placard, titled "Enemy Weaknesses," listed Iraqi shortcomings: "FM [radio] non-secure; IMINT and SIGINT [imagery and signals intelligence] not timely; C2 [command and control]; no close air support; logistical re-supply; limited night and all-weather capability." The list amounted to a catalog of military incapacity in the twenty-first century, a shorthand sketch of an adversary waiting to be crushed.

Later Friday afternoon I drove with Petraeus cross-country into the desert near Udairi airfield to watch soldiers rehearse setting up a forward refueling point, a FARP. The day was nearly perfect. Little hillocks cast blue shadows as the brilliant sun sank in the western sky. I asked Petraeus whether the attack plan seemed sufficiently audacious.

"The best of all possible worlds is that someone sidles up to Saddam and puts a bullet in his brain," he said. "How the hell can you be audacious with only one Army division on the ground and another—the 101st—still coming into the country? On the other hand, we literally could be in Baghdad in three or four days. How audacious do you want to be? It all comes down to: Do they fight? Do they drop bridges? And then, can we keep the logistics up?"

We found E. J. Sinclair with a clutch of officers watching a pair of Apaches circle overhead. With stupefying obtuseness, the military had named the FARPs for oil companies, despite Defense Secretary Rumsfeld's insistence that the invasion of a country with 112 billion barrels of confirmed reserves had "nothing to do with oil, literally nothing to do with oil." "Exxon" would be located near Nasariyah, in southern Iraq; "Shell" was to go southwest of Najaf. "Conoco," the FARP now being rehearsed, would be built three hundred miles into Iraq, less than a hundred miles from Baghdad. Soldiers had laid out a dozen nozzles and fuel hoses connected to tanker trucks. Arranged with linear precision, the twelve stations were 150 feet apart. The lead Apache leveled off before swooping in to land at one station in a monstrous boil of dust that completely engulfed the helicopter within five seconds.

"At night, wearing night-vision goggles, flying over this open desert is like flying over open water," Sinclair said. He leaned close to my ear to be heard above the rotor noise. "It's very hard to tell how high you are, or to find any landmarks to orient yourself. We've found that flying seventy-five to a hundred feet above the desert is about right—not too low to raise the dust, and high enough to give yourself time to react if necessary. But landing"—he shook his head—"landing is really hard, even in daylight."

Lieutenant Colonel Lee Fetterman, who commanded Petraeus's old battalion, the 3rd of the 187th Infantry, joined the circle of officers. He snapped a salute to the brim of his Kevlar helmet, which was draped with camouflage netting.

"I hear you're green across the board," Petraeus said. "Is that true?"

"All we need is some missiles, sir, and we'll be good to go."

"Good. Hoo-ah."

"We knew you'd be pleased, sir," Fetterman said with a faint smile. "Always better to make you happy than to make you unhappy."

Driving back to New Jersey, Petraeus turned around in the front seat to make eye contact. "It's all about risk. I cannot over-state the distance issue. We are going to go much farther than the division has ever gone before. I think the biggest challenge right now is patience. This is industrial-strength stuff that we do"—he pointed to another covey of helicopters nosing along the horizon—"and you've got to be methodical. There's a thou-sand what-ifs going through your mind."

I asked about his doctoral dissertation, and the lingering imprint of Vietnam on the U.S. Army. "More caution," Petraeus said. "Since Vietnam, when the U.S. military has opposed the use of force, it has been a virtual veto. The wariness of senior mili-tary leaders in many cases is contrary to the cigar-chomping, table-pounding, bomb-them-back-to-the-Stone-Age stereotype. Vietnam certainly appeared to have increased the caution of the military." He paused for a long moment, then added, "That's not a bad thing, and I agree with it."

As we rolled through the camp gate, I ventured the apostasy that airborne divisions had perhaps outlived their usefulness in modern warfare. Petraeus swiveled in his seat again. Rather than defend the tactical utility of such units, he stressed the type of soldiers they attracted. "There's value in having people who have confronted their fears," he said. "I think that about skydiving. It takes *something* to jump out of an airplane without being attached to anything."

Inside the TOC I pulled up a folding chair next to Petraeus at the front table and we finished the conversation. "This won't be pretty in the end," he said. "There's no way you can do what we have done in the last couple weeks and still make it pretty. In fact, I think it will be somewhat ugly for us. We'll have to brute-force our way through it.

"I think 3ID is going to race right through and get up to Baghdad in a heartbeat. They are so self-contained. They've got all the fuel, all the ammo, everything they need. They've had months to get ready and to get experience in this environment. They're like a coiled spring. They're pissed off and they just want to get out of the desert, and the way to do that is through Baghdad. The question is whether everybody else can keep up, whether we can contribute. We're coming in late, and we're inserting ourselves into a plan that already existed."

I had the sensation of watching a conjuror onstage trying to levitate a heavy object by force of will. "We've got to keep pressing forward," Petraeus said. "That's why when some people say something will be done tomorrow, I ask why it can't be done tonight."

The days seemed to accelerate, as if impending war had a gravitational pull that tugged us forward with increasing velocity.

Just before 10 A.M. on Saturday, March 15, Dwyer and I walked into the 3rd Brigade TOC, a cluster of tents half a mile southeast of the D-Main. Colonel Michael S. Linnington, the Rakkasan commander, was just concluding a pep talk to his subordinates, and he yielded the floor to his senior NCO, a handsome Samoan sergeant major named Iuniasolua Tului Savusa. After warning of snakes and rodents, Savusa said, "Lots of soldiers are getting Dear John and Dear Jane letters, and they're going to be out there sitting and thinking about it, by themselves. Be sure your NCOs are on top of this so they don't go and do something stupid."

A few minutes later, I buttonholed Savusa near the tent flap and asked about morale. "More than half the soldiers in this brigade have combat experience in Afghanistan," he said. "The biggest challenge now is maintaining the standards and discipline, and getting across to younger soldiers the dangers involved. I'm not sure they really grasp what we're about to undertake. But these guys are ready. They have confidence in their leaders. And they have a certain look in their eyes."

I made my own morale assessment with a quick inspection of several plywood latrines. Soldiers had so few authorized opportunities to articulate stress and frustration that graffiti assumed an importance larger than simply providing a doodleboard for sophomoric crudities, although there were plenty of those. "Fuck this place," one poet had written with a kind of rap exuberance. "Fuck the Rakkasans. Fuck you. Fuck me. Fuck, fuck, fuck." I also read "Bush is the Anti-Christ" and "Yea, though I walk through the Valley I will fear no evil because Thou is with me." *Is?*

Dwyer and I spent a couple of hours with D Company of the Rakkasan's 1st Battalion, which had the mission of securing FOB Shell for the kind of helicopter refueling I had seen the previous day. The company commander was Captain Corey A. Brunkow, a redheaded West Pointer and son of a telephone repairman in Concordia, Kansas. The company would drive 240 miles from Kuwait to Shell in thirty-two vehicles armed with .50-caliber machine guns, Mk-19 grenade launchers, or TOW antitank missiles. Brunkow had yet to receive any maps, and he knew nothing of his route except that it angled through lower Mesopotamia.

"You can't cover everything that's going to happen in the battlefield," he said. "And obviously with bullets flying everywhere there will be some confusion. The guys are concerned about the lack of complete support at home. We're keeping up with the news. But the bottom line really is that when the president decides to go to war, the guys are here to make it happen."

This morning D Company was practicing desert navigation and how to react in an ambush. Brunkow was sweating the details with his eighty-one soldiers as much as Petraeus was with his seventeen thousand. How many spare AA batteries should D Company carry? A rifleman in combat could use up to a dozen every twenty-four hours for night-vision goggles, laser sights, and other devices. Orders had also come down for every vehicle to carry a spare tire, but the canvas roof on a Humvee would not support the added weight and there was no place else to put the tire; Brunkow sent scrounging parties to find plywood sheets to shore up the roofs. Land mines posed a pernicious threat, and Brunkow, after careful thought, had decided to line the floors of his vehicles with a single layer of sandbags for blast protection. "You can only put so much weight on a Humvee before you start breaking axles while driving over the rocks."

Most Rakkasans, he added, would ride through Iraq in convoys of open-sided trucks. The truck beds would be lined with MRE cases, which were considered as effective as sandbags. "Ahh," Dwyer said, "a tribute to the pound cake."

Brunkow fiddled with the balky radios in his Humvee while Dwyer and I strolled down a line of vehicles parked in the sand. Every soldier wore wraparound Wiley X sunglasses. Many used a safety pin through a belt loop to skewer their foam earplugs, a bit of fieldcraft I soon took up.

"There are no distractions out here," Brunkow said when he rejoined us. "They don't have wives waiting at home at night, no PTA meetings to attend. They've got nothing better to do than train and get ready for war."

Every soldier soon received two index cards, which were to be tucked into their helmets. Both cards were dated 1 June 1966; these forms had been used to track the dead and wounded on battlefields from Vietnam and Cambodia to Panama and Afghanistan.

The first card, Department of the Army Form 1156, the "Casualty Feeder Report," included boxes to be checked for any soldier killed, wounded, missing, or captured. "Body recovered?" Yes. No. "Body identified?" Yes. No.

DA Form 1155, the "Witness Statement on Individual," was more personal, even poignant. "Date of death or when last seen." "Was he married?" "Did he have any children?" "Nickname." "Other identifying marks, such as tattoos or birthmarks."

The 101st alone had more than 550 medical professionals, including eleven physicians, twenty-five physician's assistants, and hundreds of medics. They had trained for combat on four extraordinarily lifelike mannequins, which cost $200,000 each and replicated human trauma symptoms ranging from a fluttering pulse to dilated eyes and massive hemorrhaging. Programmed to accept seventy-seven different medications, the dummies "died" if improperly treated. "Some of these kids are going to see some horrific things," the division surgeon, Lieutenant Colonel R. W. Thomas, told me. "When they see someone with a smoking stump, we want them to be able to deal with it rather than recoil. The first rule is: check your own pulse."

On Sunday morning, I found Petraeus in the division TOC studying the map, once again fighting the Medina Division in his mind's eye. "Today is going to be a good day in terms of getting almost all the rest of our helicopters out of the port, getting a huge number of vehicles out of the port and out to the camps, getting a large number of containers out of the port to the camps, and getting the rest of our ammo basic load," he said.

The Army since the end of the Cold War had fought on battlefields ranging from a desert in Iraq to a city in Somalia to mountains in Afghanistan. I asked how it was possible to avoid refighting the last war while trying to anticipate the next one. "We've learned that against an enemy who has virtually no air defense, where there's very little concealment or cover, you can absolutely hammer him with close air support. What a revelation," Petraeus said with some sarcasm. "But how would you apply that if you're trying to take down rebels in the Philippines, in triple-canopy jungle? How do you apply the lessons of one to the other?

"Coming out of the Gulf War last time, there were two types of commander. There was one type who, on the basis of a hundred hours of combat, in which his unit may or may not have had sustained fighting, was ready to make sweeping organizational and doctrinal changes. And then there were others who recognized the context, and the factors that were in play, and they were a bit more nuanced in their analysis." Petraeus laughed. "Wasn't it Mark Twain who said that if a cat sits down on a hot stove lid it won't ever again sit down on a hot stove lid, but it also won't sit down on a cold stove lid?

"When you look at the lessons of Vietnam, one of them is 'Don't rush in'—the never-again thing. On the other hand, sometimes if you intervene early you actually can prevent it from getting to that state."

Tom Schoenbeck, the preternaturally calm chief of staff who had once played wide receiver at the University of Florida, slid into the chair next to us. He handed Petraeus a draft of the Unit Status Report, a secret document used by the Pentagon to track combat preparedness. Petraeus studied the page, then pulled out his pen and marked it up with black ink. Where the draft had declared the 101st was "ready to conduct combat operations," Petraeus scratched out the phrase and substituted "continues preparation for combat operations." To Schoenbeck he said, "I don't think we can say that we're ready for combat yet."

The mess tent remained a splendid observation post, like watching wildlife from a tree blind or a glass-bottom boat. Even so, it was difficult to precisely gauge the mood in Camp New Jersey. Certainly there was jittery anticipation, a desire to get on with it. But I detected not only resignation to whatever fate held for each soldier but also a sense of inevitability that this war would lack closure, that it was simply another campaign in a perpetual state of war. "We'll never get home," I heard one soldier tell another with a sigh. "We'll just keep moving from one hot spot to another—Iraq, Korea, Iran. It'll be like World War II, hopping around."

At dinner on Sunday night, Dwyer and I sat across from a Rakkasan battalion surgeon who in excruciating detail described combat triage procedures. "If he has a head wound and most of his brain matter is gone, you're gonna to put him in the 'probable' pile," the surgeon said. "Probable" meant "probably moribund." "In a job like this you come to realize how fragile human life is. A small wound that seems insignificant can turn out to be mortal. A little bump on the head that results in a hematoma, well—" He shrugged.

"On the other hand, you'll see somebody who seems grievously wounded in a way that can't possibly be survivable, and he'll pull through." He stood and pushed back his chair. "Be safe," he said, before vanishing into the night. "I don't want to see you as a patient."

Perhaps unsettled by this tutorial in combat pathology, Dwyer and I managed to get utterly lost while walking back to our tent. We were both writing profiles of Petraeus for our respective newspapers and we were eager to get back to work quickly. It was not to be. Overcast hid the moon and darkness seemed to swallow Dwyer's flashlight beam. "Isn't that the ACP over there?" I said, pointing to a dim silhouette vaguely resembling the assault command post. "Or is that the 3rd Brigade TOC? Where the hell are we?"

Like hapless Bedouins we wandered from one tent enclave to another, asking directions to the D-Main in tones of increasing desperation. "You are about as far from where you're trying to go as you can be," one soldier told us with a sad shake of the head. Finally, after what seemed like hours in the New Jersey wilderness, we shot an azimuth along the extended arm of a helpful Rakkasan—"Just walk thataway," he advised—and stumbled back to our cots. Never had a tuberculosis ward seemed more homey.

On Monday, March 17, the White House announced that President Bush would address the nation that evening. Trey Cate promptly dispatched several soldiers to Camp Doha and they returned with the SUV full of tortilla chips, salsa, Coca-Cola, and a Samsung multisystem television on which we planned to watch the speech. Then someone calculated that the broadcast would come on at 4 A.M. local time. No one stayed up.

While we slept, Bush gave Saddam Hussein and his sons forty-eight hours to leave Iraq. "Their refusal to do so," the president warned, "will result in military conflict, commenced at a time of our choosing." A uniformed Saddam subsequently appeared on Iraqi television, wearing a holstered pistol and warning that "this will be Iraq's last great battle with the malicious tyrant in our time, and America's last great war of aggression, too."

Bush's deadline, which would expire on March 20 at 4 A.M. Kuwait time, gave the morning BUB a particular urgency. I walked into the TOC at 7:25 A.M. and found Petraeus wearing a telephone headset and scribbling notes while listening to the V Corps morning conference call. "Excellent," I heard him say. "Excellent." One of the four video screens projected a map with Medina Division units pinpointed with red diamond icons; Kuwait was covered with blue rectangles, the symbols for American units. About 130,000 American troops, including 64,000

Marines, now jammed Kuwait, along with 25,000 British soldiers. No icons signified the many Special Operations troops already filtering into Iraq, including the Army's 10th Special Forces Group in the north, and Task Force 20, operating in the western desert with the 5th Special Forces Group as well as British and Australian commandos.

A large sign in the TOC noted that the daily challenge and response passwords for sentries were, respectively, GREASE and HOUND. Staff officers quickly delivered their reports. "Got it. Okay. Got it," Petraeus said with evident impatience. Lieutenant Colonel D. J. Reyes, the intelligence chief, reported, "Our assessment is that Saddam Hussein will disperse his forces to ensure their survivability." A slide stamped SECRET/NOFORN—"no foreign distribution"—showed the locations of Iraqi Spoon Rest radar and SA-2 antiaircraft missile sites, which had been detected through communications intercepts. Meanwhile, the thirty-one meteorologists assigned to the division—weather was of more than passing concern to a unit with twenty-one dozen helicopters—had begun tracking conditions around Baghdad as well as farther south.

"Got it," Petraeus said. "Got it. Got it."

At the end of the briefing he flipped open his notebook and relayed an order from the high command. In an effort to convince Iraqis that Americans were coming as liberators and not occupiers, "no U.S. or state flags are to be displayed on any vehicles." Ben Freakley scowled, then looked at me and discreetly gave a thumbs-down gesture.

As I walked out of the tent, Trey Cate handed me a sheet of paper signed by Reyes. Security around the TOC had increased in the past two days, and the document would allow me to get in and out without alarming the sentries, while authorizing "secret-level access to all 101st Division activities."

Petraeus stopped to chat for a moment just outside the tent. He wore his helmet, pistol, flak vest, and other gear, which soldiers referred to collectively as battle rattle. Evidently he had been contemplating the art of command. Without prompting, he said, "I find this as intellectually challenging as anything I've ever done, including graduate school and working for the chairman. It's keenly interesting and complex, and trying to understand it is usually a lot of fun. A division is a system of systems, and pulling it together is hugely complicated. Army aviation is a military-industrial complex all by itself."

Vice President Richard Cheney, in another of those prewar assertions that later proved to lurk somewhere between honest error and rank mendacity, had publicly claimed that Iraq "has in fact reconstituted nuclear weapons." I asked Petraeus whether he believed Baghdad still harbored weapons of mass destruction. He put the likelihood of Iraq possessing chemical munitions at "eighty to ninety percent." The odds of attacking American troops being "slimed" with chemicals, he added, were "fifty–fifty."

I walked back to the public-affairs tent and had no sooner turned on my laptop than Cate threw the flap aside in evident agitation. His face was flushed, his eyes narrowed. "Is it too late to pull a story?" he asked. We were nearly nose to nose.

"From this morning's papers?" I glanced at my watch. "It's one A.M. on the East Coast. Most papers have been printed already, and stories have been posted on the Web. What are you talking about?"

"The CG just read Jim Dwyer's profile of him on the *Times*'s web site. To say that he's upset doesn't begin to cover it. He wants the story pulled, and if that can't happen then he wants a retraction." Cate ran through Dwyer's purported offenses, the foremost of which seemed to be that in Petraeus's view the story portrayed him as eager to win the war singlehandedly. "Will you do me a favor?" Cate asked. "Will you read this and tell me what you think?" He handed me a computer printout of Dwyer's piece. Virtually every sentence had been marked up in black ink, with many margin notes scribbled in Petraeus's swirling hand.

I sat outside on a metal chair and was only halfway through what was clearly a careful and rather generous sketch when Dwyer appeared, followed momentarily by Cate. Dwyer listened politely to Cate's complaint and scanned the scribbles across the printout. "Well, it's too late to pull the story," he said. "And I think he's overreacting."

"I think he's overreacting, too, Trey," I said. "And if he didn't like this, then he sure isn't going to like my profile of him, which also is running this morning."

Cate looked miserable as he headed back to the TOC to confess that he had been unable to stop the presses at *The New York Times* and *The Washington Post*. Dwyer and I exchanged puzzled looks. "This," I said, "is going to be a long war."

The little tempest soon blew over. Petraeus was no happier with my profile, but he swallowed his displeasure. He remained frosty for the rest of the day before regaining his good humor. I did not know it at the time, but that afternoon he told Scott Wallace, the V Corps commander, that the 101st would be ready for combat by March 21, now just three days away. He was out on a limb, and I could only imagine the pressure he felt.

"No one recognized that intense commander you profiled," Petraeus joked the next morning, then added, "You never see yourself exactly as others do."

I arrived at the mess tent at 6:20 A.M. on March 19 to find the line longer than usual and quite immobile. A soldier in front of me ticked off the possibilities: "They're on strike. They woke up late. The bus got held up." Soldiers stood and smoked, or simply contemplated the desert in what felt like the final hours of peace.

Each trooper as usual was heavily encumbered—helmet, weapon, JLIST, mask, knife, canteen, ammo belt, flak vest. Cataloging the things carried by warriors into battle has intrigued war scribes since Homer and Thucydides. Dave Fivecoat, the aide whose qualities included a born infantryman's knack for leading other men in the dark of night, provided me an inventory of his uniform and body-armor pockets:

Three pens (two black, one blue); a Chap Stick; two packets of MRE toilet paper; two identification cards; $47 and €40; packets of instant coffee, creamer, and sugar; a camera; a red penlight; a small flashlight; a handheld global positioning system; five magazines of M-4 carbine ammunition; two magazines of M-9 pistol ammo; a Silva compass; two first-aid bandages; and a cloth-bound notebook, volume XXII. In his helmet he carried two laminated pictures of his girlfriend, a piece of an emergency signal panel, and DA Forms 1155 and 1156. He wore a Timex Ironman watch, dog tags, and thick-framed Ranger glasses. He carried a buck knife, a Leatherman combination tool, the M-4 with a Surefire Tac Light and C-More red-dot scope, and, in a leg holster, his M-9. The Interceptor Body Armor and SAPI (small arms protective insert) ceramic plates used to reinforce the armor weighed sixteen pounds. Around his neck, Fivecoat wore a medal invoking St. Michael, patron saint of the airborne. I wore one, too, a gift from a beneficent chaplain.

When we finally got inside the mess tent, I sat with a two-man Stinger missile team. Corporal Joe Smiley was twenty-three and from Leitchfield, Kentucky. Private Clint Stinson, of Caledonia, Mississippi, was twenty-nine.

"I just want to do my six months here and go home," Smiley said. "I want to do what I need to do and get home safely. I've got too much going on at home to mess up here."

"When I get home," Stinson said, "I'm planning to go to Cloudmont. It's a resort in northern Alabama. It's the most beautiful place in the world. On the first tee, you drive off a thirty-foot cliff."

Smiley drained the juice from his cup. "Where I live, it's thirty minutes from Mammoth Cave, largest cave system in the world. I've never been there."

"My first wedding anniversary is next month," Stinson said, "and I'm gonna be in a war."

At 11 A.M., more than a hundred of the division's commanders and staff officers gathered in the MWR tent—morale, welfare, and recreation—for a rehearsal of the initial assault into Iraq. Yahtzee, Monopoly, and other board games were stacked on the shelves next to volleyballs and badminton sets. On the plywood floor, the lower Euphrates valley had been laid out in a terrain model measuring twenty by thirty feet. Another bad dust storm had kicked up outside. Tent ropes squeaked under the strain, and the light in the tent was sulfur colored and full of motes.

A voice called above the hubbub, "All the oh-five and oh-six commanders"—lieutenant colonels and colonels—"come up and stand in front of the map. The CG wants to take a historical photo." A dozen men and one woman—Lieutenant Colonel Kristen Shafer, commander of the 311th Military Intelligence Battalion—stood with fixed countenances, as rigid and intent as Civil War officers posing for a daguerreotype. Before they broke, Mike Linnington, the tall Rakkasan commander, flashed bunny ears with his fingers behind Petraeus's helmet.

The officers settled onto chairs and benches for the three-hour rehearsal. I turned to leave and Major Larry Wark, secretary of the general staff, handed me an envelope. "I printed out a couple e-mails my wife sent me," he said. "I want you to have them so you can see how scared the families at home are." Trudging through the blowing sand, I read Corinne Wark's anxious notes. She gave voice to tens of thousands of worried, waiting spouses and parents, children, and friends. "You are all in my every thought and prayer," she had written her husband the previous day. "I pray this is over soon and that you are all safe. You are the light of my life, and I can't wait to share the rest of our lives together."

Late that afternoon I found Petraeus standing outside the D-Main, watching seventeen five-thousand-gallon fuel tankers roll into Camp New Jersey. He looked as happy as a kid with seventeen new bicycles. "I'll tell you what," he said. "We just might pull this off."

The sun set and the wind faded. Dust hung in the air. Across the camp in the dying light, soldiers moved like armed shades, preparing for the end of peace.

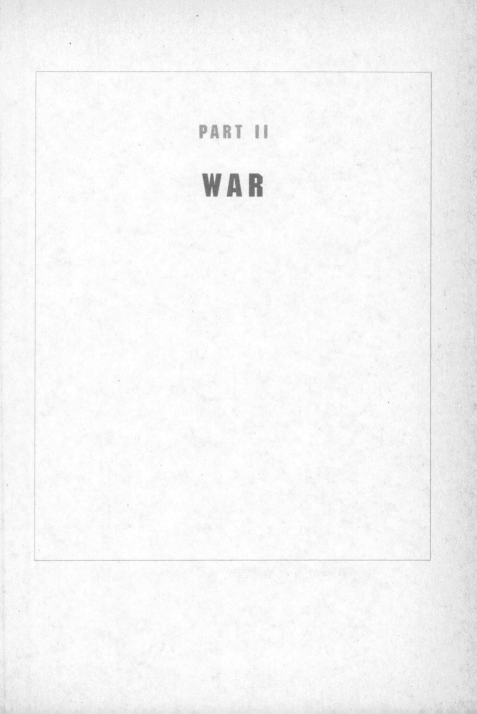

PART II

WAR

6

"THE BOLD THING IS USUALLY THE RIGHT THING"

War began when most of us were asleep, which is how most wars begin. A few insomniacs at Camp New Jersey claimed to have heard the growl of Tomahawk cruise missiles 250 feet overhead as they motored toward Baghdad before dawn on Thursday, March 20. The vast majority, however, got word through the soldier grapevine or from television: several satellite dishes had sprouted around the camp. In the public-affairs tent, Bush's announcement from the Oval Office replayed endlessly on the Samsung multisystem: "On my orders, coalition forces have begun striking selected targets of military importance. . . . We will accept no outcome but victory." Trey Cate stared at the screen and murmured, "This is going to be a weird war. We're going to live it and watch it at the same time."

More details emerged during the 7:30 A.M. BUB, where I took a canvas chair next to Dave Fivecoat and Larry Wark in a cramped corner of the D-Main tent dubbed the Skybox. U.S. intelligence had ostensibly located Saddam in a bunker at Dora Farms, a residential compound in south Baghdad; four two-thousand-pound bombs—the Air Force called them Volkswagens—and forty Tomahawks had leveled the place in a decapitation strike that perhaps surprised the Iraqis but certainly surprised the U.S. Army.

As I learned later in the day, even Lieutenant General Wallace, the V Corps commander, first heard of the assassination attempt on CNN.

Tom Schoenbeck squeezed through the Skybox on his way to the chief's seat at the front table next to Petraeus. "I'm in a state of hover right now," he said. "Things are starting to move, but it's not time to peak yet. Keep it down, keep it down." He smiled, and made a tamping gesture with both palms.

Things had indeed started to move. An electric charge snapped through the tent as officers realized that the ground attack would likely be accelerated by approximately twenty-four hours. A Predator UAV—unmanned aerial vehicle—had spotted flames shooting more than three hundred feet above an apparently sabotaged oil well near Basra. U.S. and British forces could not permit destruction of the southern fields, which generated $50 million a day in petroleum revenue. The 1st Marine Expeditionary Force, the British, and the Army's 3rd Division would attack this evening. Rakkasans from the 101st had already begun positioning near the Iraqi border in five GACs—ground-assault convoys—and it seemed probable that their battalions would soon be ordered forward to secure Exxon, the refueling base near Nasariyah, and then Shell. Petraeus would be able to redeem his promise to be ready to fight on the twenty-first: the fifth and final ship was unloading, and the division now had 120 helicopters at Udairi and another 136 at Camp Thunder.

During the BUB, reports and rumors flew around the TOC like small birds. Some seemed unlikely and soon proved wrong, such as the assertion by an American spy that Saddam would poison water supplies in towns occupied by U.S. troops. A V Corps assessment claimed that a senior Iraqi commander had "been given permission to use 30 percent of their chemicals weapons stockpile in a preemptive strike against U.S./coalition forces." Other reports, less speculative, were based on satellite imagery of Saddam Hussein International Airport, west of Baghdad, that showed Iraqi troops blocking the runways with dirt mounds to prevent an American coup de main. The Medina Division of the Republican Guard was "dispersing into urban and built-up areas for survivability," an intelligence officer reported, and that division's 14th Mechanized Brigade had prepared fighting positions along the Euphrates River between Karbala and Baghdad. Iraqi commanders still appeared to expect the main attack up three highways in the Tigris and Euphrates valleys, rather than V Corps' planned sweep to the west through the Karbala Gap.

"How good is the intelligence on those positions in terms of going after them with Apaches?" Petraeus asked.

"Sir," the lieutenant said, "we currently have eight-digit grid coordinates." A map location that precise pinpointed each target within ten meters. Intelligence also showed that Iraq's military had shrunk severely since the Gulf War. Instead of 950,000 soldiers in 60 regular army divisions, as in 1991, there now were no more than 350,000 in 17 divisions. The Republican Guard now numbered at most 80,000, down from 150,000.

Petraeus ended the morning session by reminding his staff that "General Order Number 1 has been extended to Iraq." Then, as if the occasion required a more martial declamation, he added, "We are at war."

An odd lull settled over New Jersey that morning, and I took advantage of the momentary calm to sit outside the TOC on a stack of sandbags with D. J. Reyes, the short, bespectacled G-2, or division intelligence officer. I knew that American military intelligence capabilities were extraordinary. Through a system called TENCAP—Tactical Exploitation of National Capabilities—battlefield analysts could access electronic and communications intercepts, as well as satellite imagery, from the National Security Agency, the National Imagery and Mapping Agency, the National Reconnaissance Office, and other fiefdoms within the immense American intelligence bureaucracy. What remained unclear to me was how the technological wizardry translated into warfighting advantages. What did an eight-digit grid coordinate tell you about an enemy's willingness to die for his cause? What did it tell you about how 24 million Iraqis would react to an American invasion? Would they welcome liberation? What about occupation?

"From a systems perspective, I can tell you what the Iraqis have, what they're doing, where they are, and, probably, where they're going," Lieutenant Colonel Reyes told me. "What I can't tell you is what's in their heads. Are they willing to fight? I subscribe to Sun Tzu—never underestimate your enemy. Objectively, I believe that the 14th Mech Brigade of the Medina Republican Guard Division is going to fight. Subjectively, I'm not sure how long they're going to fight. My gut's telling me that we are going to do some serious psychological damage to them as well as physical damage."

I asked whether he agreed with the conventional wisdom that HUMINT—human intelligence, or spies—remained a weak link for the United States. Reyes concurred, and pointed out that he had little personalized sense of the Iraqi enemy, not even biographical information on commanders of the Medina or 14th Mech Brigade. Ambiguity, he said, is the lot of the intelligence officer.

"I always try to remember: What is the 'So what?' That's why we say, 'Bottom line up front.' The other important point is: if you don't have anything to report, don't report."

Reyes ran a hand across his dark crew cut. "You have to be comfortable sitting in the swamp with alligators. You have to have more ass than they've got teeth. The wild card is asymmetrical tactics. Out-of-the-box thinking. I can see Saddam poisoning the water and blaming it on us. I can see him torching the oil wells, or setting fire to oil trenches, which are everywhere, around mosques, *everywhere*. I can see tactical inundations, where he blows up dams. I can see Iraqis posing as American soldiers.

"People say he'll use chemicals as soon as we cross the berm into Iraq. Naw, why would he show his hand there? I personally think he'll use them when he sees that we're definitely coming into Baghdad. I'm very concerned about Baghdad. I'm very concerned about all the urban areas. Our systems to a large extent will be mitigated or defeated if this gets into a street fight. Urban canyons allow the enemy to canalize us into ambush channels. We'll get drawn like a fly into the fire."

He shifted on his sandbag seat. An added anxiety for the 101st was the vulnerability of the division's helicopters, particularly in the MEZ, the missile engagement zone, around Baghdad; it was said to be second only to Pyongyang, North Korea, in air-defense lethality. "I lose sleep over it. Because you have to worry about everything. Roland missiles, triple A"—antiaircraft artillery—"and even iron-sight guns that have no radars associated with them. In the Mog"—Mogadishu—"helicopters were shot down with rocket-propelled grenades, RPG-7s. How do you fight that? I lose sleep over it. Every day I walk into the briefing and I wonder, What is it that I can't answer?"

I asked about working for Petraeus.

"He's very compassionate, very understanding," Reyes said. "But the man has some seriously high standards. All generals are like this. You give them something and they want more. You have to have the balls to say, I don't know but I'll find out. You also have to have the intestinal fortitude to say, This is what I think. It's an art, as well as a science. You don't get that as a lieutenant. You get it after twenty years of getting shot in the face. My good day is when nobody says anything to me."

Could this war, I asked, turn into a quagmire? What if the Iraqi asymmetrical tactics led not to a conventional slugfest, where the United States was clearly superior, but to a guerrilla campaign?

"There's some serious fog of war out here," Reyes said. "At the end of the day, the question is, Can you live with yourself? Did you give it your best? We're doing this for a reason. I don't know what it is, but I know that it's something bigger than me. Just submit to it."

I walked back to the public affairs tent and was reading e-mail at 12:25 P.M. when CNN reported that an Iraqi missile had been fired toward Kuwait. Launched from Basra, the Ababil-100—the first of seventeen ballistic missiles Iraq would shoot—had initially been detected by a U.S. Navy destroyer in the Persian Gulf. Seconds later, the wail of the Giant Voice carried across New Jersey. The siren started low in pitch, then climbed quickly to become shrill and insistent. Soldiers in the tent fumbled for their gas masks, scurrying toward a shipping container fifty yards away, which only a day earlier had been ringed with seven layers of sandbags and converted into a Scud shelter. Fumbling myself, I also headed for the container, following a debris trail of atropine injectors, chemical detection paper, and extra filters that had spilled from the soldiers' canvas creels as they tried to don their masks.

The all-clear soon sounded and I walked back toward the TOC to find Petraeus outside, smiling even though the siren had awakened him from a nap. "You're in a war," he said, clapping me on the shoulder. The initial report—proverbially, initial reports are always wrong—indicated that five Iraqi missiles had been shot down. "Know where the first shots of the war were fired?" Petraeus asked. "Camp Thunder, the Patriot battery. I fought to get those friggin' things. They weren't going to put any Patriots down there." The Ababil-100 apparently had been aimed at the four thousand soldiers and helicopter fleet at Thunder before it was intercepted and destroyed.

I asked how he felt about the effort to decapitate the regime by killing Saddam at Dora Farms. Petraeus cited an adage from General John Galvin, one of his many mentors: "The bold thing is usually the right thing."

He headed to the helicopter landing pad to pick up General

Wallace. The corps commander was coming to discuss the ground attack, which had indeed been advanced by more than a day. I sauntered back to the public-affairs tent, opened an MRE—I used the Petraeus method, slitting the pouch lengthwise as if gutting a fish—and sat on a folding chair outside. Petraeus and his entourage drove past in two SUVs, just as Wallace's Blackhawk landed several hundred yards to the south. I could see tiny figures saluting. Then the SUVs wheeled around and headed back to the D-Main.

To my surprise, the vehicles sheered away from the TOC entrance and stopped in front of me. Petraeus and Wallace climbed from the lead SUV. Heavily armed bodyguards and aides spilled from the second car. I started forward, realized that I had left my gas mask on the chair, and stepped back to retrieve it.

"He's getting back into uniform," Petraeus quipped.

Wallace removed his cavalry gloves and extended his hand. "We last met a long, long time ago," he said with a pleasant smile. "I remember a little bistro with a nice glass of wine."

We reminisced briefly about our previous meeting sixteen months earlier, at a comfortable Belgian inn during a three-day tour—organized by the Army as an educational and team-building exercise—of the Ardennes and Huertgen Forest battle-fields of World War II.

Burly and brown-eyed, with a rugged face and a voice so soft as to be occasionally inaudible, Wallace described himself as "a pretty simple guy with simple ideas." Born in Chicago and raised in Kentucky, he had graduated from West Point in 1969 as an armor officer. "Always ready to double anyone up in fits of laughter, Wally lives in a perpetual situation comedy," the acad-emy yearbook observed. "One of the best athletes among us, it has been an invaluable pleasure being defeated by him for four years." He had intended to fly helicopters but flunked out of flight school, an unexpected failure that left him briefly embit-tered as he shipped out for a year in Vietnam toward the end of the war. Much of his career had been spent in Germany with armored cavalry units, or in the Mojave Desert, at the National Training Center. His simple ideas included a conviction that "passive leadership is no leadership at all." Wallace espoused "functional discipline," which he defined as "doing what is right, all the time, even though nobody is looking." Plain-spoken and imperturbable, he had a reputation for tactical acuity.

Wallace's war plan for Iraq envisioned "five fights," only one of which directly involved Iraqis: deployment, logistics, terrain, enemy, and tempo. ("We have to have him on the ropes at all times," he declared.) Called Scott by his friends, he was not above telling soldiers that his given name was William Wallace, like the Scottish clan chieftain known as Braveheart. In an emotional talk to Petraeus's 2nd Brigade three days earlier, the corps commander had explained why he was ordering his troops into battle:

> I remember September 11. Do you? This is what this is all about. There is no place in this world for WMD, especially in the hands of a knucklehead like Saddam Hussein. . . . I want my family to be safe, I want your family to be safe. I want to know when my grandkids get on an airplane that they don't have to worry about being safe. I don't want your family to worry about being safe if they want to go to the mall. This old man is damn proud to be standing up here in front of you today.

Abruptly, the Giant Voice sounded again. We yanked the M-40s from their canvas bags, fit the masks over our faces, and adjusted the straps. I'm not certain anyone met the nine-second standard.

As we strode toward the bunker, I said, "This is going to make witty conversation difficult." My voice, already a pathetic croak from the Kuwaiti crud, sounded small and strangled through the mask.

"It's going to be a long day," Wallace replied.

Into the shelter crowded two dozen soldiers, all bug-eyed and long-snouted in their masks. "More coming. Move back," a voice called. Shipping pallets lined the inside walls for extra protection. A sticker noted that the container was made of "Superior Atmospheric Corrosion Resistant Steel." A packing slip, signed by one D. Virginia Bartholomew at Sierra Army Depot in California on December 15, 2002, showed that it had carried "mats, runway airfield landing," weighing nearly eight tons and valued at $727,650. Ms. Bartholomew had affirmed that "the packages therein are properly marked, labelled, and placarded."

Petraeus gamely tried to make conversation. The mask voice-box gave his words a metallic ping. Wallace, who was slightly deaf and disinclined to chitchat, listened tranquilly, his eyes magnified through the eyepieces. Petraeus finally gave up, muttering, "He's gonna have to pay for this."

Wallace nodded. "That son of a bitch is about to piss me off," he said. Two deep booms echoed in the distance, apparently from a Patriot battery firing a pair of interceptors at what we later learned was another Ababil-100 launched toward Kuwait City.

After fifteen minutes the all-clear sounded. We shambled from the container and peeled off the masks, our faces flushed and glistening with sweat. Braveheart seemed ready to draw his broadsword and take the offensive. He was growling, too: "I'm not looking forward to catching lawn darts for another day more than I have to." With Petraeus at his side, he lingered for a few minutes to discuss the wartime shotgun marriage of his V Corps, based in Germany, and two U.S.-based divisions that usually worked for the XVIII Airborne Corps, the 101st and the 3 ID, a union that reflected the expediency required in this expeditionary age. "You've got to learn new personalities," Wallace said, "everybody's little quirks."

I asked what the hardest part of his job was now that war had begun.

"Just the waiting. There's precious little I can do for the next twenty-four to forty-eight hours except come look Petraeus in the eye. The thing that strikes me about this whole operation is the requirement to flow forces and fight at the same time. It's a nightmare." The Defense Department's decision to abandon the Army's meticulous deployment matrix and go to war with only ninety thousand assault troops in the theater showed, in Wallace's judgment, the Army's "dexterity and flexibility."

But, I asked, did the streamlined deployment really make the process faster?

"I don't know whether it has made it faster," Wallace said. "I know it's made it harder." Among other severe shortages, including military police and civil-affairs units, V Corps had many fewer trucks than needed to move troops, supplies, and spare parts across Iraq's vast distances. Wallace recognized the shortfall but could do nothing about it, a helpless feeling he later likened to "standing there waiting to catch a safe coming out of a twenty-story window."

Avoiding a protracted battle in the cities was also very much on his mind. The previous day, Wallace had asked a group of Apache pilots, "How do you take down Baghdad? I have told commanders that we will be patient before we have to fight in the city. I pray it will not come to that. The place is as big as Boston." To me, he now added, "I'll see you downrange."

We shook hands and he drove off, trailing gunmen.

An hour later, at Petraeus's invitation, I found myself buckled into his Blackhawk, known as Warlord 457. As we looped east and then north at a hundred knots, the two door gunners slewed their M-60 machine guns at suspicious shapes and shadows below.

Petraeus studied the terrain and I wondered what the world looked like through the commanding general's eyes. Trying to parse his moods and actions had become an intriguing exercise.

He was cautious and private, and his formal statements to reporters or television cameras had a stilted, calculated timbre. Offstage, he could be tart, funny, and occasionally cynical, suggesting at one point that the expatriate Iraqi resistance in London was "trying to fax Saddam to death." His interests were broad, and our conversations ranged from Pentagon gossip and career trajectories to theology and writing. He could be self-deprecating, as when he quoted his mother as saying of his slender frame, "No self-respecting chicken would look like you." He was interested in books and ideas and minds as agile as his own, and once he apologized for turning a conversation into a monologue—a transmutation that is hardly unusual for senior commanders. Every day it became more evident that the intellectual rigor of leading a division in battle beguiled him. He badly wanted a combat patch, perhaps the only significant omission from his curriculum vitae. But I never sensed that personal ambition eclipsed his visceral awareness that seventeen thousand lives were in his hands, and that no occasion could be more solemn or profound for a commander than ordering young soldiers to their deaths.

Responsibility was heavy indeed, and Petraeus began to signal his moods by tilting his extended hand up or down. "Everyone has the full range of emotions," he once observed. "It's just a question of how fast you get there." Occasionally, when things were going poorly, he lapsed into brooding silence or snapped at an underling for infractions real or imagined. Poor Jeremy Miller, his driver, received a steady patter of rudder orders—"Go left! No, over there. Watch your speed, Ranger! Let this guy pass you." I was certain that Petraeus felt enormous pressure not to misuse the division, not to fail, not to disappoint all the surrogate fathers who had nurtured his career for thirty years. Many eyes were watching him, not only the eyes of generals he had served, but also the eyes of thousands of officers who were not going to Iraq, and who may have felt a grudging resentment toward those who were. An old Army adage held that it didn't matter which war you were in as long as it was the most recent one; since only two of the Army's ten divisions were likely to have meaningful combat roles in the march on Baghdad, that left eight divisions full of officers who would not serve in "the last one."

Ten minutes after leaving New Jersey, we touched down at Udairi airfield. Petraeus led the way into a hangar. "You boys ready to go?" he called. "Hoo-ah," a dozen voices answered. "Hoo-ah."

The Long Range Surveillance Detachment, or LRSD, served as the division's eyes behind enemy lines. Two six-man teams were to be inserted in the desert southwest of Karbala, where they would construct camouflaged "hide sites" and, for up to five days, "detect, identify, and report" Iraqi military movements that threatened helicopter refueling operations. Captain Eric Haupt, the detachment commander, explained to Petraeus that four Blackhawks, escorted by four Apaches, would haul the teams north at night, feinting several times to conceal the actual insertion locations. Special scopes allowed the teams to see six miles in daylight, almost four miles at night, and they carried an array of long-range radios.

Haupt anticipated that his men would go north in two days. Each team had been quarantined to minimize distractions and to keep them from learning details of each other's missions in the event of capture. In a pair of tents near the hangar, we inspected the kit that the soldiers had laid out on their cots, including laser optics, radios, extra ammunition magazines, chemical protective suits, knives, Energizer batteries, a five-day food supply, and eleven quarts of water per man.

"Do you feel comfortable with the mission?" Petraeus asked a sergeant who was cleaning dust from a computer keyboard with an old-fashioned shaving brush.

"Oh, yes, sir."

"What's your biggest worry?"

"Sir, my biggest worry is that there are some chemical sites out there."

Before returning to the Blackhawk, Petraeus stopped to see Colonel Gregory P. Gass, commander of the 101st Aviation Brigade. In one tent, Gass's pilots were reviewing TOPSCENE, a computer software program that combined reconnaissance photos and topographical data to create a detailed, three-dimensional video of a target area. Using a tiny joystick, a warrant officer first swooped in on two Euphrates River bridges guarded by the Medina Division's 14th Mechanized Brigade, and then "flew" just a few hundred feet above a cluster of U-shaped earthworks sheltering Iraqi armor.

In another tent, planners already were looking beyond the destruction of the Medina Division to an Apache attack against the Hammurabi Republican Guard Division, farther north. Scribbled calculations covered butcher paper on an easel. Two brigades of the Hammurabi contained 202 tanks and other prime targets, according to intelligence tallies. Demolishing half of those would effectively destroy the division. Using "probability of kill" equations that assumed a 60 percent success rate among all Hellfire antitank missiles fired, the planners figured that a volley of 161 Hellfires would be required. Since each Apache typically carried eight missiles, that meant destruction of the Hammurabi brigades would require twenty aircraft on the mission. Drawing on those calculations, planners could estimate the quantities of fuel and other supplies that would be needed.

If all this seemed detached and a little antiseptic, we were soon reminded how frayed emotions had become. Lifting off from Udairi shortly after 5 P.M., Petraeus asked the pilots to detour to the southwest before returning to New Jersey. A few minutes later, we spied Rakkasan convoys stretching toward the setting sun as it dipped toward the Iraqi border: Humvees, earthmovers, five-thousand-gallon tankers, the water trailers called buffaloes, military vans, and open-sided trucks with hundreds of riflemen packed onto benches. It was an ancient and dreadful sight: an army surging forward.

E. J. Sinclair was waiting for us as Warlord 457 set down in a maelstrom of dust alongside one convoy. The 101st and the 3rd Infantry Division were converging in a traffic jam even before they got out of Kuwait. "They're in tanks and APCs"—armored personnel carriers—"so we let them go first," Sinclair told Petraeus with a bemused shake of the head. "It has taken almost two hours to drive forty kilometers. It's going slower than we expected."

Then, a young officer who had been monitoring the radios came panting up to the command group. His words tumbled out as he saluted Petraeus. "Sir, I just got word that enemy airstrikes are coming. Everybody needs to take cover."

I looked around. The nearest cover in this flat purgatory was Jordan. Soldiers began darting about.

Petraeus looked at me and smiled. "Naw, I think that's bullshit. Those are the TLAMs"—Tomahawk Land Attack Missiles—"that are supposed to be going in at 1500 Zulu." A quick radio call to Tom Schoenbeck at the D-Main confirmed that there was no credible evidence of Iraqi aircraft. In fact, no American soldier had been attacked by enemy aircraft since the early 1950s—"a period that encompasses fully half the history of powered flight," as one retired Air Force general cheerfully noted—and Iraq in this war would fail to put up a single airplane sortie.

Petraeus seemed pleased to find that battlefield truisms are indeed true. "The first report," he said with a grin, "*is* always wrong."

A good night's sleep had been hard to come by for three weeks, and now it would be even harder. The tent usually began stirring at 6 A.M. By the time I finished reporting, writing, filing my story to the home office, and dealing with any questions from the editors, it was typically midnight or later. Trying to get a satellite-phone connection through the oversubscribed circuits had also been a high-anxiety ordeal most evenings, and in several instances I was reduced to dictating to a transcriber in Washington. In pursuit of a deep five hours, I took a sleeping tablet at one o'clock on Friday morning, March 21.

So it was that I slept soundly, first through the wailing of the Giant Voice and then through the launch of two Patriots from the battery outside New Jersey. The missiles, Dwyer subsequently told me, made "such an unbelievable roar they sounded like they were coming right through the tent."

I regained something approaching consciousness to see flashlight beams darting around the tent. Soldiers adjusted their masks and pulled on their clothes. A voice demanded, "Why the fuck are you still sleeping when we're having a goddamn Scud attack?" It took a moment to realize that the voice was talking to me. I peered at my watch and saw that it was 2:30 A.M. I wriggled into my pants but could not find my M-40. The canvas case was empty. On hands and knees I groped around the cot, to no avail. I considered lying down and going back to sleep: let them gas me and be done with it. Everyone had trooped off to the shelter except Sergeant Mark Swart, who appeared next to me in his mask.

"Did you hear that enormous explosion?" he said.

"I don't think so. I can't find my mask." I showed him the empty sack.

"Here it is," Swart said. He picked up the mask from the plywood floor where it had been lying at my feet. The all-clear sounded before I could fit the thing to my face. "Thanks, Mark," I mumbled, and lay back down. I thought of the World War II correspondents I so admired—Liebling, Shirer, Rame, Moorehead, Pyle—and hoped that they, too, at least once in their splendid careers, had known how it felt to be utterly ridiculous.

Still chagrined, I walked to breakfast by myself at dawn. The mess tent seemed empty after the departure of so many Rakkasans.

For the first time the refrigerator cases were stocked with "near beer," alcohol-free San Miguel, which seemed a little rough-hewn for breakfast. A soldier across the table railed against his sergeant, whom he repeatedly referred to as "that fucking troll." A graffito in a burn latrine asked: "Who's your Baghdaddy?"

Petraeus was in his customary seat at the head table when I walked into the BUB at 7:35 A.M. and took a chair in the Skybox. He seemed downright chipper, galvanized by war. "I hope it has settled in on everybody," he said into the microphone, "that you all are now eligible for membership in the Veterans of Foreign Wars." Then, in the same jocular tone: "How many Frenchmen does it take to screw in a lightbulb? One. He just stands there holding it and lets the world revolve around him."

The Friday-morning briefing began with a staff officer's short recitation of war news. A dozen lanes had been cut in the six-mile-wide obstacle belt that marked the border. Engineers stood on the berm, waving large American flags at the breaching forces streaming past. The 1st Marine Expeditionary Force and British troops were well into the Rumaylah oil field in southeastern Iraq, securing two refineries and a critical manifold; of more than one thousand wells in the southern fields only nine had been sabotaged, and it appeared unlikely that Iraq would be able to dump millions of barrels of crude oil into the Persian Gulf, as it had in 1991. Marines would leave the city of Basra to the British before swinging west and then north to Al Kut, angling toward Baghdad from the southeast. The day's severest losses had come in the crash of a Chinook helicopter, killing four U.S. Marines and eight British soldiers.

Although the air attack had yet to begin in earnest, U.S. intelligence estimated that 60 percent of Baghdad's 5 million people had evacuated the capital for the less vulnerable suburbs and countryside, jamming roads in central Iraq. Nearly a dozen Iraqi border posts had been hit with hundreds of artillery shells and Hellfire missiles. The 3rd Infantry Division had poured across

Kuwait's western border, meeting only light contact and killing fourteen Iraqi soldiers at the start of the blitzkrieg toward Baghdad. One Iraqi border guard died when a box of propoganda leaflets dropped from the air hit him on the head.

More than two dozen Special Forces teams had thrust into Iraq from the south, west, and north. SF troops were to seize the Euphrates bridges at Nasariyah and Samawah the next night. "They'd better hurry," Petraeus said, "or 3 ID is going to beat them there."

As for the 101st, it was ready for combat, as Petraeus had warranted. Three ground-assault convoys full of Rakkasans had moved to an assembly area near a cut, designated as Lane 11, while two other GACs were to move forward from Udairi and Camp New Jersey within the next day. Optimists on the staff believed that Exxon—a hundred miles into Iraq from Kuwait—could open by the following morning, Saturday, March 22, and that Shell, another 140 miles farther away, could be set up the day after. That would allow the Apaches of the 101st to attack the Medina Division as early as Monday night.

Another scheme, Contingency Plan Bastogne, envisioned seizing a vital highway intersection just south of Baghdad with 101st troops inserted by helicopter and reinforced with armored cavalry from the 3rd Infantry Division. Reconnaissance photos projected onto a screen at the front of the room showed the Medina's 14th Mechanized Brigade in revetments along a rail line near Musayyib, southwest of Baghdad. Intelligence analysts estimated that the Medina was at 94 percent of full strength; the Hammurabi Division was estimated at 93 percent.

Petraeus studied the photos intently. "I'll tell you what," he said, "there are some targets out there." A concurring murmur rippled through the room.

On Friday afternoon, we flew southwest from New Jersey in Warlord 457 to Attack Position Terri, where the Rakkasans were to cross the border in a few hours. Petraeus had five radio frequencies available, including corps and division networks, and he switched back and forth by flipping a console dial with his left hand.

"Boy," he said over the Blackhawk's intercom, "look at that line of vehicles." Through the left window in the passenger bay I could see a convoy longer even than the one we had seen the previous day. The cavalcade looked like a traveling circus. Desert-camouflaged Humvees, ammunition trucks, and howitzers—each with a fluorescent pink recognition panel intended to ward off fratricidal air attacks—were interspersed with fourteen Kuwaiti water trucks, purchased by the division for flushing helicopter engines and washing blades. Red, yellow, and blue disco lights outlined the cabs and beds, and each truck was stenciled with the name of the previous owner—Maskin & Transport As Singas—rather than "U.S. Army."

The helicopter set down in the usual nimbus of dust, and again E. J. Sinclair greeted us as we scuffed through the sand in a half-crouch beneath the rotor blades. Three GACs had assembled in this desolate patch eight miles from the border, each with several hundred vehicles. As one crawled forward, the other two waited their turn. The Rakkasans had donned JLIST chemical suits as a precaution, writing their last names and blood types on each tunic sleeve. In the afternoon heat, with temperatures in the upper nineties, everyone looked wilted. Soldiers dozed in slit trenches or beneath jerry-rigged sun shades next to their vehicles.

"I'm trying to get these guys not to move. Get some rest. Find some shade," said Iuniasolua Savusa, the brigade sergeant major, who had "A+" scrawled on his right arm. "After you've made these kids ride on the backs of these trucks for three days, they'll be ready to get off and shoot something."

Mike Linnington, the brigade commander, gestured to a five-ton with infantry rucksacks lashed to the sides and a placard—"Bad Motherfucker's Truck"—wired to the bumper. "Sergeant major," Linnington said to Savusa, "will you get that sign off?"

Petraeus worked the line, offering hoo-ahs and atta-boys. Soldiers answered with a desultory "Rakkasan, sir." To Lieutenant

Colonel Chris Pease, an enormous former college heavyweight wrestler who now commanded the 1st Battalion of the 187th Infantry, Petraeus said, "This is a hell of a mission for the light-infantry air-assault soldier." Swaddled in his chemical suit, flak jacket, and other gear, Pease had given his driver $100 to find a Diet Coke. "Yes, sir," he replied. "I feel like I have three layers of brassieres on me."

The only Rakkasan convoy moving forward lurched in stop-and-go fits. Sinclair and Petraeus stood beside the unpaved trail, offering high-fives and thumbs-up to soldiers who were inching toward Iraq as part of the Army's ten-thousand-vehicle invasion force.

"I'd like to get Exxon in by the morning," Petraeus told the S.

"We'll be hard-pressed," Sinclair replied. "I think it will be more like late afternoon." Forty vehicles had stalled already, although mechanics quickly swarmed over every breakdown. "We're waiting for the tail end of 3 ID to get through the berm. We can't go until they're through. You can see them out there on the horizon."

He pointed westward. Several miles distant, a procession of tiny vehicles scuttled across the desert pan, a hundred yards apart. Each trailed a delicate plume of dust.

A 101st Humvee pulling a trailer crawled past with a sign lashed to the grill: "Let the bodies hit the floor." Behind it came a truck with a Texas state flag flapping beneath the side-view mirror. Seeing a frown cloud the face of his commanding general, a soldier in the cab called to Petraeus, "I'm taking it down, sir."

As we scuffed back to the helicopter, Petraeus ruminated on how a commander had to strike a balance between oversight and meddling. "You think you're being inspirational, but most of the time you're just getting in their way," he said. "This is actually a pretty good plan. What will be required right now is a little bit of tactical patience, particularly on my part."

———

We were in the division TOC when word came that the 101st vanguard had crossed into Iraq on Route Hurricane at 8:45 P.M., bound for the seared patch of nowhere now known as Exxon. Fifteen minutes later, more than five hundred cruise missiles and hundreds of bombs began obliterating targets around Baghdad in a televised extravaganza of fireballs and billowing black smoke.

Pride and even exultation marked that evening's battle briefing. The air campaign just begun would pummel Iraq with three thousand precision-guided bombs and missiles over the next three days; planes launched from five U.S. Navy aircraft carriers complemented attacks from various land bases, submarines, and surface ships. The 3rd Infantry Division was already nearly a hundred miles into Iraq, barely twelve hours after crossing the border. Another GAC from the 101st would enter Iraq at 10:30 P.M., angling toward Shell to rendezvous with a battalion to be air assaulted by helicopter on Sunday. Though far behind the 3rd, the 101st had displayed impressive agility in mounting a major invasion only six weeks after getting the deployment order at Fort Campbell. Moreover, the Anglo-American attack had been orchestrated with power, precision, and finesse. Rather than softening up Iraqi defenses with a five-week air campaign, as in 1991, ground forces in this war had attacked first, preceding all but the improvised decapitation attack. Early reports depicted the Iraqi defenders as surprised and befuddled.

Although the invasion force was less than half the size of that mustered to liberate Kuwait twelve years earlier, commanders this time had been given a far more ambitious mission: march hundreds of miles to Baghdad, neutralize the Iraqi military, overthrow Saddam Hussein's regime, and then prevent the country from disintegrating into chaos.

Much attention had been given to the first three tasks, and Army commanders seemed confident that each could be accomplished. Virtually no attention had been paid to the last objective.

The Pentagon, sensing little urgency from the White House, had not created an Office of Reconstruction and Humanitarian Assistance until late January, and much of the subsequent planning had focused on anticipated refugee problems, rather than on looting, civil disintegration, or insurrection. As recently as early February, according to a V Corps document, CFLCC had yet to develop a plan for the postwar stabilization of Iraq in what was known as Phase IV.

American planners had made several dubious assumptions, including the premise that Iraqi civil servants would remain on the job to run essential services once Saddam Hussein and his cabal were swept away. Upon asking in one prewar conference "whether there will be a legitimate police force" in Iraq, Petraeus was told, "There are people trying to determine that." Scott Wallace had commented, "This is going to be a learning experience. . . . None of us have done this before."

Yet it hardly seemed to matter on that Friday night. The U.S. military was manifestly more lethal than it had been even a decade before, a juggernaut of shock, intimidation, and speed, well tooled for the wayfaring campaigns that had become the American way of war. Some systems that had been new in the Gulf War were now mature and fully integrated into the force— ATACMS, for example, the Army Tactical Missile System, which had a range approaching two hundred miles and was now pummeling targets around Nasariyah and Tallil air base; and JSTARS, the Joint Surveillance Target Attack Radar System, an airborne scout able to detect individual moving vehicles more than a hundred miles away.

Other munitions now falling on Iraq had been little more than a brainstorm in the early 1990s. A new generation of smart bombs, such as the relatively cheap and plentiful Joint Direct Attack Munition, or JDAM, used global positioning satellites to home in on targets. The dumb, unguided bombs that accounted for more than 90 percent of the tonnage dropped on Iraq in 1991 had been largely supplanted by twenty-two types of guided munitions, which would make up more than two-thirds of the 29,199 bombs that were to fall on Iraq in the next few weeks.

Such innovations had furthered the military's endless quest for "standoff" killing power—the ability to attack with precision, while staying outside an opponent's lethal range. No weapon better exemplified the Army's standoff capability than the new Longbow model of the Apache attack helicopter, which could fire a Hellfire missile capable of destroying a tank sitting five miles away.

"When we attack the 14th Brigade of the Medina Division, we expect to see a hundred burning armored vehicles within half an hour," Tom Schoenbeck told me as I studied the map at the front of the room.

The hiss of canned air sounded through the TOC as watch officers blew dust from their keyboards. Schoenbeck's spectacles were perched on his head, and his sunglasses hung on a cord around his neck. "Part of this is to make them sweat and wonder where the 101st is with all those Apaches they've seen pictures of," he said. "General Wallace told us, 'I want to destroy the Medina and let the Hammurabi and other Republican Guard divisions think about that. We're going to take our time, we're going to kill every one of them, and we're not going to move forward until we do.'"

Before retiring to his tent for the night, Petraeus told his staff, "This thing's about to begin for us."

Even the shrewd commanding general had no idea how right he was.

7

ENEMY IN THE WIRE

I woke to a roar so intense that concussion ghosts rippled in tiny canvas waves along the tent wall above my head. A dozen flashlight beams darted back and forth, their yellow and red shafts dancing across the ceiling. At first I thought the ungodly noise was a jet directly overhead, perhaps an A-10 Warthog. Then I realized that it was a Patriot scorching past, launched from the battery beyond the mess tent.

The wail of the Giant Voice supplanted the receding din of the missile. I pulled on my gas mask and started to lie down, then remembered the danger of suffocation. I depressed the switch on the small blue penlight attached to my Swiss Army knife and studied my watch: 3 A.M., Sunday, March 23.

Half-dressed soldiers tromped around the plywood floor or whisked through the tent flaps, mumbling incoherently in their masks. The all-clear soon sounded. I pulled off the M-40, carefully wrapped the elastic straps around the eyepieces, and slipped the mask back into the case; I was no longer cavalier about packing the damned thing for the next occasion.

Several unmasked soldiers stood near the foot of my cot, their faces slick with sweat. A sergeant's voice abruptly brought me to full consciousness: "There's been some sort of attack at the Bastogne TOC. They don't know what's going on." Bastogne was the nickname for the 1st Brigade, bivouacked a few miles north at Camp Pennsylvania.

Slipping on my boots and jacket, I tromped a hundred yards across the sand to the opening in the concertina wire, where skittish sentries in the D-Main security tent scrutinized my badge and waved me through. A dozen cardboard boxes stacked next to the checkpoint contained newly printed street maps of Karbala and other cities in central Iraq.

Despite the hour, the command post was fully manned. A huge map of greater Baghdad was posted at the front of the room, along with diagrams showing the defensive configurations for Exxon, Shell, and Conoco. Another map showed the leading edge of the 3rd Infantry Division, now 150 miles into Iraq, nearly halfway to Baghdad. A placard listed the daily challenge, MATCHBOX, and countersign, VALET, and suddenly the pass-words seemed more than a Hollywood convention. A six-foot time line labeled "Graphic Execution Sketch" plotted a schedule of events for the next twelve days. Nowhere did it mention an attack on Camp Pennsylvania.

Petraeus stood behind the head table. Strain etched his face. A new haircut, inflicted by the headquarters' amateur barber on Saturday, had left his scalp nicked and patchy. I sidled up and he told me what he knew, which was not a great deal. After a busy if oddly routine day at New Jersey overseeing the division's initial surge into Iraq, he had been awakened shortly before 2 A.M. by a report that 1st Brigade was under attack from grenade and rifle fire. Suspicions that infiltrators had penetrated the Pennsylvania perimeter, or that turncoat Kuwaiti translators were responsible, had now yielded to a belief that the attack was self-inflicted, a fragging. A sergeant was in custody, a Muslim convert who had been guarding ammunition in a convoy that was preparing to decamp for Iraq. The casualty total had reached at least thirteen; several soldiers were critically hurt, and the brigade commander, Colonel Ben Hodges, had been lightly wounded.

Petraeus's voice dropped to a low monotone as he unspooled this tale of carnage and betrayal. I sensed his disbelief that the division's first casualties could come in such a hideous manner. "Fragging": even the word was poisonous, connoting indiscipline, and lost causes, and an Army unhinged by Vietnam.

I thanked him and stepped outside the tent to call Washington on my satellite phone. It was just after 4 A.M. I dictated seven paragraphs, which were posted on the newspaper's Web site at 8:27 P.M. Saturday, EST, and updated several times until the deadline for Sunday's newspaper had passed. As I finished the call, an officer walked out of the TOC. At least one wounded soldier had died, he told me. "This is bad," he added. "This is really, really bad."

It took months for a comprehensive account to emerge of the incident at Camp Pennsylvania, and the mystery of fratricidal murder would never be satisfactorily solved. But accounts from 1st Brigade in the thirty-six hours after the attack, and my conversations with witnesses during a subsequent visit to Bastogne with Petraeus, gave me a reasonably clear picture.

Sergeant Asan K. Akbar had been born Mark Fidel Kools in the Watts neighborhood of Los Angeles. His mother changed his name when he was a boy and the family converted to Islam. After graduating from high school in southern California, he attended the state university at Davis for nine years, eventually earning degrees in aeronautical and mechanical engineering. Joining the Army in 1998, he had won several promotions despite evidence that he was something of an odd duck in a military culture that prized conformity. Comrades later described him as "scatterbrained," "incompetent," and "a headache." He slept badly at night and sometimes dozed during training. Once he was spotted doing karate kicks while sleepwalking, and soldiers began to call him Crouching Tiger, after a popular movie that featured extravagant displays of martial arts.

Shunted between units over the past several years and given minimal responsibilities, at the age of thirty-one, Akbar had ended up in Bravo Company of the 326th Engineer Battalion, a component of 1st Brigade. Several senior sergeants tried to block his deployment from Fort Campbell to the Middle East. "I was told, 'You will take him. We need the numbers, and we need to take full strength into Kuwait and Iraq,'" Sergeant First Class Daniel Kumm later testified. The only Muslim in his company, he seemed unsettled at the prospect of war with an Islamic country, particularly when he overheard crude joking among soldiers about rape and plunder. After arriving at Camp Pennsylvania, his platoon lieutenant observed, Akbar seemed "possibly depressed or suicidal." To his mother he complained, "Mom, nobody in my platoon likes me."

Saturday, the twenty-second, had been frantically busy for the Bastogne brigade, which was about to follow the Rakkasans into Iraq. There were maps to issue, ammunition to distribute, and hundreds of vehicles to organize into assault convoys. By 1 A.M. Sunday, most brigade staff officers had crawled into their sleeping bags for a few hours of rest. The Bastogne TOC occupied a large tent in the center of Camp Pennsylvania. Two red fire extinguishers stood near the entry flap, where a sign noted, "Threat Con Delta, Weapons on Amber." Another sign, tacked to the sentry's plywood desk, asked, "Who Else Needs to Know?" Gravel walkways lined with green sandbags led from the command post toward a large concrete culvert used as a missile shelter. Concrete barriers protected a sand courtyard around the TOC, separating it from neat rows of sleeping tents fifty yards away.

At 1:20 A.M. the brigade sergeant major, Bart Womack, was just settling for the night in the tent closest to the TOC. The lanky Bastogne commander, Ben Hodges, was sprawled on a nearby cot, already in a deep sleep. Womack switched on a small television connected to a satellite dish, and flipped to the Golf Channel. Suddenly a hand pulled open the tent flap and an incendiary grenade bounced across the plywood floor in a shower of sparks followed by a searing white flash. Hodges, astonishingly, remained asleep until a second grenade—this one a fragmentation model—clattered across the floor and detonated with an explosive pop. "We're being attacked!" Womack bellowed. "We're being attacked!" Hodges woke just as two metal shards punctured his right forearm, causing bloody but superficial wounds.

Officers in two adjacent tents were less fortunate. Major Verner Kiernan, the brigade fire-support officer, was sitting at a small table, tapping out an e-mail on a laptop computer. He jumped up at the sound of the initial explosions in Hodges's tent next door, slipped on his boots, and grabbed his pistol for what he assumed was a training drill. A soldier pushed aside the tent flap and said, "We're under attack, sir." A few seconds later, Kiernan heard a grenade clatter across the floor. The explosion ripped apart cots, vinyl partitions, and rucksacks. Flames licked at the rear wall and smoke billowed through the tent. Kiernan was unhurt, but Major Gregory Stone, a forty-year-old from Boise, Idaho, with two young sons, was grievously wounded in the neck and abdomen. He would die of his injuries two days later.

In the third tent, the detonations woke Captain Mark Wisher, an Air Force liaison officer. Leaping from his cot, he had begun to dress when a soldier appeared in the tent entryway. "Sir, we're under a ground attack," the soldier warned. The notion struck Wisher as absurd. How could the Iraqis mount a ground attack in the middle of Kuwait? Other officers scrambled to their feet, grabbing helmets and weapons. Wisher was reaching for his boots when he heard an ominous thud as an object hit the plywood floor, bounced heavily, then rolled for a moment and stopped. He crouched to make his body as small as possible and clawed at a seam in the tent wall in an effort to break the Velcro seal. The grenade blast blew him through the canvas, seeding his right arm, shoulder, lung, diaphragm, and liver with fragments. Hot steel tore into both of Captain Terence Bacon's knees and ripped at several other officers as they bolted for the doorway.

Pleas for help and shouts of alarm swept the encampment. One soldier used a bayonet to cut his way out of a burning tent. Radio calls carried across Pennsylvania. "Enemy in the wire! Enemy in the wire! We're under attack!" Hodges's tent was blazing, and terrified soldiers swarmed in confusion or lay bleeding in the sand. Major Kenneth Romaine, the brigade executive officer, had been working on battle plans for the morning departure and managed to get out of Hodges's tent uninjured after the second grenade detonated. Pistol drawn, he saw movement from the corner of his eye and wheeled to fire when a single rifle bullet struck both his hands, deflected into his left thigh, and blew out the back of his leg. First Sergeant Rodlon Stevenson also ran outside and saw Captain Christopher Scott Seifert, a twenty-seven-year-old intelligence officer from Easton, Pennsylvania, running with a gas mask in his hand when a soldier with a rifle, wearing a brown T-shirt and desert camouflage trousers, shot Seifert in the lower back, point-blank. Stevenson rushed to Seifert's side. "You can't go this way," Stevenson told the dying officer. "You gotta fight for your family. You got a newborn baby."

The killer had flushed the men from their tents with grenades, then stood outside to pick them off with his M-4 rifle. After shooting Romaine and Seifert, he had melted into the night.

The shooting stopped, the screams ebbed. Troopers extinguished the fires and administered first aid. Ten soldiers were bundled into evacuation helicopters and flown to combat hospitals at Udairi and Kuwait City. Chaplains circulated through the camp, offering trauma counseling. Two Kuwaiti interpreters, whom Colonel Hodges had interviewed about possible employment earlier in the evening, were seized, then later freed. A brigade officer called Petraeus, who ordered the staff to determine whether any grenades were missing from their caches and to compile a list of disaffected soldiers.

It took less than an hour for Sergeant Akbar's name to surface. Until midnight, when his shift ended, he had been guarding the ammunition in a Humvee scheduled to leave for Iraq in the morning. Seven grenades were missing from that stockpile. As the alarm spread and the guard was doubled, Akbar had joined sentries peering for enemies around the perimeter of the brigade command post. Now he was missing.

No sooner had the uproar begun to subside than the camp missile siren sounded, part of the same alert that at that moment woke me at Camp New Jersey. Soldiers clawed at their mask bags and took shelter in concrete culverts. With a fantastic roar a Patriot leaped from its launcher and angled up on a golden pillar of flame. But the Patriot was befuddled. Instead of targeting an Iraqi Ababil-100 or Al-Samoud 2, the missile had locked onto a British Tornado fighter-bomber flying south.

Lieutenant Colonel Christopher P. Hughes, a battalion commander whose command post was on the far side of Pennsylvania, had managed to reach Hodges on the radio. "I got knocked on my ass," Hodges told him. Now Hughes arrived at the brigade TOC just as the Patriot detonated overhead in a white flash, followed by a concussive boom. Hughes looked up to see aircraft and missile debris raining down; the wreckage included two dead British crewmen. By the glare of the explosion, he spotted the silhouette of the destroyed Tornado's wingman, streaking south.

In the concrete shelter outside the TOC, Sergeant Major Womack discovered Sergeant Akbar, who was dragged out and flex-cuffed with his face in the sand. Three grenades were discovered in his gas-mask case in the shelter, and investigators soon found three empty grenade cannisters and a pair of safety clips in his JLIST bag near the flagpole. "You guys are coming into our countries," Akbar was quoted as saying, "and you're going to rape our women and kill our children." Three spent M-4 shells were discovered near the sleeping tents; investigators soon matched the casings to the bullet removed from Captain Seifert's abdomen during his autopsy. To intensify the havoc, someone apparently had turned off the brace of outdoor lights before the attack began. Akbar's fingerprints were found on a generator outside the demolished tents.

Inconsistencies and uncertainty would persist. Two witnesses told investigators that Akbar did not resemble the man they saw shoot Seifert. One soldier thought he saw gunfire come from a second shooter. Akbar soon was transferred to a stockade in Mannheim, Germany, before being flown to the United States. No American soldier had been prosecuted for the murder of another soldier in wartime since Vietnam, and no soldier had been executed in wartime since Private Eddie Slovik was shot for desertion in 1945. In June, a military hearing officer would find sufficient grounds to try Akbar for murders committed during "a surprise attack executed by stealth." Under military law, a final decision on whether to convene a court-martial, and whether to declare the Pennsylvania massacre a capital crime, punishable by death, rested with the accused soldier's division commander. Petraeus, recognizing the emotional cross-currents, exercised his legal discretion to refer the case to higher authority for disposition.

A long, sad night stretched into a long, sad Sunday morning. A profound sobriety descended on Camp New Jersey, supplanting the adrenal excitement of the past three days. Seifert's comrades had the somber task of packing up his books, personal photos, and uniforms. Many soldiers were unsettled and would sleep badly for weeks; that the accused killer was Muslim provoked mostly a careful silence in the ranks. War had come inside the division headquarters with unanticipated savagery. One staff officer wrote in his journal: "The first fragging of the war. Is this the next Vietnam?"

Before the morning BUB, Larry Wark gave me an accounting of the sixteen soldiers killed or wounded at Camp Pennsylvania. The 1st Brigade staff had been decimated, with key officers probably out for the duration of the war.

Why the Patriot had misfired at the Tornado remained unclear; ten days later, another Patriot destroyed a U.S. Navy F/A-18C Hornet flying from the USS *Kitty Hawk* over Karbala, killing the pilot. The United States had invested $3 billion to fix serious flaws discovered in the Patriot during the 1991 Gulf War, repairs that should have precluded the system from confusing a friendly aircraft with an enemy missile, even if, as some air-defense experts believed, the British crew had improperly set the "identification friend-or-foe" transmitter intended to prevent such blunders. Air-defense logs indicated that the Patriot battery manually fired a single interceptor after radar symbology indicated an approaching antiradiation missile nine miles downrange at 18,300 feet, traveling at 511 knots. Some experts speculated that the proliferation of Patriot batteries protecting various Army camps had caused the radars to confuse one another.

At 7:40 A.M., Tom Schoenbeck, who had commanded Bastogne before Ben Hodges, stood with the cordless microphone. "Attention in the TOC. We're going to start the BUB in five minutes, so get your last-minute things together. We're going to do this quickly, so be very concise and give the CG only what he needs to know to make decisions."

Officers shuffled sideways through the narrow aisles to their seats, murmuring "Excuse me"s and trying not to trip over snarled computer cables. The day's challenge and password were posted on the front partition: BOTTLE and EGGS. Petraeus ducked through the tent flap and removed his helmet. He looked remarkably fresh for a man who had slept very little. "Okay," he said, "let's go." The war news was good. Rakkasan troops on Saturday had reached Exxon, which was now a full-service gas station with eighty thousand gallons of fuel on hand. The 3rd Infantry Division, two hundred miles into Iraq, had bulled north through the region where Shell would be built and was clearing Objective Rams, southwest of Najaf.

Tonight, after Rams was secure, the V Corps' 11th Attack Helicopter Regiment planned to stage there and launch an Apache attack against the Medina Division between Karbala and Baghdad. Another unit from the 101st, the 3rd Battalion of the 187th Infantry Regiment, was ready to air assault by Blackhawk from Udairi to Shell this afternoon. That would provide a base for 101st Aviation Brigade Apaches, now scheduled to conduct additional attacks against the Medina on Monday night.

A large video screen in front of Petraeus showed dozens of bright blue icons from Blue Force Tracker, a new system that allowed commanders to track battlefield movements precisely, through satellite transponders placed in selected tanks, helicopters, and other vehicles. Like lapis beads on a string, the icons stretched from the Kuwaiti border up the Euphrates valley to within a hundred miles of Baghdad. The sight was breathtaking.

"The Iraqi 11th Division is now considered combat ineffective," an intelligence officer reported. "There are reports of Saddam Fedayeen remnants in the vicinity of Nasariyah. The word is that they are using women and children as human shields." The Fedayeen—irregular militia, often with ties to the ruling Baath Party and supposedly controlled by Saddam's elder son, Uday—had begun harassing American convoys in armed pickup trucks. Reports later suggested that several thousand Fedayeen were heading south from Baghdad.

"Okay, got it," Petraeus said. "Got it." On the tent's cathedral ceiling, a black-and-white television image from an aerial drone somewhere over central Iraq flickered like a silent movie. More staff officers delivered their reports. "Got it. Got it. Next."

Petraeus scanned the list of planned movements by the division into Iraq. "This goes this afternoon. This should go this afternoon. This goes tomorrow. Tomorrow." The 101st Apache attack on the Medina's 14th Mechanized Brigade faced complications from a brewing storm. "Tomorrow night," Petraeus said. "Weather permitting."

At 7:55 A.M., the green field phone connected to V Corps chirped on the front table. Petraeus listened for a minute, then turned in his chair and announced that the Army staff in Washington would "provide the personnel to backfill those we lost last night. Pretty good indicator of our Army's support for us."

The rest of the agenda flashed past. Trey Cate summarized media coverage of the fragging: "Sir, a lot of negative press out there, but that's to be expected. It's a negative situation."

The briefing ended half an hour after it began. Petraeus stood to face his staff. He paused to collect himself, then said in a loud, crisp voice, "Okay, we had a real tough night last night. To lose a Screaming Eagle is a terrible thing. To lose one the way we lost one last night is a real tragedy. The best way we can honor those who were hurt is by driving on and accomplishing the mission. Air assault!"

"Air assault!" the officers answered in unison.

We spent the day preparing to break camp. Petraeus had decided to move directly to Shell by helicopter on Monday morning, with stops at Pennsylvania and Exxon. Sergeant Miller had already left with the Humvee and most of our gear. Ben Freakley also had gone ahead by helicopter, with Dwyer in tow, to set up the assault command post. Most of the headquarters would follow by ground convoy over a three-hundred-mile trail, and it would likely be at least a week before we again saw Schoenbeck and most of the staff.

The 3rd Battalion's leap into Shell on Sunday afternoon went well, and I could see the headquarters regain some of its swash. "That was the longest air assault in the history of the U.S. Army, more than four hundred kilometers," E. J. Sinclair told the staff. "That airfield at Udairi was jammed, but today it's so empty that you'd feel like the Maytag repairman. Now it's time to go blow something up."

Lieutenant Colonel Rick Gibbs, the G-3, or division operations officer, agreed. "Yes, sir. Time to go kill something."

At 7:30 A.M. Monday, March 24, I donned my desert camouflage JLIST, shouldered my travel kit, and headed for the TOC. Suspenders kept the pantaloons from falling around my knees, and the long sleeves on the tunic were folded back in elaborate cuffs. I felt more like Bozo than Audie Murphy.

Petraeus emerged from the tent as I arrived. His tan backpack was slung over his shoulder, and his face seemed drained, his expression fretful. Without his usual buoyant greeting, he looked me directly in the eye and said, "I think we've got a war here."

We climbed into the SUV with Fivecoat and Miller and rode out to the helipad. Something else bad had happened, but before I could inquire, Petraeus picked up the handset to take a radio call. Fivecoat leaned over and murmured, "The 11th Attack Helicopter Regiment mission didn't go very well last night." At least one Apache had been shot down, another had crashed in the dust, and Iraqi defenders appeared to have sheltered in urban neighborhoods, which was precisely the sort of city fighting the Army hoped to avoid. That boded ill for the Apache attack by the 101st planned for that night. Also, Fedayeen marauders had attacked more convoys. Petraeus looked somber as we tossed our bags into the back of Warlord 457 and buckled ourselves in.

The flight to Pennsylvania took ten minutes. Soldiers from 1st Brigade stood in serried ranks outside the TOC, where an M-4 had been shoved bayonet first into the gravel next to the flagpole. I walked over to Chris Hughes, the battalion commander who had watched the Tornado disintegrate overhead. "I taught antiterrorism for three years at the Pentagon, for all the services,"

Hughes told me. "But I don't know how you could see this one coming."

Chris Seifert's helmet with its silver captain's bars hung by the chin strap from the rifle butt, and a pair of desert boots was neatly aligned in the sand. "Father God," a chaplain intoned, "into your hands we commit this child." He read from the 121st Psalm: " 'I lift up mine eyes to the hills, from whence cometh my help.' " Battle ribbons fluttered in the breeze. I picked out *Dak To, 1966* on the guidon of the 2nd Battalion, 327th Infantry.

Ben Hodges, whose right forearm was swathed in white bandages, spoke briefly. "There are two messages I want to give you this morning. Chris Seifert was an outstanding officer. And I'm extremely proud of how well and how quickly you responded the other night. I am not a cheerleader, but there is nothing that's going to stop the Screaming Eagles. There is nothing that's going to stop us."

The *whomp-whomp* of three Chinooks carried on the wind from the south. "There is a time for everything under the heavens," the chaplain continued. "A time for war, and a time for peace."

An honor guard fired three volleys. A bugler played "Taps." Soldiers blotted their tears on their JLIST sleeves, then dispersed to make final preparations for the march north.

Hodges walked with us out to the helicopter. The Blackhawk engines began to whine. I pointed to his bandaged arm and asked how he was feeling. "It's nothin'," he said in his pleasant Florida drawl, then added, "Helluva thing." He saluted Petraeus and turned back to the tents.

We had almost reached the helicopter when Petraeus stopped and gave me another of those searching looks. "I think," he said, "that this thing may be overstretched." We climbed aboard and rose in a golden cloud of dust, then swung west toward Iraq. The time for peace had passed.

8

THE CRY OF BEASTS IN
THEIR DESOLATE HOUSES

We crossed the border at 9:55 A.M. The obstacle belt marking
the boundary included a berm, a tank ditch, two fences, another
berm, another ditch, and a third berm. The landscape was flat
and vast, a great brown pan occasionally stippled with tuft grass
and scarred every few miles by a sand trace that passed for a
road. Bedouins waved from their tents, closely watched by our
flinty-eyed door gunners. Sheep loped away from the rotor
noise, but camels stood fast, working their cuds. Rusting tank
hulls and blown turrets from the last war littered the dunes,
where American forces sweeping out of Saudi Arabia in the so-
called Left Hook had obliterated Iraqi defenders in February
1991. The terrain was as inhospitable as anything I had seen
elsewhere in the Middle East or in North Africa, where I
recently had researched a history of the U.S. Army's punishing
Tunisian campaign in 1942–1943. We flew at ninety knots and
at an altitude of seventy feet until crossing a stretch so barren
that the pilots—Warrant Officers Marc Daniels and Travis
Gronley—eased up a bit in an effort to discern where sky ended
and ground began. Severe weather was closing fast, and Petraeus
wanted to reach Shell before the storm arrived.

We were in Mesopotamia, and the very concept seemed

fraught with history and calamity. The civilizations of five millennia had piled one atop another—Sumerian, Babylonian, Assyrian, Ottoman—in a jumble of potsherds and incinerated cities. "It was here that man formed the first farming communities, discovered gods, and later God, developed written symbols to convey ideas, made money and a system for its use, built the first planned cities, invented laws and learned how to brew beer," the journalist Michael Kelly had written in *Martyrs' Day*. It was also where we derived our superstition about black cats, our partition of clock faces into twelve segments, and our inconstant conviction that fate can be divined in the movement of stars. (Petraeus, I noticed, preferred to knock wood, frequently.) The Assyriologist Samuel Noah Kramer once tallied more than two dozen cultural firsts that originated in this wizened place, from the first love song and the first tale of resurrection, to the first historian and the first recorded incidence of apple-polishing. It was a land of the plow, of the irrigation canal, and of mass murder on an epic scale. It was where seven angels had poured the chalice of God's wrath over the Euphrates so that "wild beasts of the islands shall cry in their desolate houses and dragons in their pleasant palaces." Or so claimed Isaiah.

It was also where Western armies went to die, an aspect of its history that seemed not entirely irrelevant to those of us aboard Warlord 457. The last expeditionary force to tramp north toward Baghdad got within twenty miles of the capital, retreated in disarray to Kut, and there surrendered in April 1916. Of the twelve thousand British and Indian troops taken prisoner, four thousand died in captivity from what Parliament decried as "the dead weight of Asiatic indifference and inertia." Total casualties in the British Tigris Corps during the campaign exceeded forty thousand. The losses in the Black Watch Regiment—794 of 842 men—were not atypical.

"We started eating horse flesh. It's not bad, but I prefer beef. We are going to try starling on toast tonight," a lieutenant in the 104th Wellesley Rifles had written. "Fleas bite hard—are in the thousands. The men are dying off fast now from starvation, scurvy, pneumonia, etc. . . . I am pretty fed up with Mesopotamia." The British general Stanley Maude had eventually seized Baghdad from the Ottomans, but expired there of cholera while trying to compose sundry Muslims, Kurds, Jews, and independent tribesmen into a nation consonant with British notions of civilization. "The Arab is generally intelligent, quick and impressionable," observed the British official history, *The Campaign in Mesopotamia.* "But he is slovenly and uncreative in practical matters, and is lacking in the power of co-operation. . . . He has a natural bent for intrigue. . . . The Arab is used to continual warfare of the guerrilla type." A cautionary tale of empire-building if ever there was one.

At 10:30 A.M., Forward Operating Base Exxon materialized below us, an abjectly barren outpost with a dozen refueling nozzles next to a rock quarry. Fighting positions had been dug around the perimeter, and vehicles were arranged like spokes on a wheel with their noses pointed out, giving the camp a wagon-train-in-Indian-territory ambience. For half an hour, while the Blackhawk refueled, we sat in a command-post tent that still carried the manufacturer's label: "Custom Canvas." A map on a plywood board showed Exxon as a goose egg in the middle of nowhere. A huge Hewlett-Packard copier and a map-making laminator occupied one corner; cases of hand grenades had been stacked near the tent flap. "We've got 3 ID in front of us and they pretty well ate up the road," Lieutenant Colonel Chip Preysler, commander of the 2nd Battalion of the 187th Infantry, told Petraeus. "The tracks are so rutted that our bumpers are pushing sand. It took about sixteen hours to get here after we crossed the border." Sergeants had walked up and down the convoys, banging on vehicle doors to keep the drivers awake.

Petraeus seemed pensive as we reboarded the Blackhawk shortly after 11 A.M. for the eighty-minute flight to Shell. From the commander's seat in the right rear, he looked across the bay to where I was, as usual, wrestling with the octopuslike seat harness (it involved four straps, a circular buckle, and a radio headset that I kept forgetting to remove before bounding off the helicopter). Corporal Stephen Glasier, one of the MP body-guards, reached over and helped untangle me as the Blackhawk lifted into the air.

Petraeus watched Exxon quickly recede until it had been swallowed by the desert expanse. "This is not only going to take determination," he said over the intercom, "but *sheer* determination."

"That's the best kind," I replied, affecting a phony buoyancy.

"I'm really proud of what we've done at Exxon, the fact that they did this as effectively as they did. That's an achievement," he said. "I *do* think this thing is overstretched. But to be fair, they didn't expect this kind of resistance." Referring to Colonel Greg Gass, who commanded the Apaches scheduled to attack the Medina Division's 14th Brigade that night, Petraeus added, "Destiny Six may have that same look in his eyes as some of those guys you write about in the early days of the North African campaign."

I barely had time to wonder what he was talking about—wasn't the 3rd Infantry Division more than halfway to Baghdad? Why should Gass be unsettled just because the 11th Regiment had lost a couple of helicopters the previous night?—when the fair weather abruptly vanished. Dust thickened and within five minutes the helicopter seemed wrapped in cotton batting. The pilots slowed down, picking their way.

At 11:30, Petraeus radioed the D-Main at New Jersey, using his call sign, Eagle Six. "Get hold of Destiny and Thunder"—his two aviation brigades—"and tell them not to launch any more aircraft west. The winds are picking up and conditions are marginal."

Peering out the left rear window, I thought his description was generous. The sun floated above us like a gold lozenge in the haze, but the world below had become vague and opaque. An occasional smear of green drifted past, only to be swallowed by the relentless brown.

"Eagle Six, this is Victory Six." Scott Wallace's serene voice came through my headset. He was already at the V Corps advance command post, north of Shell at Objective Rams, not far from Najaf. "We will not conduct a mission tonight." Search-and-rescue teams were hunting two Apache pilots missing from the 11th Regiment's mission the previous night. "Other things," Wallace said, had also intruded to scrub the 101st's attack on the Medina.

"Victory Six, Eagle Six," Petraeus answered. "Roger. High winds are forecast."

"We'll talk later," Wallace said.

"I am en route from Exxon to Shell," Petraeus added. He rubbed the window with a white cloth, as if to wipe away the murk. "The weather is marginal. Recommend against launching Chinooks with bridging equipment."

"Roger," Wallace said. "Thanks for that. I concur."

At 11:45, the chief pilot, Marc Daniels, told Petraeus over the intercom that we had reached the point of no return. The Black-hawk had sixty-five minutes of fuel remaining. Shell lay thirty-three minutes ahead at our current pace. If we were to return to Exxon—flying into the wind—we had to do it right now. Petraeus wiped the window again, and advised the crew to push on.

"Roger. Bad enough to scare, but not bad enough to make yourself turn around," Daniels said with admirable sangfroid. Visibility now was perhaps a couple of hundred feet. Daniels climbed to three hundred feet, following an azimuth and relying on instruments. The door gunners, Sergeants Christopher Marchand and Patrick Croff, leaned out of the bay, watching for other helicopters, as well as uncharted hills and power lines. I tried to block out an insistent image of the Blackhawk cart-wheeling across the desert in a cataclysm of broken blades and burning fuel. My palms were moist and my pulse had quick-ened. Petraeus was very quiet, and I wondered if he felt as unsettled as I did. From his seat in the forward bay, Fivecoat fiddled with the Blue Force Tracker screen, which showed our position relative to Exxon and Shell.

More radio reports came over the corps network. At Rams, visibility was under a quarter mile. A protracted gunfight had occurred at Nasariyah, the Euphrates River city not far from Exxon and about two hundred miles south of Baghdad. Iraqi forces had ambushed the 507th Maintenance Company, a support unit traveling by convoy at the rear of the 3rd Division. At least fifteen soldiers were missing—among them, as we later learned, Private First Class Jessica Lynch. Survivors reportedly had taken refuge at Tallil air base, where they were said to be "looking for their parent unit." Three Iraqi artillery pieces had been spotted in Nasariyah "250 meters from a children's hospital." We heard Wallace ask for the grid coordinates. After plotting them on a map, the corps commander advised, "That is a legitimate target. Use as precise a munition as possible."

Petraeus looked at me across the helicopter bay. I cocked an eyebrow. Nasariyah was a Shiite Muslim stronghold with 300,000 people who were supposed to welcome the American liberators. A phrase heard from Washington in recent weeks was "Expect parades."

Visibility had dropped to fifty feet. Petraeus wiped his window. The pilots eased Warlord 457 up and down, climbing when they glimpsed ground through the blowing dust, then easing back down when the ground vanished.

At 12:23 P.M. I spied a rectangular patch of green, then another, and another. Tents. Vehicles. FARP Shell. I felt a sweeping sense of salvation, and gratitude to our crew as the pilots settled the helicopter onto the first available spot. The thin sand crust gave way beneath the wheels and the helicopter lurched sharply to the right. The engines died as we scurried out into the warm wind.

We trudged half a mile through swirling dust to the ACP, the assault command post: Petraeus, Fivecoat, the two military police bodyguards, and me. In the bulky JLIST, burdened with my

Right: Maj. Gen. David H. Petraeus (right), commander of the 101st Airborne Division, and Lt. Gen. William S. Wallace, commander of the U.S. Army's V Corps. *(Joshua Hutcheson, U.S. Army)*

Left: Brig. Gen. Benjamin C. Freakley, the assistant division commander for operations, often referred to in the 101st simply as "the O." Freakley, who at times grew restless at the division's deliberate pace, was a force of nature, an old fashioned warfighter with a big heart and five sons.

Right: Brig. Gen. Edward J. Sinclair, the assistant division commander for support, known as "the S." An Apache attack helicopter pilot from Montana and a former West Point basketball player, Sinclair was large and cheerful, with a broad, open face, the sort of man whom other men instantly like. *(Public Affairs Office, 101st Airborne Division)*

Right: Col. Ben Hodges (right), commander of 1st Brigade, with Petraeus in Najaf on April 1, 2003. A few hours before Hodges was to lead the brigade into Iraq from Kuwait, two of his officers were murdered and more than a dozen soldiers were wounded in a midnight attack, allegedly by a disaffected sergeant.

Left: Col. Joseph Anderson, commander of 2nd Brigade, standing near crates of Iraqi ammunition discovered in a Baghdad amusement park. A New Yorker and a West Pointer, Anderson at forty-three was bald and forceful, with long eyelashes and a tendency to lean forward when speaking until he was inches from his auditor.

Right: Col. Michael S. Linnington (left), commander of 3rd Brigade, with Petraeus on April 6, during planning for the attack on Hilla. A tall, buoyant veteran of Afghanistan, Linnington had listed his priorities in a green, cloth-bound notebook on his knee, beginning with "Tactical patience."

Left: Udairi air field in northern Kuwait, where seven of the Army's fifteen Apache attack helicopter battalions were based by mid-March. "I wish Saddam Hussein could just see that, see them lined up out there, all that killing power," Petraeus said. Brig. Gen. E. J. Sinclair moderated the "tape vs. paint" debate in the rectangular building on the far right, thirty yards from the open hangar door. *(Public Affairs Office, 101st Airborne Division)*

Right: Camp Victory, Kuwait, on March 7, when a vicious sand storm knocked down seventeen tents. Hundreds of homeless soldiers piled rucksacks, weapons, and MRE cases on their exposed cots to keep them from blowing away. Others huddled in sleeping bags for protection, or sheltered in a shower trailer.

Below: Early afternoon, March 29. Soldiers from 2nd Brigade, having just air assaulted 250 miles from Kuwait, trudge across Objective Jenkins in the timeless waddle of the overburdened infantry, heading for the Euphrates River town of Kifl. Near this spot a few hours earlier, a suicide bomber killed four 3rd Infantry Division soldiers.

Left: Special Forces vehicles, ignoring the prohibition against flying American flags, pull into the southwest corner of Najaf on April 1, followed by an Army Humvee (left). The beginning of what would become a large, welcoming crowd is gathering on the street.

Right: An Iraqi family hurries south on Highway 9, fleeing the gunfire in Najaf on April 2. Pushing a cart loaded with a battered suitcase and a propane tank, the man sobbed great, heaving sobs. "He's worried about his kids," an Iraqi translator said, "that they're going to die."

Left: An Iraqi military terrain model, discovered in a bathroom stall in Najaf, depicts the plan for the city's defense. Green toy soldiers, representing Americans, stand below the escarpment on the southwestern approach to the city. Red toy soldiers, representing Iraqis, occupy revetments along the perimeter avenues. The model includes plastic cars, palm trees, and donkeys.

Above: Inside the tactical operations center, known to 101st Airborne Division wits as the TOC Mahal. Secret maps and projector screens line the front of the large tent (not visible to the left), while officers occupy folding tables on risers, their staff positions denoted by white signs on the laptop lids.

Left: Lt. Col. Stephen M. Schiller, commander of the 2nd Battalion of the 17th Cavalry, seen here in a chicken processing plant in southern Baghdad. Schiller's Kiowa helicopters, long overshadowed by the more lethal Apaches, proved invaluable in urban combat. "We don't hover, we stay low, and we're very small," one pilot said. "That's a big advantage over towns."

Below: Air assaulting infantrymen from 2nd Brigade spill out of a Blackhawk on the southern edge of Karbala on April 5. *(Public Affairs Office, 101st Airborne Division)*

Left: Capt. David G. Fivecoat at Forward Operating Base Shell on March 29. A thirty-one-year-old West Pointer from Delaware, Ohio, Fivecoat was a smart, sinewy towhead serving his second tour as Petraeus's aide, an experience his peers teasingly suggested he record in a memoir to be titled *Success Through Pain.*

Below: Soldiers from 3rd Brigade roll toward Hilla on April 8, unaware that Iraqi ambushers are hidden in a mulberry thicket a few hundred yards ahead, near the grain elevator at Objective Hippo. Shooting erupted less than a minute after this photo was taken.

Left: Petraeus (right) and Freakley examine the crude field camp of Iraqi ambushers on the western outskirts of Hilla on April 8. The owner of these boots lies dead, in his stocking feet, on the far side of an adjacent road.

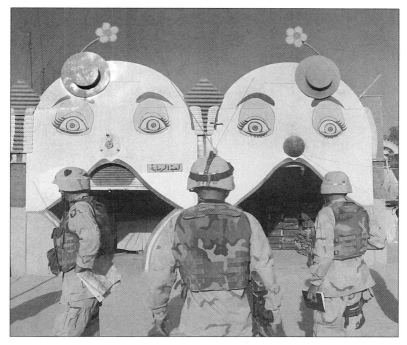

Above: Col. Joe Anderson (left) and other officers examine ammunition hidden in the beanbag toss at an amusement park in south Baghdad.

Right: Captured by an artist in better days, Saddam Hussein beams over the Al Qadisiyah State Establishment, a munitions plant in south Baghdad where the 101st put its headquarters in mid-April before moving to Mosul in northern Iraq. "Think Safety," a placard in one of the factory workshops urged. "Every Thing Has Its Place."

Petraeus overlooking the ruins of ancient Babylon on the left and the reconstructed palace of Nebuchadnezzar on the right, a few miles from downtown Hilla. He stands atop one of Saddam's many palaces, an empty four-story limestone monstrosity erected on a man-made hill.

satellite phones and laptop, I was soon soaked in sweat and coated in grime.

"That may have been the worst flight I have ever had," Petraeus told me. He smiled.

Shell was to be our home for the next ten days, and my first impression of the place made me pine for New Jersey. The camp was utterly barren, flat as an ironing board, with no vegetation, no running water, no nothing. Three burn latrines stood sentinel, one with a missing door and another, missing both the door and a side wall, that soon was dubbed the Room with a View. "The only difference between this place and the moon," an apt graffito noted, "is a little gravity."

A small cluster of tents circled the ACP, which consisted of a couple of tents melded together with a small anteroom where entering soldiers dropped their helmets and weapons. Shell had only existed for a day, and the command post was a work in progress. Half a dozen men were stringing communications wire, extension cords, and computer cables. Others wiped off the folding tables with splashes of bottled water and towels from a gargantuan box of Total Wipes II. Two soldiers carefully taped together several map sheets of the hundred-mile stretch between Shell and Baghdad. Dust filtered through every seam in the tent. A small Saddam Hussein doll dangled from a hangman's noose tied to the tent frame. As if to compensate for the tension and appalling conditions, everyone was elaborately polite.

I took a metal chair next to Major Len Kircher, the ACP chaplain. His vehicle was parked outside, with "God Squad" written in dust on the side. "Most of us came on the GAC from—well, it was *not* from heaven," he told me. "We left Camp New Jersey on Wednesday night, got here last night. Four days. To stay awake, guys were taking the little packets of Taster's Choice that come in the MREs and eating the freeze-dried coffee without bothering to add any water."

Ben Freakley walked in. He was a reassuring sight, exuding his usual energy and humanity. Kuwaiti crud had reduced his voice to a raspy whisper as he briefed Petraeus on the latest combat news. Warlord 457 was among the few helicopters to get through to Shell this afternoon. More than a dozen others had been forced down by the weather, and two more made emergency landings after running low on fuel. Blackhawks and Chinooks littered the southern desert. Among those marooned were division battle-staff officers who'd been traveling behind us, including Rick Gibbs, the G-3, and D. J. Reyes, the G-2. (Reyes later told me that his helicopter landed so hard that one dozing passenger believed they had been hit by a missile.) Several helicopters sling-loading equipment had been caught by high winds, and the pendular effect had threatened to bring them down. A couple managed to set their loads onto the desert floor, but one crew had simply cut loose a large crate of Apache spare parts. No one knew where the container was, or whether any of the equipment had survived the two-thousand-foot fall.

"The next good weather is sixty hours from now," Fivecoat reported.

"We're not doing an air assault for at least seventy-two hours," Petraeus said. "Call Exxon and tell them not to launch anything else out of there."

Iraqi technicals—pickup trucks sporting machine guns—were swarming out of Najaf to harass the V Corps logistics base at Rams. Since Friday afternoon, Iraqis had been attacking suicidally, often with rocket-propelled grenades. Some 3rd Division troops had run short of ammunition and were fighting with scavenged AK-47s. Wallace wanted Mike Linnington's 3rd Brigade to bolster security around Rams.

Freakley and Petraeus sat on the floor at the front of the ACP, studying the map; to read details at the bottom, they both stretched out full length, their noses pressed close to the acetate. The 3rd Infantry Division had traveled roughly three hundred miles, a prodigious feat of blitzkrieg audacity. But twenty-nine

Americans had been killed near Nasariyah on Sunday, and seven others remained missing. Contrary to expectations, the mass capitulation of Iraqi units had not occurred. Task Force Tarawa, a Marine force five thousand strong, held key bridges over the Euphrates and the Saddam Canal. Bitter fighting persisted on a stretch of Nasariyah roadway known as Ambush Alley, and a half-dozen Marines had been killed by friendly fire from an Air Force A-10. Unexpected resistance also continued against Marines and British troops in the southeast at Um Qasr and Basra. The Army's logistics trail stretched from Rams back to Kuwait like a long, frayed tether. A figure who looked and sounded like Saddam Hussein had appeared on Iraqi television with the advice: "Cut their throats and be patient."

"Maybe," Fivecoat murmured, "these people don't want to be liberated."

Lieutenant Colonel Hank Arnold, an ACP staff officer, pointed to several cities along the western lip of the Euphrates valley: Najaf, Kufa, Hilla, Karbala. Each stood uncomfortably close to the supply line that would sustain an attack on Baghdad. "Sooner or later," Arnold told me, "the corps commander is going to have to go in and clean out these pockets."

Just before 1 P.M., commanders and other senior officers from the three Apache battalions filed into the ACP and sat at the three rows of tables. The folded cowls of their bulky chemical suits made them look like monks at vespers. Wallace had arranged for his pilots from the 11th Regiment at Rams to discuss, in a conference call by satellite phone, their star-crossed mission the previous night. Freakley and Greg Gass were to moderate the discussion; Petraeus remained outside, attending to the division's movement into Iraq. Over a black speaker box on the front table came the tired, disembodied voice of Gass's counterpart in the 11th, Colonel William T. Wolf, who was soon joined by other senior pilots. Their account was disjointed, even jumbled, as they tried to make sense of a disaster—the Army called it "a failure chain"—that had occurred less than twelve hours earlier. I soon realized why news of the mission so unsettled Petraeus while we were still in Kuwait.

Sixty Apaches had flown 230 miles from Udairi to Rams on Sunday afternoon to stage for the attack that night. Their ambition was to shred three Medina brigades and the division artillery, expediting the 3rd Infantry Division's drive past Karbala into the southern approaches to Baghdad. U.S. intelligence had a precise count of Iraqi equipment—eighty-seven guns in the Medina artillery, and 291 combat vehicles in the three brigades, of which half were to be destroyed—but rather sketchy notions of how that equipment was arrayed northeast of Karbala and south of Baghdad. Instead of specific grid locations for specific targets, the 11th Regiment's pilots for the most part received only vague, give-or-take-a-kilometer locations of Iraqi company positions. The attack therefore required what the Army called a movement to contact—groping for the enemy—rather than the deliberate attack preferred by marauding helicopter units.

Other problems had accumulated. The speed of the 3rd ID's advance and an approaching storm caused the Apache mission to be advanced by twenty-four hours, and compressed preparation time in aviation is rarely a catalyst for success. But pilots worried that if they failed to fly on Sunday night they might not get into the war; poor visibility already had caused the regiment to scrub one mission, against an Iraqi infantry division three nights earlier. Nine possible attack routes had been proposed for the Medina, with 11th Regiment planners favoring a flanking approach from the west rather than the obvious avenue out of the south. Yet V Corps had approved only three southern routes, denying the western approaches because of concern that they would intrude on airspace allocated to the 101st, and particularly because such routes required establishing a vulnerable refueling point southwest of Karbala. A last-minute appeal from Rams to amend the routes was also denied.

Meanwhile, ground convoys with fuel and ammunition trucks bound for Rams from Kuwait had been delayed by traffic jams and soft sand. So little fuel was available that at the last minute Wolf was forced to scratch one of his three squadrons from the attack, while another squadron—equivalent to a battalion—left behind an additional five helicopters. Darkness and billowing "moon dust" further hampered refueling along the mile-long flight line, and the mission was delayed two hours and fifteen minutes. Crews swapped helicopters at the last minute in an effort to get key combat leaders into the air.

At 1:15 on Monday morning, thirty-one Apaches lifted out of Rams and turned north for the fifty-mile flight. The night was very dark, and the helicopters kept fifteen rotor lengths apart, flying one hundred feet off the ground at 110 knots. One Apache crashed during takeoff, the crew disoriented by the dust. As the pilots described their routes over the speaker box, Ben Freakley pointed to various towns and phase lines on the large map at the front of the room. As I later learned, U.S. intelligence eavesdroppers had detected fifty cell-phone calls made by Iraqi observers as the helicopters pressed north; the same simple but effective early-warning system had been used by Somali militiamen in Mogadishu. One Iraqi, believed to be a major general in Najaf, supposedly used the speed-dial feature on his cell phone to alert defenders.

"This is urban terrain up there. I don't think we appreciated it, but it's really suburbia from Baghdad to the Karbala Gap," said a voice from the speaker box. "In reality, when we turned to the west it was much more urban than anything we'd seen in map analysis. And then large, *very* large-caliber triple-A started coming at us."

Senior U.S. commanders had considered bombing the Iraqi power grid, but ultimately chose to leave the lights burning in an effort to minimize reconstruction requirements. On this mission, the decision backfired. As the Apaches arrived overhead, all of the lights in a large area—including the towns of Haswah and Iskandariyah—were extinguished simultaneously by a master switch. Two seconds later, the lights came back on, a signal for hundreds of Iraqis with small arms to fire into the air. The helicopters flew into a wall of lead.

One commander subsequently described ground fire punching through three of his Apaches. Some rounds pinged, like gravel thrown against sheet metal, while others struck with sledgehammer violence. Iraqi gunners trained their fire above the power lines, where the exposed helicopters had to pull up to two hundred feet to clear the wires. "There were eight or ten heavy streams of fire coming out of the city," he added. "We never really had contact with enemy tanks or artillery." Another troop commander's radios were knocked out as he entered the target area, leaving him mute and deaf through the battle, one of many communication problems plaguing the mission. In the Apache known as Palerider 16, Lieutenant Jason King was shot through the neck; his crewmate in the rear seat could hear breathing over the intercom, but King was unable to talk with a throat full of blood.

Fire came "from all directions, front, back, left, right. We detected no emitters whatsoever," another voice added, which meant that no sophisticated air-defense radars had been employed, just fountains of unguided "iron sight" fire from rifles, machine guns, rocket-propelled grenades, and simple anti-aircraft guns. Pilots in the backseat, using the Apache's thermal night-vision system, which revealed heat-radiant objects such as tanks and humans, could not see the Iraqi tracers. Those tracers were all too visible to copilots in the front seat, wearing night-vision goggles that amplified the ambient light; only the back-seaters, however, controlled the 30mm chain gun, so the front-seater had to laboriously direct the back-seater's gun onto the target with instructions over the intercom.

Freakley worked a large wad of gum between his jaws. "It's our supposition," he said, "that they must have a very extensive visual observer network."

"Absolutely, sir."

"What was the separation between your SEAD and your attack?" Freakley asked. Suppression of enemy air defenses—SEAD—was a vital prelude to any air attack, and typically involved choreographing long-range artillery, Air Force and Navy counterradar bombing, and electronic jamming.

"We planned thirty minutes' separation." Eyebrows arched throughout the ACP. Petraeus and others had insisted that any attack on Republican Guard targets be launched almost the instant that the SEAD lifted, before the defenders had time to recover their wits. In fact, SEAD for the 11th Regiment had been a debacle. Artillery and Air Force units apparently were not notified of the two-hour delay in launching the Apaches. Thirty-one long-range missiles, ATACMs, were fired long before the helicopters left Rams, and many pilots believed "it acted more as a warning than a suppression." Fighter-bombers had also left the area by the time the Apaches arrived, so that the 11th, as the Army later concluded, "went in alone and effectively unsupported."

Gunfire had erupted from rooftops, cars, balconies, alleys, backyards, and trees. "Their suburbs are not like our suburbs," one pilot said. Another added, "The volume of fire intensified with each subsequent troop cycling in, and it got heavier the farther north we went. Most of it came from housing areas." Some pilots had been reluctant to fire back for fear of killing civilians. "But after a few hits," a pilot later said, "you get less reluctant." Several Iraqi buildings had been destroyed, including one believed to be a school. "But that's where the fire was coming from."

Gass sat hunched in a folding chair, listening intently and asking an occasional question. He was a compact man, with fine cheekbones and thin lips. He had grown up in Knoxville, and had once told me that before coming into the Army in 1980 he wanted to be a dentist. In the best of times he smiled infrequently. Now, as Petraeus had anticipated, Destiny Six indeed had the somber look so common in North Africa during the grim winter of 1942–1943. His subordinates looked equally glum, their eyes downcast or fixed on the map. No one made eye contact.

Not many pilots from the 11th got close enough to engage the Medina; one squadron aborted before ever reaching enemy entrenchments. Few Hellfire missiles were fired. A single troop made it to Highway 1 below Baghdad, but failed to find any of the thirty Iraqi T-72 tanks reportedly in the area. Ground fire set several rocket pylons ablaze, forcing pilots to jettison them before flames spread to the fuselage. Half of the 30mm guns in one squadron reportedly jammed, possibly because of defective ammunition. The damage inflicted on Iraqi armor targets was estimated at a half-dozen armored vehicles and three trucks. U.S. intelligence still put the Medina Division at a robust 88 percent of full strength.

"Target fidelity may have been there, but we didn't have time to engage," one pilot said. Gunfire had severed the hydraulics in Vampire 12, an Apache flown by two warrant officers, David S. Williams and Ronald D. Young, Jr., who were forced down. "When I went over there to see if I could see them," a pilot said, "I came under heavy fire. The crew was not recovered."

Freakley leaned close to the speaker as the pilots offered a few more observations in voices that sounded increasingly strained.

"There's a lot more trees out there than you would think."

"They could see us fairly well. We think maybe light was bouncing off the clouds and illuminating us from above."

"We're going to have to deliberately clear those urban areas," another pilot said. "If we were to loosen up on the ROEs"—rules of engagement—"I would definitely use MPSM. But I don't think that's an option right now." Multipurpose submunitions were cluster bomblets fired on rockets; highly lethal, they also left enough duds to be problematic in urban areas.

Apaches limped back to Rams, some without functioning navigation equipment or sights. At least two narrowly avoided a midair collision. Of the twenty-nine aircraft that returned safely, all but one "sustained some damage." "The sun came up and it was eerie," one captain later recalled. "You had never seen helicopters so muddy, so many canopies with holes in them." Stunned pilots sat slumped in the cockpits or on the Apaches' stubby wings. On average, each helicopter had fifteen to twenty bullet holes; one took twenty-nine hits. Sixteen main rotor blades and six tail blades were damaged enough to require replacement, along with six engines and five drive shafts. Forty-six other blades needed repairs.

Freakley's eyebrows lifted again. The regiment had been shot to pieces in exchange for less than a dozen Iraqi vehicles. Two $20 million helicopters had been lost; in one squadron, only a single helicopter was still considered mission capable, and a month would pass before the entire regiment was fully ready to fight. The battle calculus hardly required elaboration.

The conversation meandered to a close. Clearly, the regiment had underestimated the small-arms threat, Iraqi ingenuity, and what Wallace would call "the urbanization of nonurban areas." Just as clearly, the Iraqis had learned something during twelve years of repeated attacks on their air-defense systems by American and British pilots enforcing the no-fly zones. "There's a very different threat out there than what we expected," one pilot said. "What we went through last night is something we didn't anticipate. I guess we believe that what we've been training for, for a long time, is not going to work here."

Gass thanked Colonel Wolf for his time and signed off. "All right, Greg," Wolf replied. "Lots of luck to you. Out here."

The 101st pilots filed out of the ACP. No one said much. The wind howled outside.

The bad news kept coming. Young and Williams, the two missing Apache pilots from the 11th Regiment, appeared on television that afternoon in Iraqi custody, along with a grizzled farmer who claimed to have shot down their helicopter with his rifle.

At 2:30 P.M., a distant boom rolled across the ACP. Something had exploded twenty-five yards from the Patriot missile battery protecting Shell, hitting the same hard-luck unit involved in the mauling of Jessica Lynch's company at Nasariyah and the Tornado shootdown at Camp Pennsylvania. Fragments severed the Patriot radar's hydraulic lines, leaving the camp and dozens of parked helicopters vulnerable to Iraqi missiles. At first an Iraqi mortar round was suspected, but soon a soldier walked into the ACP with several large, metal shards extracted from the Patriot wreckage: the battery's radar had been hit with an antiradiation missile mistakenly fired by a confused F/A-18 pilot.

I now understood that Petraeus knew, from his conference call with V Corps at seven this morning, how poorly the Apaches had fared. Surprise had been lost, obviously, and surprise is the essence of deep attack. The vulnerability of the helicopter had again been revealed: of twelve thousand helicopters used during the Vietnam War, more than five thousand had been destroyed by enemy fire and assorted mishaps, according to the Vietnam Helicopter Pilots Association. I could already imagine the naysaying in Washington, including gibes from the sister services: the Army's premier deep-attack weapons system, and certainly the one most extolled by Army aviators, had been outgunned by peasants with muskets. Had anything really been learned since Mogadishu, where the destruction of two Blackhawks had led to eighteen dead Americans, a thousand Somali casualties, and the end of American involvement in the Horn of Africa?

If this was bad for the 11th Regiment, in some ways it was worse for the 101st, boding ill for a division that had staked much of its combat reputation in this war on the lethality of deep attacks. Wallace had concluded, as I eventually learned from Army documents that recorded his reactions, that "deep operations with the Apaches, unless there's a very, very, very clear need to do it, are probably not a good idea." Plans to have the 101st clear a zone around Baghdad's international airport were now, in Wallace's words, "in the trash can." At a minimum,

Apache tactics would have to be radically revised. Pilots in the 101st were reluctant to second-guess their brethren in the 11th, but already I had heard puzzled exchanges. "Why didn't they just pull back when they started taking that much fire?" one officer had blurted. The American technological advantage—all those eight-digit target coordinates, and Top Scene, and fire-and-forget Hellfires—seemed less imposing, less decisive, less relevant.

I tracked down Greg Gass in the ACP and asked his thoughts.

"My biggest concern about all this is the maps that we have," he said. "We naturally want to avoid built-up areas. The map shows us areas that are free to maneuver in, but what you've really got is urban sprawl all over the area south of Baghdad. It's much more extensive than we appreciated. It's really hard on pilots when somebody's shooting at them from a house. The most accurate weapon we have is a Hellfire. The quickest weapon is the cannon, but it causes the most collateral damage, and you want to avoid that."

I wondered, but did not ask, how the nation could spend more than $30 billion annually on intelligence and still be unsure where there were towns and where there were not towns.

"The other issue is the accuracy of the fire at night with what we call iron sights," Gass continued, alluding to guns without radar guidance. "That tells me that they could see us in the dark. I don't know if it was because of the clouds reflecting light from above and actually silhouetting the helicopters, or because they had, as guys in the 11th Regiment believe, night optics of some sort.

"The weather isn't helping, that's for sure. We're checking engine intakes for clogging, and we're tying down blades so they don't flap in the wind and cause damage to the rotor systems. The Apache is a finicky beast, and you have to continually maintain it."

I asked how the 11th Regiment's travails would affect his pilots. Gass sighed. "Any time you hear about somebody going down, you get a knot in your stomach that makes you nauseous."

Petraeus was outside, blinking hard against the grit that swirled like fog through the camp. His countenance had changed, perhaps because he sensed that the war had changed. The convoys in southern Iraq had been attacked almost hourly. In a brief conversation before we ducked back into the ACP, he noted the long, vulnerable supply lines and the need to consolidate combat power, while pressing the offensive to retain initiative. Somehow Army logisticians had to deliver 2 million gallons of fuel a day, more than twice the amount used by two Allied armies in France in the fall of 1944. Petraeus wondered whether more forces would be needed in Iraq, perhaps a lot more, "to secure the LOCs," the lines of communication extending from Kuwait. The decision by Secretary Rumsfeld and the senior military leadership to attack with a much skimpier force than originally proposed seemed bolder than ever. "We all told them this," Petraeus said.

At 5:20 P.M., he met inside the tent with Freakley, Mike Linnington, and the ACP staff. Each subordinate wrote in a green, cloth-bound notebook, standard accoutrement for every Army officer. Much discussion was devoted to securing Shell and Rams. Should the perimeters be contracted? Expanded? Reinforced? The Long Range Surveillance Detachment missions and all helicopter flights had been scrubbed by bad weather, so seeing the enemy was difficult. Of more than twenty LRSD teams throughout V Corps, only three had been inserted behind enemy lines; one of those was immediately compromised by Bedouin dogs, and the team of six men spent forty-eight hours covered with a camouflage sheet in a hole eighteen inches deep until they could be extracted.

Two white pickup trucks had been spotted nearby, possibly casing Shell. "I wonder if those are the same two that have been reported elsewhere," Petraeus mused. He nibbled on a slice of flat wheatbread from an MRE packet. He and his men might have been Civil War officers poring over a map by candlelight, although in this command post CNN chattered from the adjacent communications van.

At 5:40 P.M. there was a flurry outside and someone bellowed, "Gas! Gas!" We donned our masks, and the conference continued. There was no gas. We removed our masks.

The session finally ended shortly before 7 P.M. "The problem is that the only part of Iraq we own is here at Shell," Petraeus told the staff. "We've got to be very, very careful. They have eyes all up and down the road. They know where we are."

The wind had died at sunset, and the sky gradually cleared. Stars jammed the heavens, as many stars as I had ever seen: an astrologer's paradise. The night was bitter cold. I found Dwyer, who had been off somewhere with Freakley's driver. I was terribly glad to see him. Sergeant Miller arrived in the Humvee, pulling a small trailer with my bags aboard. Thirty yards from the ACP, on a cot in the open next to Dave Fivecoat's, I spread my sleeping bag and crawled inside. Parachute flares, seething with magnesium brilliance, drifted to earth along the edges of the camp, where sentries watched for white pickup trucks and other hobgoblin disturbers of the peace.

9

"A MAN JUST SORT OF EXISTS"

At dawn on Tuesday, March 25, the skies again began to cloud. By midafternoon the weather was not only worse than it had been on Monday, it was worse than it had ever been in the long, sorry history of Mesopotamia, or so we preferred to believe. A fierce storm that, like this one, blows out of the south is known as a *turab,* but everyone in the 101st Airborne Division insisted on calling it a *shamal*—which is a wind from the north— perhaps because *shamal* has a plague-of-frogs ring. Begoggled soldiers pulling guard duty sat in burrows with neck gaiters pulled up around their ears. Helicopters flew briefly before being grounded again, and even vehicle traffic all but ceased as visibility dropped and the odds of getting lost shortened. Except for the grumble of generators, the normal racket of an Army bivouac faded, overwhelmed by creaking tent ropes and the shrieking wind.

As Camp New Jersey had made me nostalgic for Camp Doha, so Forward Operating Base Shell made the Garden State seem Edenic. The ACP was primitive but at least it afforded the battle staff some shelter; for most grunts, however, living conditions were primeval. Ernie Pyle had called infantrymen the "mud-rain-frost-and-wind boys," but that sobriquet omitted dust. Life at

FOB Shell—soon known, inevitably, as FOB Hell—was lived in a four-inch layer of brown talc, a fifth element to accompany fire, earth, air, and water. Even in a dead calm, the stuff rose in spinning dust devils beneath every footfall. In a gale, the air became saturated with grit and was transformed from a gas to a solid.

I was reminded of Pyle's description of World War II infantrymen in Tunisia in 1943: "There are none of the little things that make life normal back home. There are no chairs, lights, floors or tables. There isn't any place to set anything or any store to buy things. There are no newspapers, milk, beds, sheets, radiators, beer, ice cream or hot water. . . . A man just sort of exists." Those of us who just sort of existed at Shell soon adopted a defiant motto, or call it a war cry: "Embrace the suck."

Until the weather improved, there was no place to go and little to do except talk; I took advantage of the interlude to chat up various staff officers. The little Saddam doll swung from its noose in the ACP, where the day's challenge and response passwords—respectively, PANTS and QUILL—had been posted on the map along with the latest disposition of U.S. forces. Thirty miles north of Shell, 3rd Infantry Division units had moved north and east of Najaf to prevent Iraqi reinforcements from entering the city. But forward movement had been stalled by the storm and by fanatical, if mostly ineffectual, attacks by Baath Party irregulars and the Fedayeen using technicals, rocket-propelled grenades, and sniper tactics. U.S. intelligence had presumed that these forces would be used to suppress insurrectionists in the Iraqi population, not to challenge the American Army. "We really did not know where they were," a brigade intelligence officer later observed. "People did not want to hear about the Fedayeen. It was an undefined enemy. So we ignored it. . . . If you cannot put a name or a face to an enemy, then why dedicate combat power to them?"

I asked Lieutenant Colonel Hank Arnold, who was on duty as an ACP watch officer, how he thought the week would play out. Arnold was short, bald, and fine-boned; his wife, Susan, was a judge advocate general officer in the D-Main. "Once these guys realize that it's a myth that American soldiers won't fight in the cities, they'll get the message," he said. "Right now they'll crawl up to our positions and if you catch them, they'll surrender. If they get close enough to fire their rifles, they'll exchange a few shots, then surrender." This, I suspected, was hardly the case in Najaf or Nasariyah, where at least some Iraqis appeared to be fighting to the death.

"Yesterday, 3 ID was short fifteen thousand gallons of fuel," Arnold said. "Then several hundred thousand gallons got to Rams. So we have plenty of fuel to go to Baghdad. All we need now is good weather. And when the weather clears, instead of having just one battalion of the 101st up here, we'll have almost three brigades."

On the other side of the command tent, I found two staff officers who had finally reached Shell before the weather again halted helicopter operations, D. J. Reyes, the G-2, and Lieutenant Colonel Doug Gabram, an Apache pilot who was the deputy G-3 for air operations. Both were still puzzling over the 11th Regiment's mission and its implications for the 101st.

"They went into an urban area and you can't do that with attack helicopters," Gabram said. "The number one killer, through the entire history of attack helicopters, is small arms and rocket-propelled grenades."

Reyes agreed. "The Iraqis are smart guys. They've probably seen *Black Hawk Down.* It's obviously very decentralized. Everyone assumed that Saddam was controlling everything tightly from Baghdad. But these paramilitary forces clearly have the authority to engage on their own."

I donned my goggles and went outside. Soldiers plodded through the wind with their chins tucked into their chests, as if braving a blizzard. To keep my precious cot from blowing away, I had dragged it into the lee of Miller's trailer and weighted it with my bags; cot and bags alike were caked with talc. While I was calculating whether more ballast was required, Ben Freakley walked up. A brown film coated his eyeglasses, and his face looked as if Pan-Cake makeup had been applied with a trowel. He accepted my invitation to have a seat on the cot, and we turned our backs to the gale.

"We're still choosing to attack where we want and when we want," Freakley said, his croaky voice raised above the wind. "Instead of bypassing the Fedayeen, we're going to have to attack them. The key to the operational art"—the use of combined-arms forces, usually with at least a corps—"is getting all your assets into the fight. We need to reverse his efforts to resort to asymmetrical warfare, by using our tanks, our Apaches, our infantry, all of our assets together."

U.S. intelligence about the Fedayeen was obviously wrong—Freakley disdainfully called it blobology. The division would have to conduct more of its own reconnaissance and surveillance rather than rely on inadequately analyzed information provided by higher authority, much of it obtained from satellites, UAVs, and electronic eavedropping. "We need better intelligence, a better appreciation of the terrain, and we need to understand that the enemy threat is not, as we thought, a sophisticated air defense with radars and missiles, but a pretty sophisticated network of alerts through cell phones, which gets the populace to fire RPGs and automatic weapons on cue. They obviously have observers who are reporting the headings, speed, and altitude of our helicopters."

In a tactical adjustment, Wallace was giving the 101st a tank battalion—with forty-four Abrams M1A2s and Bradley Fighting Vehicles—to reinforce the division's light infantry. And instead of charging into Iraqi strongholds, the Apaches would be used to coax the enemy into revealing himself; once pinpointed, targets could be struck with bombs from less vulnerable Air Force and Navy jets. "See how long they can take *that*. What matters is that the enemy dies, not *how* the enemy dies," Freakley said. "The adversary who adapts his tactics fastest typically wins in combat.

I don't want to underestimate the enemy, but I don't want to make him a giant, either. They're thugs. They're not soldiers, they're thugs."

He was working himself into a fine wrath, and his jaw was set the way I imagined Stonewall Jackson's jaw was sometimes set. "We just need to gather ourselves, and the soldiers need to get their blood up. There's something about an American soldier that makes it hard for him to believe that someone is actually shooting at him."

Freakley's eyes softened. He looked around through his dirt-streaked spectacles and seemed to realize for the first time that we were sitting in my bedroom, such as it was. "Is this where you're sleeping?" he asked. "Why don't you pull your cot into my tent over there and stay with me?"

I protested the intrusion on his privacy, but Freakley insisted, and when he strode off to fight his war I wasted not a minute before dragging my gear into his small tent next to the ACP. A large box of candy sat on his cot, open but uneaten. The O had given up sweets for Lent.

Two hours later I went next door to the plans tent. Rick Gibbs, the G-3, had generously found me a place to work so that I could get my laptop out of the dust, which had clogged the keyboard and every port. Thirty officers and enlisted planners jammed the tent, working on maps and logistics and various battle schemes, all of them top secret. Sergeant First Class Bill Endsley cleared a spot at his table, next to the coffee urn, then said cheerfully, "I just want to tell you one thing, and that's this: if you publish anything that you see in here without permission, you *will* go to jail. Welcome." Over a map at the front of the room I heard Gibbs say of Iraqi troops, "I want those fucking bastards to know that if they move they're going to die."

At 5 P.M. there was a commotion outside. I pushed through the tent flap in time to see a towering black storm wall bearing down from the south, kicking a brown cloud of debris before it. I retreated inside and moments later the tent shuddered, as if given a great swat. The wind shrieked at fifty knots and a gritty miasma filled the tent; I swept my keyboard with a small paintbrush only to see it coated again within two minutes. Then sheets of rain lashed the camp, each drop congealing with the suspended dust. A soldier, spattered from helmet to boot heel, pushed into the tent and exclaimed, "It's raining mud!" A few minutes later I looked outside again. Not only had the sky turned red from the setting sun refracting through the dust, but the very air was crimson, as though the atmosphere itself was hemorrhaging. It all seemed ominous and biblical.

"That was the nastiest thing I've ever seen," the division sergeant major, Marvin L. Hill, told me later in the evening. "When the air turned red like that, I put eyedrops in. I thought I was having vision problems. You just have to accept that the wind's gonna blow, the tent's gonna collapse. Just find a place to lie down and wait it out."

That seemed like sage advice, and when I turned in to the Hotel Freakley for the night I was glad to see that Dwyer, too, had been given sanctuary. The three of us were wedged like sprats in a tin. "Embrace the suck," we bade one another before falling asleep, for there was nothing good to say about this night.

The next morning dust lay drifted in windrows *inside* the tent. After moderating slightly at daybreak, the wind picked up with redoubled howling. Humvees and helicopters appeared to have been dipped in milk chocolate. I arrived in the ACP at 7:30 A.M. to find Petraeus on the phone with Wallace. His face was drawn, as if he had slept poorly. An intelligence officer, Lieutenant Jeanne Hull, told me that orders had come down overnight banning the term "Fedayeen," which means "men who sacrifice themselves for a cause," because it ostensibly invested those fighters with too much dignity. They were to be referred to as paramilitaries. (Later the approved phrase would be "terroristlike death squads.") Hull estimated that there were nine to twelve Fedayeen battalions in Iraq, each with roughly six hundred fighters, including a battalion in Najaf. In a small blow against Orwellian excess, most officers continued to call them Fedayeen.

Petraeus hung up and ordered Fivecoat to get the Humvee ready for a trip to the V Corps command post at Rams. He pushed back from the table, snapped the chin strap on his helmet, and shrugged on his flak vest. "Want to step outside and chat for a minute?" he asked.

We stood fifteen feet beyond the tent flap. I blinked at the dust, and felt grit between my molars. When Petraeus turned to face me, I was alarmed to see how troubled his blue eyes were. "This thing is turning to shit," he said. "The 3 ID is in danger of running out of food and water. They lost two Abrams and a Bradley last night, although they got the crews out. The corps commander sounds tired."

A scheme to parachute the 82nd Airborne Division into the Karbala Gap had evaporated. Two battalions had their jump gear rigged at Kuwait International Airport, but the proposed drop zone was discovered to be perilously rocky; also, it was uncertain that ground reinforcements would reach the paratroopers in time to forestall substantial casualties. Instead, the 82nd would be used to secure supply routes around Nasariyah, a move Petraeus considered sensible.

I was reminded of a decision by General Maxwell Taylor in September 1943 to abort a planned jump by the 82nd Airborne into Rome, an episode Petraeus knew well. That act of prudence sixty years earlier probably had averted a massacre.

"The bold move is usually the right move," I said, trying to lighten the mood by reciting the adage Petraeus liked, "*except when it's the wrong move.*"

He smiled. The dust was blinding. I had misplaced my goggles and it was difficult to see without squinting hard. I suggested that we move behind his small tent, which was adjacent to the ACP, but when dust pursued us there we stepped inside.

Petraeus noted that the Pentagon had finally abandoned all hope of pushing the 4th Infantry Division into northern Iraq through Turkey. The flotilla of ships carrying the division kit—including the Army's most technologically advanced mechanized equipment—would sail from the Mediterranean through the Suez Canal, around the Arabian Peninsula, and up the Persian Gulf. "You know how long that will take," Petraeus said.

U.S. forces had yet to encounter the Republican Guard, but Iraqi irregulars seemed much more aggressive than anticipated and the Shiite south hardly had welcomed the invaders as liberators. The battlefield was nonlinear, with only a vague distinction between the front and the rear.

"No one really saw this coming, did they?" I said.

"No," he replied. No prewar estimates had anticipated a defense of Najaf by Iraqi regular army or Republican Guard troops, nor did those estimates predict stiff resistance from paramilitary forces. "We did worst-case scenarios, where the enemy really put up a fight, but no one took it very seriously. We need to get lucky. The CIA really needs to pull one out."

Capturing or killing Saddam Hussein seemed a wan hope, and I said as much. Petraeus agreed. "Hell, we couldn't find Noriega for four days in a country that we owned," he said, alluding to the frustrating hunt for the strongman Manuel Noriega in Panama in 1989.

"It's possible, even probable that we'll hold in place for a while," he continued. "The original timeline called for us to be at this point in forty-seven days, so we're here far ahead of schedule in that sense."

"Do the Iraqis have the ability to counterattack?" I asked.

"They do. Their losses would be very high. But we're in danger of running out of artillery ammunition."

Resupply was difficult because of the weather and insecure convoy routes. One Marine unit supposedly was down to a day's supply of food. The 101st had fifty-seven thousand gallons of fuel at Shell, but without additional stocks a concerted Apache attack against the Medina Division's 14th Brigade later in the week would be problematic. The 3rd Infantry Division had ample fuel, but had not been resupplied with food or water since leaving Kuwait and was "black"—dangerously low—on those necessities as well as on ammunition; on Tuesday, the division's commanders had reported prolonged, ferocious combat, with nearly a thousand Iraqis believed killed in the Euphrates valley around Najaf.

Even if the Chinooks could have flown, they had limited cargo capacity. And with helicopters grounded, the 101st was largely immobile because many of the trucks the division needed for transport remained at sea. The Pentagon decision to abandon the Army's meticulous force-deployment plan, coupled with the urgent need to squeeze additional units through the Kuwait City bottleneck, was bogging down logistics and transportation.

The weather, Petraeus said, was "about as nasty as anything I've ever seen." Nonbattle injuries had begun to appear in the ranks—eye irritations, nosebleeds, respiratory ailments. "At least," he added with a fleeting smile, "it's not cold."

He hooked his thumbs into his flak vest and adjusted the weight on his shoulders. "Tell me how this ends," he said. "Eight years and eight divisions?" The allusion was to advice supposedly given the White House in the early 1950s by a senior Army strategist upon being asked what it would take to prop up French forces in South Vietnam.

"You're really into something now," Petraeus added, as he pushed through the flap to find Fivecoat and the Humvee.

"So are you," I said.

At 4 P.M. on Wednesday, March 26, Petraeus returned from V Corps, and we resumed our conversation in his tent. A Ziploc bag full of Pop-Tarts—his favorite breakfast food—sat on a folding table, coated in dust. The discussions with Wallace seemed to have gone well. At the end of the conference, Petraeus reported, the corps commander had thanked him. General David McKiernan, the CFLCC commander, had joined the discussion by speakerphone. Wallace was sleeping badly and had lost his voice, but Petraeus thought he had seemed resolute. The 3rd ID, still known as the Rock of the Marne for its World War I exploits, reportedly had killed hundreds more Iraqis the previous night in heavy fighting near the Euphrates River town of Kifl, north of Najaf. The division was scattered over a swatch of Iraq measuring roughly 140 by 40 miles. "I'll tell you what," Petraeus said, "there are some fighting Muldoons in that outfit." The diversion of the 82nd Airborne to secure lines of communication in southern Iraq seemed smart and necessary, although the division had but a single brigade in the theater. Wallace had sent a handwritten note to Major General Chuck Swannack, Jr., commander of the 82nd, suggesting the urgency of the task: "Get your ass up here."

The corps would pause to gather itself, although it was unclear precisely how or when the offensive would resume. Iraqi units were becoming so jumbled that Wallace considered the enemy defensive scheme confusing and Iraq's order of battle "incomprehensible." The corps commander was unsure, as he later put it, "how to fight an enemy that does not appear to have a plan." His own plan was changing by the hour, including his long-held belief that the 101st and 3rd ID would subtly switch roles as the corps closed on Baghdad, with Petraeus's infantrymen playing a bigger role in capturing the capital, supported by Marne troops. For now, V Corps still intended to build firebases outside the capital and gradually reduce the city with raids from those bases.

Petraeus rocked on the balls of his feet. "We can't get Samawah or An Najaf to fall yet," he said. "We can blast through the Karbala Gap, but then what? And by the way, there's nothing between us and the Marines to the east. There's a pretty substantial gap.

"When do you consolidate what you've got? On the one hand,

it has been a breathtaking success. That's the plus. But the minuses for the logisticians have been substantial. They're pushing tons of stuff up, but you've got to build mountains of supplies, and you're moving those mountains four hundred kilometers deep into enemy territory across supply lines that are not secure." A historian had once referred to the territory between an armored spearhead and the logistical rear as "the void," and, as Petraeus knew, this particular void was uncommonly vulnerable. "There are so many second- and third- and fourth-order effects. Tell me when you've built up a ten-day supply of fuel, water, ammo—you just go down the list. There's a tremendous fog in trying to figure out who has what. Right now it's just a bunch of guys with trucks out there driving around."

The deep attack by the 101st Apaches against the Medina's 14th Mechanized Brigade would occur Friday night, if the dust settled. Today, for the first time since leaving Fort Campbell, the entire 101st Airborne was "green," ready to fight across the board. In an effort to prevent Republican Guard units in northern Iraq from repositioning toward Baghdad, a thousand soldiers from a U.S. Army airborne unit based in Italy would parachute into the Kurdish-controlled north in a few hours; what the Army called LGOPPs—little groups of pissed-off paratroopers—would soon be scattered along a drop zone ten thousand yards long. An armored cavalry regiment also was en route to Kuwait to help safeguard supply routes.

"But each time you bring in one of these forces you exacerbate your logistics problem," Petraeus added. "And let's say you throttle An Najaf. Then you've got six hundred thousand people you're responsible for providing with food, water, and medical care."

I asked why the Army could not simply cordon off centers of resistance like Najaf, and bypass them. (I habitually dropped the Arabic article "An," while the Army doggedly preserved it.) "That was the theory, that they might not welcome us but that they wouldn't resist us," Petraeus said. "There's been much more tenacious resistance than expected. It would cost us a lot of troops to cordon it off. There are still hundreds, if not thousands, of enemy soldiers in An Najaf.

"If you can't get An Najaf to fall, you probably aren't going to go much farther," he added. "I made that point to Wallace. It's a Shia holy city, and it's important." Wallace had wanted to avoid Najaf "like the plague" because of its religious significance, but now he had no choice. The corps commander also subscribed to the military adage that "nothing good ever happens in a pause." Recapturing the initiative was vital, but he insisted that several conditions be met before the attack resumed: five days' worth of supplies stockpiled; the logistics base at Rams secured; and the Medina Division whittled to half strength by air attacks and long-range artillery.

As the conversation drew to a close, Petraeus held up his left hand.

"It's the darnedest thing," he said. "I've lost my wedding ring. I guess it just slipped off my finger somehow."

We rummaged about for a couple minutes, searching the tent floor and cot, without success. Petraeus shrugged and headed for the ACP. "Okay," he said, "see you later."

I tried to sort out the ruminations of Petraeus, Freakley, and other senior officers. Was the Army taking counsel of its fears? I didn't think so. Calling a pause in the pell-mell rush toward Baghdad seemed sensible, particularly since air attacks would continue mostly unabated, even if overcast skies made it difficult to gauge with satellite cameras and reconnaissance planes precisely how badly the Iraqis were hurt. The Air Force on Tuesday had flown fourteen sorties against the Iraqi 14th Mechanized Brigade alone; the Air Force also estimated that in twenty-four hours it had destroyed thirty-two T-72 tanks and seventeen armored personnel carriers, mostly in the Medina Division. Wallace had planned to halt for several days anyway, as his forces gathered themselves below Baghdad. Petraeus was worried, and like everyone else he felt the oppressive effects of the weather. When I had asked what Wallace wanted at this point in the war, Petraeus answered, only partly in jest, "A thirty-five-day air campaign"—similar to the one waged in 1991 before the ground offensive began.

I knew that Petraeus had mused to Freakley and others about whether it made sense to pull back the Army's lines in order to consolidate and reinforce the attack. Yet he recognized the insuperable political price of such a move. I realized that not only did he see the tactical challenges—securing supply lines, defeating the Fedayeen, eviscerating the Republican Guard—but also he was beginning to sense the strategic obstacles in subduing and then occupying a huge country where a significant portion of the population was willing to wage an urban-based guerrilla war. "Easy money, boss," Petraeus habitually answered when given a task by his superiors, but there was nothing easy here. Having been to Somalia three times and Bosnia twice, I knew how ugly urban combat could be, with houses and buildings providing the concrete equivalent of triple-canopy jungle.

Even after sunset, the wind remained so intense that I could not set up the three-panel antennae required by the Nera satellite phone. Instead, I typed a memo on my laptop in Freakley's tent. At 9 P.M. I stumbled outside and sat on a sandbag, holding the computer and a flashlight, with a black trashbag pulled over my head and torso to keep the dust out. Shouting above the maelstrom, I dictated through another, handheld sat phone that refused to work in the tent. My colleague in Washington, Tom Ricks, who was the *Post*'s senior Pentagon reporter, had detected disquiet among senior generals, and our joint story on Thursday's front page, under the headline "War Could Last Months," would begin:

> Despite the rapid advance of Army and Marine forces across Iraq over the past week, some senior U.S. military officers are now convinced that the war is likely to last months and will

require considerably more combat power than is now on hand there and in Kuwait, senior defense officials said yesterday.

After half an hour of baying over the phone, I pushed my way back into the tent. Dwyer sat typing, with a paper respirator strapped across his nose and mouth. Dust made his eyebrows and hair appear to be carved from alabaster. "I'm fifty years old and a modestly successful author," I told him. "I have a beautiful wife, lovely children, a comfortable house, a dog. And I just spent the last thirty minutes sitting through a sand storm in a place called Hell with a trash bag over my head."

Dwyer chuckled and turned back to his keyboard.

The article apparently struck a nerve in Washington. President Bush, asked by reporters for *his* assessment of the war's duration, snapped, "However long it takes to win." The ever helpful president of France, Jacques Chirac, observed, "They underestimated Iraqi patriotism. They would have been better off listening to us."

The skies finally cleared on Thursday morning, March 27, bringing to an end a storm that had lasted for three days. I expected to see a dove beating toward us with an olive branch. Soldiers crawled from their burrows and the camp came to life as they whacked the dust from their sleeping bags, hung out their laundry, and queued up for haircuts.

At 11:45 A.M. I flew with Petraeus and Fivecoat in Warlord 457 to the edge of Shell to rendezvous with Colonel Ben Hodges. The 1st Brigade commander had just arrived after the long road march from Camp Pennsylvania, and we found him next to an unpaved road with a map spread across his Humvee hood. The day could not have been lovelier; it felt as though we had emerged from a long, filthy tunnel.

Petraeus gave Hodges a quick progress report on the war.

"The map does not do justice to the urban sprawl here," he said. "There are bad guys all over. This is really rugged terrain. What I want to emphasize is that this is a serious friggin' enemy. They've been fighting big-time here. They don't stop until they're killed. If you see somebody with a weapon, kill them. They're actually using white flags to feign surrender."

Hodges had arrived expecting his brigade eventually to move northwest of Baghdad to seize Objective Bears, one of the three potential Army firebases outside the capital. But, Petraeus said, "the plan has changed two or three times in the past twenty-four or thirty-six hours as corps has reassessed things." In addition to protecting Rams and Highway 28, the vital north-south road known as Alternate Supply Route (ASR) Boston, the 101st likely would be asked to subdue Najaf, with 1st Brigade—reinforced by the tank battalion—squeezing from the south, and 2nd Brigade air-assaulting by helicopter to attack from the north.

Hodges nodded. His eyes were calm and alert.

"The challenge is the logistics," Petraeus continued. "Those are building, but the question is: Do we have business going farther if we're challenged right now? I tend to think not. We're in a long war here, as I think you realize. I want to keep our guys from getting killed in large numbers. That's the bottom line. I hope that this is the dying gasp of a regime on the ropes, as it's being cast in some quarters. But I'm not so sure."

At 12:30 P.M. we bundled into the Blackhawk and headed north so that Petraeus and Hodges could compare mental images confected from maps and reconnaissance photographs with the Mesopotamian reality. Three Kiowas followed as bodyguards, skittering single file in our wake like a cracking whip. Soon, greening wheat and barley fields rolled beneath us at ninety knots, framed by dikes and canals. Egrets tiptoed through a reedy marsh. After so many days of unremitting brown, the pastoral scene seemed hallucinatory. A woman dressed in black flicked a switch at a pair of donkeys. Outside a hamlet of half a dozen flat-roofed mud houses, three farmers looked up from a gushing water pump and raised their arms. "They're waving," Hodges said over the intercom. "That's a good sign."

"Sir," pilot Marc Daniels called, "we're up even with the city. There on the ridge, you can see it." Two miles to the east, crowning a stony escarpment lined with palms, I spied the troublesome city of Najaf. Minarets poked above a skyline of apartment buildings, and sunlight shattered against the gold dome of the Tomb of Ali, the burial shrine of Muhammad's son-in-law who had died in the seventh century. Empty Iraqi infantry trenches squiggled across the desert, and the charred wreckage of antiaircraft guns stood like mileposts along the two-lane blacktop of ASR Boston. Tanks, Bradley Fighting Vehicles, Humvees with TOW missiles, and artillery tubes could be seen ringing the western approach to the besieged city. The Blue Force Tracker icons on Dave Fivecoat's screen showed that they belonged to the 3rd Infantry Division.

"Sir, I really don't want to go near the town," Daniels said.

"Nor do I," Petraeus replied.

We followed Boston across the fissured escarpment. Empty Army supply trucks rolled south on the long voyage back to Kuwait for new loads. Near the limit of the American advance, southeast of Karbala, we turned around.

"Wait. Stop, stop," Petraeus suddenly called. "Turn around. Looks like someone is waving his arms."

Someone *was* waving. Blinded by a dust devil, the driver of a heavy truck towing a fuel trailer had plowed into an oncoming Bradley. Warlord 457 landed just as the badly injured driver was being eased onto a back board by medics from the 3rd ID's 15th Infantry Regiment. Blood spattered the crushed truck cab, a reminder that war zones held a thousand hazards besides enemy bullets. I toed the debris scattered from the wreck: a crumpled ammo box, a can of Mountain Dew, two JLIST overshoes, Power Duster in a spray can. The stink of JP-8 fuel saturated the air like the precise odor of misfortune.

While Fivecoat flew in the Blackhawk with the injured soldier to an aid station, I sat in the sun with Hodges and Petraeus on a small hillock a hundred yards from the road.

"Everybody's frame of reference is changing," Hodges said. "The enemy always gets a vote. You fight the enemy and not the plan. I personally underestimated the willingness of the Fedayeen to fight, and maybe overestimated the willingness of the Shiites to rise up. Now we have to focus on securing our lines. We talk about how you should find, fix, and finish the enemy. That's what we've got to do."

Petraeus interrupted, as if remembering something he had neglected to mention. "If you see a pickup truck with a machine gun in the back, kill it. There are no friendlies with pickup trucks and machine guns."

"Not a question," Hodges said.

"If you see somebody with a machine gun," Petraeus repeated, "hose 'em."

Five minutes later a white pickup truck sped south on ASR Boston. A .50-caliber machine gun was mounted in the bed. "Look at *that*," I said. A captured pickup? Special Forces? Enemy infiltrators? The three of us stared as the vehicle disappeared over the lip of the escarpment. Petraeus rolled his eyes.

On the flight back to Shell, Hodges said over the intercom, "Wonder why they're making such a fight for An Najaf? Why didn't they wait until we were closer to Baghdad?"

Petraeus stared out the window for a moment before replying. "I don't know. That's a good question. It might have been smarter to suck us in some more."

A few minutes after we returned to Shell, Wallace arrived by helicopter. Aides set up a folding table and gray folding chairs behind Freakley's tent, where the corps commander sat with Petraeus and the O for nearly an hour. I kept an eye on the little conference, and when it broke up at 4:30 P.M., Dwyer and I sauntered over to Wallace. "Can we talk to you for a minute?" I asked.

Wallace smiled and playfully came to attention, bracing like a West Point plebe about to be hazed by upperclassmen. As usual, he wore his Wiley X sunglasses and cotton cavalry gloves. The smile quickly faded when I asked him to analyze V Corps's progress.

"I'm appalled by the inhumanity of it all," he said. "We've got reports of Saddamists giving out weapons and forcing people to fight, threatening their families. The attacks we're seeing are bizarre: technical vehicles, with fifty-calibers and every kind of weapon, charging tanks and Bradleys. It's disturbing to think that someone can be that brutal. It's also very disturbing that the people have put up with this for twenty-five years. I think the people are numb."

U.S. commanders had expected some Fedayeen opposition, he continued, but not the ruthless fanaticism. "The enemy we're fighting is different than the one we'd war-gamed against, because of these paramilitary forces. We knew they were here, but we did not know how they would fight."

This assessment over the coming days would be widely quoted, debated, and—in some instances—denounced. But as Wallace spoke, his analysis seemed reasonable, and even obvious. We asked what he expected from the Apaches at this point.

"We've got a buttload of Apaches, but we need to reconsider our tactics," he replied. On a positive note, many of the damaged 11th Regiment helicopters had been repaired or would soon return to the fight, and the durability of the Apache under intense fire had reinforced pilot confidence.

"A buttload?" Dwyer said.

Wallace smiled, but again the smile quickly evaporated. "We're dealing with a country in which everybody has a weapon, and when they fire them all in the air at the same time, it's tough."

"Does this mean the war is going to last longer than antici-pated?" I asked.

He cocked his head. "It's beginning to look that way."

Throughout the conversation he spoke so softly that Dwyer and I both leaned close as we scribbled in our notebooks. Later I would learn that Wallace believed he and Petraeus had subtly different views of how the war should proceed at this point. Petraeus thought Najaf was decisive, a "center of gravity" in Iraq's opposition. Wallace considered the city important, but secondary to Saddam's regime in Baghdad. V Corps, Wallace warned, would not be given "the luxury of being very precise and very slow in dealing with what was a lesser problem than the Baghdad problem." The generals concurred that subduing Najaf likely would occupy the 101st for weeks; they also agreed that if the U.S. Army could not, as Wallace later put it, "solve the problem of Najaf, a city of five hundred thousand in southern Iraq, then we were not going to be able to solve the problem of Baghdad, a city of five million."

Wallace studied the cloudless blue sky. "We knew we'd have to pause at some point to build our logistics power," he told Dwyer and me. "This is about where we expected. I've got to give my best military judgment. Right now, I think the situation is that given the weather, the long LOCs"—lines of communication—"and the fact that we've got to bring up our logistics, we're got to take this pause. We're still fighting the enemy every night. We're doing things to keep him operating at a higher tempo."

"How much pressure are you feeling from General Mc-Kiernan to get on with it?" I asked.

He shook his head. "We're both products of the same institution, which says that that really cool plan we made isn't going to survive once we cross the LD," the line of departure.

Wallace strolled back to his Blackhawk and took off.

"What'd he have to say?" asked Petraeus, who had been chatting with another reporter. Dwyer and I read back our notes.

"Well," Petraeus said, "that's pretty candid." Dwyer and I agreed, then went to write our stories.

———

At the 7 P.M. BUB, a Special Forces liaison officer reported that four teams from the 5th Special Forces Group were identifying targets and gathering intelligence in Najaf, along with "OGA" operatives. "Other Government Agency," or OGA, was field vernacular for the CIA.

"We saw a white pickup coming down the road this afternoon with a machine gun in the back," Petraeus said.

"Yes, sir. Most of ours are white Tundra pickups."

Petraeus turned around, eyebrows raised. "Gotta think about the young soldier with the Mk-19 who is worried about guys from An Najaf coming at them in white pickup trucks with machine guns in back."

"Sir," the SF officer said, "about eighty percent of our guys are driving white pickup trucks, rubbed down and painted crazy like the Iraqis do."

"I'm very concerned about that," Petraeus said. "We've got to work that."

At 11 P.M., Freakley ducked into his tent and found Dwyer and me typing away. I had written a short feature on our helicopter ride above Mesopotamia, and now had nearly finished another piece on Wallace's comments. Freakley removed his helmet, body armor, and uniform shirt before using an electric coil to heat a pint of water, which he then poured into a stainless steel bowl. "It's always better to shave at night in the desert," he told us. "Know why? Because the oils in your skin can be replenished while you're sleeping. Your skin doesn't dry out as fast." He lathered his cheeks and swiped them with the razor.

"Have you noticed that your cuticles are cracked?" he asked.

I *had* noticed, and in fact it was painful to reach into my pockets.

"That's a sign of dehydration," he said. "You need to drink more water."

I sensed that he had more on his mind than desert fieldcraft. How had the meeting with Wallace gone? I asked.

He gave a noncommittal shrug as he slipped off his boots and slid into his sleeping bag. The 101st would lend its battery of six 155mm guns to the 3rd Infantry Division. Originally, the division was just going to provide extra ammunition, but Freakley said he had urged Petraeus to give the 3 ID the guns themselves, which had seen little action with the 101st.

"What a smart command structure does is that at the tactical level, you adjust the plan. At the operational and strategic level, you adjust the plan. The strategy originally was 'Get to Baghdad as rapidly as you can, change the regime, bring in humanitarian aid, and declare victory.'

"Now," Freakley said, "it's going to take longer. In the Civil War, the strategy for the North at first was 'On to Richmond.' That evolved into 'Kill the enemy army.' "

I said I hoped that the adjusted war plan in Iraq wouldn't take four years, as the Civil War had.

Freakley rattled off the 3rd ID's exploits—this brigade attacking here, that brigade attacking there—but two-thirds of the division was now tied up containing Najaf and Samawah. The 101st so far had been relatively quiet. For an officer as aggressive as Ben Freakley, that subsidiary role was galling. To Petraeus he had suggested, "Sir, we might want to get more of the division into the fight." To Ben Hodges he had advised, "The best way to protect is to attack." There were intelligence reports that the Fedayeen in Najaf might break out to the north in an effort to escape the tightening American noose. It would be a shame if they got away, Freakley said.

"I wish we could offer more to General Wallace," he added. "I feel like the corps is punching with one arm."

He turned over and soon was fast asleep.

At 9:30 A.M. on Friday, March 28, I intercepted Petraeus outside the ACP as he was returning from the Room with a View. After a four-day delay, forty of the division's Apaches were to attack the Medina Division near Karbala that night in an operation code-named DESTINY REACH, and I was curious to gauge his temper.

"I'm a little concerned about the campaign of rising expectations," he said. "If we take our time, things will be okay. My concern is that we're trying to rush. Transportation is our Achilles' heel. We can't transport dismounted soldiers right now."

I thought of the motto of one truck company I had seen: "We may not be the best, but without us the best would walk." Trucks and other support vehicles from V Corps were still trickling into Kuwait, and probably would not reach the division in substantial numbers for another two weeks.

"When do we get to the point where we can easily move soldiers and supplies around?" Petraeus asked. "We can do it with helicopters, but even in good weather you want to minimize landings in this dust."

The deep *whomp-whomp* of helicopters cut him short. A flight of Blackhawks swept over us, bringing in another infantry battalion from Kuwait. Petraeus craned his neck and extended his right arm with a thumbs-up. Shielding our eyes against the brilliant sun, we could see troops in the bays: in each helicopter, sixteen heavily laden soldiers were wedged so tightly that after the long flight they would walk with a cramped waddle until circulation returned to their legs.

"The Iraqis are driving pickup trucks into tanks," Petraeus continued. "If people are willing to impale themselves on you, that implies a certain degree of commitment."

I asked how long the campaign was likely to last. Without hesitation he posited that it might take weeks to reduce Najaf, and months to subdue all of Iraq.

"Really?" I said. "Do you think you could be at it all summer?"

"Summer!" He grinned. "We'll be lucky if it's just summer."

Tonight's attack would be the first chance for the division's new Apache Longbows to see action. After the 11th Regiment's debacle five nights earlier, many pilots believed the Apache had something to prove, even as Wallace and Petraeus debated whether to permit further helicopter deep attacks. In the modern military, every campaign, every firefight, was freighted with political and financial implications. Some officers even suspected that the future of Army attack helicopters was at stake in Iraq. Failure, or just the perception of failure, could fortify fixed-wing advocates who argued that the billions spent on rotary aircraft would be better diverted to less vulnerable systems. Bang-for-the-buck skirmishing never ended in Washington—interservice rivalry and a thousand lobbyists guaranteed perpetual conflict on Capitol Hill—and no battlefield was too remote for the budgetary consequences of those clashes to be sensed.

"The guys really want to do it tonight, they want to get going. You have to take that into account. You can't leave them sitting forever," Petraeus said. "But we really have to look at the intelligence. We cannot have a repeat of Sunday night. The dilemma is, okay, what if we go in and turn around under fire? What does that say? Or, what if you go out and don't kill anything, and take fire anyway?"

And then there was simply the hazard of taking off and landing in the dust at night, which one aviator had told me was like "a Navy pilot trying to execute a carrier landing in rough seas at midnight."

"The Apache is a great system," Petraeus said, with another sardonic grin, "when you're not in the desert."

An hour later Petraeus ducked into the plans tent to review the intelligence for DESTINY REACH with Gass, Freakley, and other officers. Helmets were stacked in a pyramid on a floor locker, and an air conditioner clicked on every few minutes with a low roar. Petraeus sat on a gray folding chair, stripped to a black long-sleeve T-shirt with a two-star insignia. "Things have changed," he cautioned. "The idea that they're going to collapse, and that air defenses around Karbala are relatively weak, is out the window."

A slide flashed onto a screen at the front of the room: "14th Mechanized Brigade/Medina Republican Guard Armor Division. Intel update. 280800Z March." The attack plan called for the 2nd Battalion of the 101st Aviation Brigade to fly north from Shell toward Karbala, arousing and distracting Iraqi defenders before pulling back to allow attacks by close-air-support planes. The brigade's 1st Battalion would veer northwest for sixty miles across the large, shallow lake called Razzaza, before looping out of the north above Karbala to attack the Medina's 14th Brigade from the rear while Iraqi attention was diverted south by the 2nd Battalion. The mission was designed to destroy defenders plugging the Karbala Gap, the narrow neck between the city and the lake. Barely a mile wide, the gap was a convenient and obvious gateway to Baghdad that mostly avoided the rivers and irrigation ditches threading other approaches; if the 3rd Infantry

Division could knife through, the Americans would be difficult to stop short of the capital.

Half a dozen briefers, each wielding a red or green penlight laser, stood in sequence to tell Petraeus what they knew about the enemy: the Iraqi brigade consisted of an armored battalion and three mechanized battalions, which were outfitted with armored personnel carriers. The Medina Division was now assessed at 76 percent of full strength although, after more than a week of relentless air attacks, the tank battalion of the 14th Brigade was listed at 14 percent, with only five T-72 tanks left. A number of artillery tubes had also been destroyed. The brigade headquarters had been identified twenty miles northeast of Karbala in the town of Musayyib, where a tank platoon and two mechanized companies guarded the highway bridge across the Euphrates.

A PowerPoint map showing Iraqi air defenses popped onto the screen. The lethal radius of various guns and missiles appeared as broken red circles, while blue lines depicted the communication links to Iraqi "vis obs"—visual observers equipped with telephones. Roland missiles had been detected yesterday in Najaf. A Low Blow radar, typically linked to SA-3 missiles, was operating west of Karbala, and a Spoon Rest radar had appeared north of the city this morning. At least nine S-60 gun positions could be counted around the 14th Brigade, each with a range of several miles. Pilots were advised to stay below fifty feet to escape radar detection.

"The enemy," D. J. Reyes told Petraeus, "recognizes that our main effort is being pushed toward the Karbala Gap."

Another slide, titled "Collection Emphasis D+9," listed the intelligence systems currently operating over that patch of Iraq: JSTARS, Hunter and Predator drones, Global Hawk, RC-135 Rivet Joint, EP-3Z Aries II. The division would receive real-time signals intelligence, electronic intelligence, and MTIs—moving target indicators from JSTARS aircraft tracking Iraqi vehicles.

The briefing broke up. As he exited the tent, Petraeus told me that he was pleased, although chagrined that so few armored targets could be identified. Air Force, Navy, and Marine warplanes apparently had gutted the brigade, and during the sandstorm survivors had repositioned in palm groves and Karbala's neighborhoods. Pickings were slim, but he was inclined to launch the attack.

"We need to find out whether we can do it," he said, "or whether we can't do it."

I was surprised to learn in a satellite-phone call from Washington that Wallace's comments the previous day had caused a brouhaha. Both the Pentagon and Central Command officers in Qatar had reacted defensively or, in some cases, belligerently to suggestions that the war was not unfolding precisely as anticipated. "I'll give you a definitive statement," General Richard B. Myers, chairman of the Joint Chiefs of Staff, told Pentagon reporters. "I think it's a brilliant plan." President Bush was described by the White House as "irritated." Wallace, who was mystified by the uproar, later told me that he had been cautioned by McKiernan. "Scott, about the article. It's caused a great deal of concern at the highest levels of government," the CFLCC commander told him in a terse radio call. "You just need to stay away from the press for a while."

To those of us in the field, the corps commander appeared to be articulating the obvious. He had publicly given voice to what many officers were saying privately about the complications of bad weather, vulnerable supply lines, and tenacious Iraqi paramilitaries. His original war plan had called for bypassing southern cities during the blitzkrieg to Baghdad, on the presumption that the Fedayeen and other irregulars would remain on the defensive. Moreover, the Army in Iraq lacked the infantry legions that military planners believed necessary for protracted urban operations. "Stay out of the cities," Wallace had repeatedly insisted. Not until the Iraqi military had been defeated and the capital captured had Wallace intended to enter the cities, as part of an effort to stabilize the country; the corps commander had been loath before then to join what he called, in his earthy argot, "a broke-dick, big-ass urban fight."

Now that had changed. It could be argued that a plan predicated on enemy passivity was flawed. But Wallace could not now risk leaving Iraqi marauders in his rear, shooting up fuel and ammunition trucks and capturing more Jessica Lynches. Corps planners had expected thirty-five thousand Iraqi prisoners in southern Iraq, but nowhere near that number had been captured. Moreover, recalcitrant Fedayeen were preventing Iraqi army units from capitulating as U.S. commanders had hoped. If the cities were providing havens, as Najaf and Nasariyah were, then the cities must be subdued and probably occupied. Clearing a room, a building, a block, a town, required both muscle and deliberation. Every officer trained in MOUT—military operations in urban terrain—knew that difficult tactical and psychological questions obtained. Siege warfare, if required, could be ethically convoluted.

"We're not going to catapult diseased cattle into the city or anything like that," Major Bill Abb, one of Petraeus's senior planners, told me on Friday afternoon while studying a map of Najaf. "But there's a question of what you *can* do and what you *should* do. We might be able to knock out the electricity in a city, but do you want to see pictures on CNN of the baby who died because power to the incubator was cut off?"

Much had gone right in the past week, including things that were mostly invisible from ground level at Shell or Rams. Thousands of Special Forces troops, secretly operating in western and northern Iraq, and from the town of Ar Ar in northwest Saudi Arabia, had run roughshod over Iraqi outposts. Ten thousand air sorties had battered Iraqi targets everywhere. U.S. casualties remained minimal, and Iraqi civilian casualties seemed light. The 3rd Infantry Division was almost to Karbala. No chemical or biological weapons had been used, or, for that matter, found. (Today, in fact, ten Iraqi tanker trucks suspected of carrying the choking agent phosgene had been destroyed by the Air Force north of Najaf; neither phosgene nor any other toxin was detected in the wreckage.) Iraqi oil fields had been spared. No Scuds had been fired at Israel in an attempt to widen the war, as had happened in 1991.

But the political imperative of waging a short, decisive campaign increasingly conflicted with the military necessity of girding for a longer, more violent, more costly war of attrition. None of the people in Washington who had led the nation into a preemptive attack by a small invasion force nearly bereft of allies wanted to believe that the conflict could drag on for months, perhaps tying up most of the Army's ten divisions and bleeding the nation of money and manpower.

In speaking about his battlefield challenges, it seemed to me, Wallace had been speaking truth to power. When I mentioned to an officer at Shell that Secretary Rumsfeld seemed testy in answering reporters' questions about Wallace's comments, the officer snapped, "Let Rumsfeld come out here and try to do a better job of commanding the corps."

Just after 4 P.M., Petraeus again met Freakley and Gass in the plans tent for the requisite "conditions check" that would determine whether to launch the Apache attack. A meteorologist led off by noting that the moon would not rise until 4:30 A.M., hours after all the helicopters had returned. Fifteen-mile-per-hour winds were expected to die at sunset. "Sir, the weather is a go across the board. There shouldn't be a cloud in the sky. Visibility should be more than four miles."

D. J. Reyes then stood to voice concerns about a surface-to-air missile ambush—he called it a SAMbush, without smiling—northeast of Karbala. SAM batteries and other key targets would be struck with eighteen long-range ATACMS rounds, each spewing hundreds of lethal bomblets. SEAD, suppression of enemy air defenses, would cease less than four minutes before the Apaches struck, compared with more than two hours for the 11th Regiment on Sunday night. To make themselves as difficult to hit as possible, pilots intended to constantly vary their airspeed and altitude.

"What obstacles are en route? Are there any high-tension lines?" Freakley asked.

"Yes, sir," Gass replied. "There are high-tension lines."

"Are there vis obs along those wires? One of the issues with the 11th Attack Helicopter Regiment was that they felt they were a little exposed when they climbed to get over the wires," Freakley said. "How do you feel about these routes versus the routes flown by the 11th AHR?"

"I feel much more comfortable with ours," Gass said.

Petraeus ran through a checklist, asking each staff officer in turn for recommendations.

"Intel is a go," Reyes said.

"Fire support is a go."

"Air defense is a go."

"Command and control is a go."

Petraeus stood to face the staff. He would call Wallace momentarily to obtain final approval. "My recommendation to him at this point is that we go. Just so you know, here's my thinking. One, the crews have drilled this real well. Two, we need to do a mission. If you dip your toe in and the water's too hot, you pull back. I feel that we have to do something, not for the sake of doing something, but to get our feet wet without plunging all the way in. Okay, that'll do it. Thanks very much. Air assault!"

Petraeus, Freakley, and the battle staff had taken their chairs in the ACP when I entered at 8 P.M. Nine maps covered the walls. The voltage in the room reminded me of ringside before a prize-fight. I took the only seat available—on the floor, against a map board—and studied a two-page "execution checklist." Alphabetized female names, beginning with Alexandra, Bonnie, and Carol, provided code words for significant events that could be transmitted by radio without betraying vital information to Iraqi eavesdroppers. "Carrie," for example, signified the formal authorization of the attack by Wallace, at 4:42 P.M.

"I guarantee you there's a little adrenaline running through some cockpits right now," said Chief Warrant Officer Brendan Kelly, the Apache brigade's tactical operations officer, who was sitting next to me. The screen saver on Kelly's laptop showed a tidy brick house with a sprinkler watering the lush lawn. Across the aisle, an officer tracking Iraqi air defenses poured himself a cup of coffee from a stainless-steel thermos, then took a swig from a can of Red Bull. "EA-6 on station now," someone announced, referring to a Navy electronic jamming plane.

"Attention in the TOC," Petraeus called. "You can see an awful lot of aircraft up there." He flicked his penlight at a radar screen. Green blips represented aircraft bombing Iraqi targets around Karbala, including F-14 Tomcats from an aircraft carrier and Royal Air Force planes, which were hammering S-60 antiaircraft guns. Another screen showed ghostly images of empty rooftops near Karbala, broadcast by a television camera mounted on a drone.

At 8:30 P.M., "Glenda" signaled the takeoff of eight helicopters from the 1st Battalion's B Company, bound for the lake and then Karbala's northern precincts. Others departed Shell in quick succession: Gretchen, Hannah, Heather, Heidi. I knew that somewhere out there Greg Gass—Destiny Six—was trying to orchestrate the attack despite balky radios in a command-and-control helicopter behind the lead company.

At 8:43 P.M., a voice announced, "Apache down south of Shell. Cause unknown." Alarm and imprecations rippled through the tent. The helicopter had crashed during takeoff. "What the fuck?" muttered Doug Gabram, who was coordinating the attack in the ACP.

Helen. Hope. India.

"Julie, with six aircraft." Another company had taken off.

"Come on, boys," pleaded Warrant Officer Kelly, "get into the fight." The officer across the aisle drained his Red Bull.

Lucy, Maddie, Marjorie, Millie.

Just before 9 P.M., D. J. Reyes relayed warnings of enemy aircraft near Karbala, which seemed improbable, and of impending Baath Party attacks on all American forces and installations in Iraq, which seemed even more improbable. Petraeus, who had been brooding over the downed Apache, waved away the reports as "a little premature."

Molly, Nancy, Noel, Norah. The radio calls grew fainter as the Apaches pressed north, but Blue Force Tracker showed their progress as bright blue dots on a screen. Three icons, representing three companies of the 1st Battalion, inched across Lake Razzaza before skating over the salt flat north of Karbala. At 9:20 P.M., we watched as the lead company began its attack run to the southeast, following a canal into the heart of the suspected 14th Mechanized Brigade positions. "Lot of CAS up there right now," Petraeus said, circling the radar tracks with his laser. "Damn! Look at that."

A barrage of ATACMS missiles ripped through Iraqi targets four minutes in front of the lead helicopters, close enough for pilots to see the detonations and smoke swirling from demolished vehicles. "Hey," one pilot in the 2nd Battalion radioed, "there are people on the roof and they are waving at us." Another answered, "Dude, they ain't waving."

The lights of Karbala winked out momentarily, but this time the subsequent ground barrage proved ineffective. Most Iraqi fire appeared concentrated in the south, where the 2nd Battalion danced out of range, firing back from four miles away at targets along Highway 9.

Patty, Rita, Sally, Samantha.

Just before 9:30 P.M., someone reported another Apache down

at Shell. The helicopter was said to have flipped over while landing in the dust. A staff officer in the ACP clicked on a crew list stored in his laptop, then matched the tail number to the names and call signs of the two pilots. The blue icons on the screen were suddenly transfigured into mothers' sons. Petraeus pursed his lips. He looked grim, and later he would tell me that at that moment, for the first time in the war, he felt his blood pressure spike.

At 9:36 P.M., a frantic message warned that 3rd Infantry Division soldiers were taking fire from Apaches. "We're not hitting any friendly troops, right?" Rick Gibbs asked in a loud, fretful tone. "Hello? Hello?" The report soon proved spurious.

Shortly before 10 P.M., the 2nd Battalion began pulling back toward Shell. As planned, the battalion had diverted Iraqi attention to the south. Radar tracks showed American and British warplanes continuing to pummel defenders who had revealed themselves by firing at the helicopters. North of Karbala, the 1st Battalion pressed the attack down the canal before swinging west to escape over the lake. The ACP grew subdued, then oddly silent.

Sandy, Shelly, Suzie, Uma.

"I wish I knew what was going on up there," Kelly said. "It's feast or famine in the deep attack. It's gratifying to hear that they're not getting shot up, and that the enemy has flexed to the south like we hoped."

He studied the electronic map at the front of the tent. "We had the benefit of learning from the 11th AHR. Ultimately they were the sacrificial lambs and we took our cues from them. The Apache was not designed to go into an urban environment. It's designed to fight in open terrain, or maybe in a wooded area. There's got to be a better way to fight in cities. Maybe it's UAVs with infantry. But Saddam has studied Somalia and the Balkans, and he is not going to put his armor forces out in the desert again like he did in 1991."

We soon learned from reports trickling in that above Karbala the 1st Battalion had found few traces of the 14th Brigade despite thirty minutes of trawling. As suspected, Iraqi forces that had survived a week of Air Force pummeling had repositioned during the storm; at least the 101st would be able to tell the 3rd Infantry Division that resistance in the Karbala Gap was likely to be light. The tally eventually claimed by the two Apache battalions and their supporting fires included a dozen armored vehicles, eleven air-defense systems, three artillery tubes, and twenty trucks; the official Army tally amounted to ten armored vehicles, five pickup trucks, a fiber-optic facility, and twenty Iraqi fighters. Whatever the actual figure, the destruction hardly approximated the hundred tanks and armored personnel carriers that had burned so furiously in the imaginations of many Apache pilots.

The two crashed helicopters turned out to be total losses, at $20 million each. Both had been downed by dust rather than enemy fire. Weighing more than nine tons, a fully armed and fueled Longbow was indeed the finicky beast described by Gass, particularly during takeoffs and landings. In its death throes, one Apache also had nicked a parked Blackhawk. Human casualties proved minor: a broken leg was the worst of it.

Petraeus put a positive spin on DESTINY REACH. His division had been blooded, and was in the fight for the duration.

"It was a good mission, actually, using good coordination between the Apaches and the U.S. and British fighter-bombers," he told Dwyer and me as we stood next to the front table. "I feel real good about how all the assets were brought together. This is setting the eventual conditions for resuming the ground offensive."

The final Apache company reported leaving the target area at 10:39 P.M. Adrenaline seeped out of the ACP. The tent canvas seemed to sag ever so slightly, and staff officers began to slip away in search of a little sleep.

Wendy, Yolanda, Zandra, Zoe.

11

AN ARMY OF BONES

Najaf was the black pearl of the Shiite Muslim world. Here was buried Ali ibn Abi Talib, son-in-law of the prophet Muhammad, who had been stabbed to death while praying at a nearby mosque in A.D. 661; we had spied the gilded dome of his shrine during our helicopter excursion on Thursday. For thirteen centuries, Ali's sacred bones had lent Najaf a cachet enjoyed by few Arab cities. Muslims unable to make the long haj to Mecca often traveled instead to Najaf as an earnest of their piety, while burial within the vast necropolis around Ali's tomb was so coveted that the so-called corpse traffic became a booming business in central Mesopotamia, the way beaver pelts once dominated commerce on the Missouri River. Proximity to Ali was said to ameliorate the ordeal of the grave, and to abridge the interval between death and resurrection. One imam calculated that, in terms of religious efficacy, burial in Najaf's Wadi al-Salam for a single day exceeded seven hundred years of prayer. By the early 1900s, twenty thousand bodies a year were shipped to Najaf from Iran and other Shiite strongholds. Shroud weaving and tomb building boomed. As a gateway to the vast desert that stretched toward Saudi Arabia's Empty Quarter, Najaf also became a trade center for camel skins and wool, attracting Bedouins from Araby and

Syria who then converted from Sunni to Shia Islam. Najaf so embodied the Shia spirit that it was described as "a world within a city," drawing Shiite scholars as Rome draws Catholic theologians. No fewer than nineteen religious schools had been established by the early twentieth century, and the Iranian revolutionary Ayatollah Khomeini had enjoyed a contemplative if scheming exile here for sixteen years.

True, Najaf routinely fell on hard times. Water shortages grew so severe by the late sixteenth century that only thirty inhabited houses remained in the city. That parched condition was reversed after 1803 by construction of the Hindiyya canal, which diverted enough water from the Euphrates to sustain pilgrims and corpses alike. New hygiene regulations in the 1920s curbed the cemetery trade again, and half of Najaf's population was unemployed by 1938. In the 1980s, Najaf suffered another reversal when Iranian pilgrims were barred during the Iran-Iraq war.

A few years later the city ran afoul of Saddam Hussein during the star-crossed Shiite revolt that followed the Persian Gulf War. Insurrectionists chanted, "There is no god but God, and Saddam is His enemy." Baathist officials were hunted down and executed, and rebels smashed even the traffic lights as symbols of Saddam's autocracy. Loyalist troops answered with tanks bearing a counterslogan: "No more Shiites after today." Thousands died, and most of Najaf's eight thousand theology students fled to Iran. Bullet holes in the mosques had since been patched, and structures razed by artillery rebuilt. More than a decade later, Najaf was a quiescent if not precisely obedient city of 560,000. It was said that only three images hung on the walls of Ali's shrine: a picture of the tomb itself, the family tree of Saddam Hussein, and a portrait of Saddam at prayer.

The 101st Airborne Division now prepared to pounce on this holy place with all the firepower the U.S. Army could muster. Najaf by the last weekend in March seemed to have become a linchpin in the entire campaign. Seat of the most fanatical resistance, it straddled a vital northbound route—Highway 9—and was almost within artillery range of ASR Boston to the west, which the Army had chosen in a deliberate attempt to skirt the city. Despite ferocious fighting all week, Najaf remained unbowed. Some V Corps intelligence analysts also worried that American control of the place would give Saddam Hussein an irrefutable signal that the Army was intent on seizing Baghdad, perhaps triggering Iraqi chemical attacks or other desperate measures.

The 3rd Infantry Division had battled all around Najaf for five days without ever entering its inner neighborhoods. Unable to bypass the city as planned, because of Fedayeen marauders, Marne troops had isolated Najaf beginning March 25 by seizing Euphrates bridges to the north and south. Fending off suicide attacks through the morning of the twenty-seventh, often in near zero visibility, U.S. forces on the city's southern perimeter alone estimated that more than two thousand Fedayeen had been killed and at least a hundred technical vehicles destroyed. An Iraqi brigadier general captured Friday afternoon, March 28, reported that eight hundred fighters continued to shelter in central Najaf.

Now General Wallace ordered the 3rd ID to position farther north for a drive through the Karbala Gap, and the eventual assault on Baghdad. The 101st would finish the job in Najaf, initially throwing up another loose cordon and then, perhaps, clearing the city. Precisely how and when to accomplish the latter remained uncertain. Petraeus intended to squeeze the city with two brigades, Hodges's 1st from the south and Colonel Joe Anderson's 2nd from the north, cutting off escape routes, blocking Iraqi reinforcements, and protecting the approaches to Rams. Substantial improvisation would be required. No one was eager to fight door to door, block to block, in what Hodges called "a Stalingrad kind of city fight."

On Saturday morning, March 29, Ben Freakley told me he had

a scheme for reducing the city, although he had not yet proposed it to Petraeus. The O was irate at division planners for what he considered their sluggish, uncreative thinking about Najaf.

"We broadcast and drop leaflets, urging the Shia to help the Americans, or at least remain neutral, and we promise the Saddamists that if they don't surrender by nine A.M. the next day there will be dire consequences," Freakley said. The untouched box of sweets sat next to his cot, awaiting the end of Lent. "Then, at 9:01 A.M., we level ten targets. Repeat the next day, and stir. Keep repeating until they comply."

At noon I met Petraeus outside the ACP for the short walk to Warlord 457. I was about to ask him about Freakley's prescription when he said, "Four Marne soldiers were just killed by a car bomb." An hour earlier, a taxi being searched at a checkpoint north of Najaf had exploded when a soldier opened the trunk. The blast blew the vehicle fifteen feet across the road. Petraeus quickened his stride toward the helicopter. The implications for the 100,000 American soldiers now in Iraq hardly required elaboration. Iraq had instantly been shown to have the makings of Beirut or the West Bank.

Only half of the Republic of Iraq was desert, but after five days at Shell it seemed inconceivable that more hospitable terrain existed in this benighted country. Yet as we flew northeast, the other half began to reveal itself. Spear grass and saltbushes demarcated the boundary between brown and green. Below Najaf's escarpment—a sheer, 250-foot cliff that angled northwest from the city—a shallow lake several miles long had been carved into rice paddies. A 3rd Infantry Division artillery battery perched next to a small quarry. What might they mine here? I wondered. Uranium? Phosphates? Hope? A peasant woman in black robes carried a large tub on her head. Petraeus waved. She waved back. Flat-roofed adobe farmhouses grew more numerous, flanked by gum trees, and by greenhouses with plastic canopies.

The Blackhawk crossed a four-lane highway and skimmed over a date plantation framed by canals. Iraq had 22 million date trees, almost a tree for every Iraqi, and before the Gulf War the country had supplied 80 percent of the world's dates. I had read that female trees bore up to a thousand dates each season and could remain fertile past the age of one hundred. Such details seemed comforting, suggesting a sane Iraq, an Iraq of husbandry and date-nibbling, an Iraq that was more than dust and malevolence.

Chickens scattered into the brush as Warlord 457 and our two Kiowa bodyguards carefully threaded the telephone wires and touched down on a two-lane blacktop a few hundred yards from where the car bomb had detonated that morning. Objective Jenkins, as the Army called this place, occupied the western bank of the Euphrates, fourteen miles north of Najaf. The road continued another eight hundred yards, then crossed the last bridge spanning the river before a great, south-flowing fork in the Euphrates. Beyond the bridge lay the town of Kifl. In this place the Old Testament prophet Ezekiel, humorless and God-besotted, had preached to the Jews during their Babylonian captivity in the sixth century B.C., foretelling the restoration of Israel. The 3rd ID recently had battled through Jenkins and into Kifl, and I spotted a couple of dozen dead Iraqis in body bags stacked under the palms. Here, at least, the corpse traffic still thrived.

Colonel Anderson, the 2nd Brigade commander, waited for us with an open map. More than nine hundred of his soldiers had just flown by helicopter 250 miles from Kuwait in what the division deemed the longest air assault ever. They were to secure the bridge, which still stood because Iraqi engineers had improperly rigged their charges and botched the demolition during the 3rd ID's assault on Tuesday. The brigade would then seal the northern approaches to Najaf.

I watched as one company rose from the tall grass and trudged down the road toward Kifl in the timeless waddle of the overburdened infantryman. I read their name tags: Osbourne, Lee, Martinez, Peek. They lumbered past in a column, sweating beneath the weight of body armor, canteens, smoke canisters, knee pads, antitank weapons, rifles, night-vision goggles, M-249 light machine guns, gas masks—all the accoutrements of modern combat. One soldier stumbled crossing a ditch and lay on his back, helpless as a flipped turtle, until his buddies yanked him onto his feet. On the dusty side of a Humvee someone had scribbled "FUBAR," an acronym I recognized from Mogadishu: Fucked Up Beyond All Recognition.

"For some reason, the Iraqis want this town," Anderson told Petraeus, gesturing vaguely toward Najaf. "They're fighting for it. It's not like there's a million dollars in gold here. But they want it. There's a cement factory over there with some smokestacks. That's where these guys seem to be marshaling."

Anderson, like Petraeus, was a New Yorker and a West Pointer. At forty-three, he was bald, sinewy, and forceful, with long eyelashes and a tendency to lean forward when speaking until he was inches from his auditor. "Nothing keeps me awake nights," he had once told me, and I believed him.

Smoke curled from the chimney of a nearby farmhouse. Four Apaches drifted overhead. Petraeus stared toward the tree line, and I knew that he was thinking about the car bomb. An Iraqi official had warned in a television appearance that such attacks would become "routine military policy." I believed that, too.

"The key is stopping something before it gets close to you," Petraeus told Anderson.

Anderson nodded. "We're waving at them to stop, and if they don't stop they get what's coming. White flags mean nothing out here." Some Iraqi troops reportedly had swapped their uniforms for civilian clothes, and GIs were to keep an eye peeled for military boots beneath *dishdasha* robes.

At 1:35 P.M., a convoy of five Humvees came down the road, trailed by a Bradley. Wallace climbed out with Major General Buford C. Blount III, commander of the 3rd Infantry Division. For half an hour they stood on the road with Petraeus and studied their maps. Blount was keen to plunge on toward Baghdad, but Wallace insisted that he wait until all three of the 3rd ID infantry brigades were gathered above Najaf; only today was the 82nd Airborne supplanting Blount's 3rd Brigade at Samawah, where Army intelligence estimated that five hundred entrenched diehards were coercing another fifteen hundred Iraqis to fight through executions and extortion.

I heard the dull *crump* of a mortar round detonate on our side of the Euphrates. A minute later Army 105mm howitzers barked in reply, dumping fifteen or twenty counterbattery rounds across the river.

Wallace drove off with his entourage. We reboarded the Blackhawk and angled east before swinging south. The lovely green ribbon of the Euphrates scrolled past Kifl, which lay badly smashed on the far bank. Ezekiel's tomb stood somewhere in that desolation. "There was a noise, and behold a shaking, and the bones came together, bone to bone," the prophet had written. "And the breath came into them, and they lived, and stood upon their feet, an exceeding great army."

Among other tasks on this Saturday afternoon, Petraeus sought a better place to park the division's helicopters, and we examined several possible alternatives to dusty Shell, which had already claimed two Apaches. To his frustration and to my surprise, finding a site proved impossible. Even irrigated barley fields had a thin topsoil crust that turned to powder at the least disturbance. "Well, sir," pilot Marc Daniels observed, "the green stuff looks as dusty as the brown stuff." Solid ground closer to the Euphrates was insecure, either too close to populated areas or within Fedayeen mortar range.

I realized that yet another prosaic logistics issue had critical combat consequences. The Army had purchased portable, reusable landing pads made from rolls of synthetic material called Mobi-Mat. To construct a large helipad—ninety-eight feet by fifty-five feet—required twelve mats, pinned together with spikes that resembled long tent pegs. But those twelve mats weighed more than two tons; with the Army short of food, water, fuel, and artillery ammunition, Mobi-Mat necessarily took a lower priority on transportation manifests. Moreover, despite a surge in production the matting was in short supply, and by late March there were fewer than 150 Mobi-Mat helipads for the entire Army, of which the 101st had a couple of dozen. "Without logistics you might be able to fight," a warrant officer at Shell had told me, "but you won't fight for long."

"I'm not sure the perfect place exists," Fivecoat said as we scrutinized yet another dust trap.

"I don't think so, either," Petraeus muttered. "It's like hunting for the right house."

At 3:30 P.M., Warlord 457 touched down three miles south-west of Najaf, on the flats below the escarpment. Ben Hodges led us into an abandoned elementary school where 1st Brigade had set up its command post. A faded blue and red frieze covered the stucco walls of the one-story building, and an Arabic inscription promised, "Plan well and the results will be good." Beyond the concertina wire that snaked around the TOC perimeter, refugees from Najaf plodded along the dirt road. Women in their billowing black *abaya*s resembled walking rain clouds.

Inside Classroom No. 5, soldiers had tacked up a chart labeled "March Madness 2003." The names in the brackets tracking the NCAA basketball tournament seemed drawn from another world: Syracuse, Marquette, Texas, Kansas. The Bastogne Brigade banner, sky blue for the infantry, hung near the door, and a large National Imagery and Mapping Agency street map of Najaf pinpointed gas stations, the power plant, and a theater. Najaf New Airfield, which featured one of the longest hard-surface runways in Iraq, stretched southeast of the city and no doubt had been vital to the pilgrim trade. A 101st intelligence map highlighted roughly four hundred protected, "no fire" sites to be avoided in Najaf. Blue dots designated a stadium, schools, an amusement park, and grain-storage facilities. Black dots indicated mosques; yellow dots, hospitals; green dots, markets. An oversized circle marked the Tomb of Ali, nestled against the sprawling, L-shaped cemetery that ran along the escarpment. Much less certain was where the Iraqi defenders had holed up, or how many remained.

"We've moved into blocking positions south of the city," Hodges said, pointing on the map to Highway 9. "This intersection is called Checkpoint Charlie. We've blocked the highway to vehicle traffic in and out of An Najaf here, except for one ambulance that had an arrangement with 3 ID to enter and leave the city. We search it any time they want to come through our lines."

"Keep a watch on those taxis," Petraeus advised.

Hodges led us outside to a small convoy of Humvees, and we drove east. The city loomed to our left, dominated by Ali's glinting dome. South of town, the fields were blanketed with discarded plastic bottles and acres of other litter. Waterbirds high-stepped through the shallow ponds. A driver flicked his whip at a donkey pulling a two-wheeled tumbrel; a little boy stared from the cart bed.

Checkpoint Charlie was held by a company of Abrams tanks from the 2nd Battalion of the 70th Armor Regiment, a unit from Fort Riley, Kansas, now attached to the 101st. Three miles south of Najaf's heart, this had been the limit of the 3rd Infantry Division's advance. Shot-up cars and a charred city bus had been pushed to the highway shoulders. A dozen prisoners, all in civilian clothes, squatted in a semicircle. Unconfirmed intelligence reports indicated that Fedayeen were coercing other Iraqis to fight by threatening to execute their families. Petraeus sidled over with his short, rotund translator, whom everyone called Lieutenant Joe and who once had been an Iraqi army colonel before displeasing the regime, which reputedly yanked out all his fingernails and toenails. Joe had escaped to Oregon, where he ran a limousine service in Portland. Now he was back in uniform and back in his homeland as part of a U.S.-sponsored émigré militia known as the Free Iraqi Fighters.

Joe quizzed a flex-cuffed, snaggle-toothed prisoner wearing a white turban and green jacket. "He says someone from the Baath Party came this morning from Baghdad to tell them to fight hard. He says they have planted mines in Najaf." The white-turbaned man spoke urgently, his eyes wide and bloodshot. Another prisoner, a tall, mustachioed man wearing sandals and a black robe, interrupted with a long burst of Arabic. "They know that we are going to assault this town," Joe said. "Their morale is down." A third prisoner, wearing a gray caftan, carried documents indicating he was a member of al-Kuts, an organization equivalent to the National Guard. Joe translated his lament: "I hate this life. I hate the army. I hate Saddam Hussein."

Baathists in Najaf claimed that the U.S. Army would soon pull back, the prisoners reported, forsaking the Shiites as they had been forsaken by the United States during the 1991 revolt. Hodges planned to counter with his own propaganda broadcasts, but his psychological operations team at the moment consisted of Spanish speakers.

"They got a hard lesson from 1991," Lieutenant Joe told me. "They are watching now. When they see that the forces of Saddam Hussein are going to be defeated, and that the Americans are serious this time, they will welcome us."

I was skeptical about both the welcome and its duration. I asked Joe what role he hoped to play in the new, liberated Iraq. "I am from this area. My mother still lives near here," he said. "But I would like to be mayor of Baghdad. Good nightclubs there. Here, there's not much. Baghdad would be fine."

Before Joe could elaborate on the capital's charms, Lieutenant Colonel Marcus DeOliviera, one of Hodges's battalion commanders, appeared. "This will be a good first baptism of fire for my soldiers. *Much* better than a night assault into Baghdad," he said with a knowing look. Like many Army officers, he referred to his Iraqi adversaries not as Fedayeen, or paramilitaries, but as knuckleheads. "What these knuckleheads are doing is launching RPGs up into the air. They'll come racing down the highway, jump out of the car, fire an RPG, and jump back into the car." Several tanks suddenly took off up the highway toward Najaf in an effort to flush out Iraqis from a suspected assembly area. They stopped half a mile away, their turrets pivoting left and then right, as if sniffing for knuckleheads.

We got into the Humvees and returned to the Blackhawk for the flight to Shell. "This is a very tough place for leaders," mused Petraeus. "They have to make difficult decisions, and they have to make them quickly."

On Sunday afternoon we were back in Najaf, this time after an hour's Humvee drive from Shell. The constriction of the city had begun in earnest, with a tighter cordon by 2nd Brigade from the north and 1st Brigade from the south. Still, the division was feeling its way, trying to pinpoint Iraqi redoubts and gauge the resistance. I had heard no more about Ben Freakley's aggressive scheme to coerce submission through ultimatums and bombing. Some staff officers, I knew, believed that to throw two brigades at Najaf was excessive, and precluded having a force in reserve to deal with unforeseen events, including a sudden regime collapse in Baghdad.

Petraeus had been in a sour mood, snapping at staff officers when a fan that was switched on during Saturday night's BUB blew dust around the ACP. The car-bombing deaths nettled everyone. "We cannot afford a damned bunker complex," Freakley told me in his tent early Sunday. "I don't want our soldiers being picked off every day by snipers and car bombers, cheap kills for the enemy. We can't let that happen."

By the time we arrived at Checkpoint Charlie at 3 P.M., Petraeus had regained his humor. The 3rd Infantry Division to the north and Marines to the east were about to resume the offensive. The relentless air campaign was carving up Iraqi units across Mesopotamia. "I think this thing is starting to regain some momentum," he said as we sat in Petraeus's Humvee with Five-coat and Miller, waiting to rendezvous with Wallace. "But it has to be deliberate. I'm feeling somewhat rejuvenated." Army intelligence believed that Iraqi resisters in Najaf now numbered in the hundreds, not the thousands. Cleaning them out, stronghold by stronghold, Petraeus said, was likely to be "a company fight, a platoon fight really."

I asked about the four hundred "no-fire" sites and whether it was difficult to get permission to hit targets believed to be sheltering Iraqi diehards. Depending on the sensitivity of the target and the potential for collateral damage, some sites required petitioning for authorization up the chain of command, even to the secretary of defense.

"My sense is that they're getting easier to get approved now," he said. "The process made sense when we thought we were just going to roll through them, I guess. But with car bombers and the other things they've been doing, the enemy is taking the gloves off. Our gloves are coming off, too."

Several pickups with machine guns in the beds stood near the intersection. Leaning against the trucks were a dozen soldiers with longish hair and idiosyncratic uniforms: baseball caps with T-shirts and desert camouflage trousers were popular, as were brushy mustaches and stubbly cheeks. Various flavors of SF—Special Forces—were buzzing around Najaf, including troops from the "white" world, such as the Operational Detachment Alpha (ODA) teams of Green Berets, and others from the "gray" or "black" worlds, like the Army's counterterrorism 1st Special Forces Operational Detachment Delta, better known as Delta Force. The shadowy unit called Task Force 20 was hunting Iraqi leaders and illicit weapons. And of course there was OGA, that Other Government Agency. Special Forces described their missions as SR (special reconnaissance), DA (direct action), UW (unconventional warfare), CBT (combating terrorism), CP (counterproliferation of weapons of mass destruction), HA (humanitarian assistance), and so forth. I recalled that the Sumerian script five millennia ago had comprised an unwieldy two thousand characters, but surely that was simplicity itself compared with the SF argot in Iraq.

Petraeus nodded at the desperadoes loitering around the pick-ups, each man bristling with weapons. "They're such caricatures," he said in a tone of amused affection. "Everybody wants to be somebody else. White wants to be black. Rangers want to be Delta, or OGA."

Freakley soon joined us, and at 3:20 P.M. Wallace drove up with his retinue. The intersection began to resemble a bazaar. The corps commander, Petraeus, and Freakley bent over a map, while various horse-holders milled about. On a bullet-chewed concrete bus shelter, someone had scrawled "Rat Bastards." Across the highway from the SF gaggle, Iraqi pedestrians walked to and from Najaf with the easy stride of people accustomed to hiking long distances—slender, elongated Giacometti figures, bent forward at the waist like rods of angle iron. Soldiers at the checkpoint frisked them, patting down *dishdasha* or *sayah*, the suit jacket worn over a tieless shirt and long skirt that is a relic of British colonial days.

Four hundred yards up the highway, an infantry company darted in and out of the Najaf Agricultural Institute. Earlier that morning, an Abrams tank had blasted a hole in the southern wall, and troops had spent the day rooting Fedayeen out of the compound, dodging occasional mortar rounds. "Don't get stuck in the city," Petraeus had warned Hodges, but clearing the institute drew fire from adjacent compounds, pulling the brigade deeper into Najaf.

"That's why we're here, to kill these dudes down," Specialist Ryan Miller, a twenty-one-year-old from Missouri, told me as we stood near the Humvees. "Heck of a job. No other job like it."

Without warning a mortar round exploded forty yards to the southwest, very close to the SF gun trucks. Amazingly, no one was hurt, perhaps because the sand absorbed most of the blast. I ducked between two Humvees, while the three generals made a conspicuous show of nonchalance. "Getting fucking close, huh? Better get out of the friggin' intersection," an SF soldier bellowed with what struck me as penetrating if unheeded wisdom. Fivecoat picked up a shell fragment but tossed it away after concluding that the steel shard would "bring me bad karma if I kept it." Later, he noted in his green notebook the importance of looking "cool under mortar attack when around the SF."

Counterbattery radar had picked up the mortar round's trajectory and pinpointed the probable location of the Iraqi crew. We watched as a pair of Kiowas darted above a walled compound a mile north of Checkpoint Charlie, radioing detailed descriptions of gunmen on rooftops to a forward air controller. Moments later a pair of F/A-18s streaked overhead, silver specks more easily heard than seen, and the compound erupted in flame and smoke. Three more fighters dumped their payloads. I caught a glimpse of the fifth and final missile, a tiny, hurtling needle. Gray clouds churned from a trio of burning buildings.

Petraeus and Wallace watched through their field glasses, murmuring encouragement like trifecta bettors at a racetrack. "This is a very good combined-arms operation," Petraeus said. "We're very proud of the tankers, the Kiowas, the dismounted infantry, close air support." As Wallace turned to leave, I mentioned that *The Washington Post* editorial page that morning had applauded his public candor. He smiled, thinly. "I'll put it on my résumé," he said.

Back at Shell shortly before 6 P.M. the Humvee jounced over the sandy trace that led to the ACP. Petraeus turned in his seat and held out his hand with the palm inclined, a gauge of his mood. The day clearly had been galvanic for him, even though much of his time was spent idly standing around, which seemed to be the role of senior commanders in tactical scraps. "We've lived a lifetime each day out here recently," he said.

Najaf was unfolding as he wanted it to unfold, with prudence and deliberation bordering on the ponderous. Freakley's impulse to issue ultimatums and answer noncompliance with obliteration did not comport with the Petraeus way of war. An operation to isolate the city was evolving into a deliberate attack, partly because of Iraqi provocations, partly because clearing Najaf now seemed the only sure way to subdue it, partly because war was a beast of momentum.

No Screaming Eagles had been killed. (Petraeus again made the knock-wood gesture, rapping his knuckles on his helmet.) Ali's dome still stood. Hit-and-run attacks on supply lines had diminished. Battle rhythms are important, both for units and for commanders, and Petraeus sensed that he had found a good one for himself: attending to logistics and administrative details in the morning, circulating among the brigades through the afternoon, then returning to the ACP in time for the evening BUB, further planning, and a decent night's sleep. That pattern had emerged over the past several days; it was to persist almost without interruption for the rest of the war.

Under Army doctrine, a division commander was supposed to anticipate and plan the battle seventy-two to ninety-six hours in advance, while his subordinates orchestrated the immediate fight. I saw how difficult that could be, given the fluidity of the battlefield, the frequent change in orders from corps, and the hypnotic lure of the action.

"Some of this is about just feeling it," Petraeus said, rubbing his fingers together, "and having a tactical awareness. It's like hearing the radio. Some people can hear it across the tent, even with all the other noise around—their ears are somehow tuned to it—and others just can't. As a battle develops, you have to look through different eyes—armor eyes, dismounted infantry eyes, aviation eyes. For example, how long does it take to move from Checkpoint Charlie to the airfield by tank? On foot? By helicopter?"

He got out of the Humvee, his eyes bright. "It's really a war now," he said, and I thought of Robert E. Lee's melancholy insight, about how fortunate we are that war is so terrible, or men would grow too fond of it.

There was no mess hall in which to eavesdrop, alas, but Shell still afforded opportunities to hear soldiers talk about soldiering. At the piss tubes, or on the barber's stool, or while writing homemade postcards sliced from MRE cartons, veterans often discussed the relative demerits of the various hellholes they had occupied, and there was general consensus that among Somalia, Bosnia, Rwanda, Haiti, Kosovo, and Afghanistan, the Iraqi desert was nonpareil in its wretchedness. Even the Iraqi sand seemed godforsaken: a division engineer reported that it lacked the requisite static charge to make concrete. Better sand would have to be imported.

"It's funny when you get into an environment like this," Major Len Kircher said, without a trace of a smile. "You parse your day into activities that you don't even think about when you're back home. Okay, *now* I'm going to shave. *Now* I'm going to eat. *Now* I'm going to get a cup of coffee." Sergeant Bill Endsley, whose table I shared in the plans tent, told me, "When soldiers first leave home, they talk about all the things they want most when they're at home: pussy, a beer. Then, when they've been here awhile, it's a shower, or a bed, or wondering what it's like not to wear the same uniform for a month."

Najaf had been squeezed for several days, but now it was about to be throttled. At 9 A.M. on Monday, March 31, we left Shell in the Humvee and again drove to Checkpoint Charlie. Mortar rounds continued to pepper the agricultural institute. Petraeus gestured toward the dense neighborhood across the highway from the institute. "You get one little BB shot from any of these houses," he ordered, "level it."

We followed a circuitous route for two miles past the power plant to the western lip of the airfield, known as Objective Cat.

A company had formed a picket line with bayonets fixed on their M-4s. Great black clouds of smoke rolled over Najaf to the north. Lieutenant Colonel Stephen M. Schiller, commander of the Kiowas—the 2nd Battalion of the 17th Cavalry—landed his helicopter next to the Humvee and hurried over.

Schiller pointed to another smoky fire raging between the air-field and the river. "There's a building over there with a huge ditch, and boxes and boxes stacked in the ditch, maybe ten feet high and thirty feet long, full of weapons," he told Petraeus. "We put HE"—high-explosive rockets—"and fifty-cal on them. The roof on the building was gone and inside we could see hundreds of boxes with weapons. Then we saw a truck camouflaged with palm fronds. When we hit it, missiles twelve to fifteen feet long ignited and came off the front end of the truck, at least a dozen of them."

"I don't want you to push too fast," Petraeus said. "I'm not sure about flying at night."

"They don't seem to be on the rooftops like they were yes-terday," Schiller said. "We feel a lot safer flying at night, to be honest. They can't see us."

"What size helmet do you wear?" Petraeus asked. The gleam in his eye left little doubt that he was bent on taking a look for himself from Schiller's helicopter.

"You have a small head," Schiller said. "I'll get my S-3. He has a small head."

As Petraeus and Schiller scouted the riverbank from above, the battalion executive officer, Major Ken Hawley, sang the praises of the Kiowa, which had long flown in the shadow of the bigger, more lethal Apache. "We don't hover, we stay low, and we're very small. That's a big advantage over towns," Haw-ley said. "Anything that small above sixty knots—and that works out to about seventy miles an hour—is very hard to hit with small-arms fire."

After Petraeus returned, we drove through an onion field to

the eastern edge of the airfield. A pair of mammoth D-9 bull-dozers lumbered down the runway, clearing debris with their blades and accompanied by a skirmish line of dismounted infantry. Petraeus ruminated aloud about how the advantages of having a beautiful concrete runway for his helicopters stacked up against the disadvantages of being within Iraqi range.

As we watched the D-9s, Freakley's voice came over the radio. Anderson's 2nd Brigade had been ordered by V Corps to conduct a daylong feint toward Hilla, fifteen miles above Kifl, to draw attention away from the 3rd Infantry Division's movements near Karbala. Two companies of Abrams tanks had attacked at dawn, a mile apart up the east bank of the Euphrates, while artillery batteries leapfrogged up the west bank. Iraqi defenders, including unexpected reinforcements from the Nebuchadnezzar Republican Guard Division, answered with concentrated artillery and small-arms fire. The tank's commander, Lieutenant Colonel Jeffrey Ingram, radioed for attack helicopter support as he pushed to within a mile of Hilla's southern perimeter.

Eight Apaches had been hit, Freakley reported. All eight returned safely to Shell, but two had been seriously damaged in a fusillade by small-arms, rocket-propelled grenades, and 57mm antiaircraft guns from palm groves along Highway 9. One pilot, a company commander, was wounded. And the division had lost its first soldier: Specialist Brandon J. Rowe of Roscoe, Illinois, a 2nd Brigade infantryman, had been killed by shellfire. He was a week shy of his twenty-first birthday.

Petraeus stared across the airfield as he replaced the radio handset. He looked grim, as if he were in physical pain. Later he told me that he had felt his blood pressure spike for the second time in this war. Iraqi losses would prove substantial—the Apaches claimed more than two dozen guns destroyed, and Ingram's tankers estimated 250 Iraqi troops killed—but the Apaches' vulnerability and the defenders' tenacity were clearly preying on the commanding general's mind.

Shortly after 1 P.M., Wallace landed in his Blackhawk on the cleared runway and walked over to the Humvee. He listened to Petraeus's battle summary: Anderson, finishing the feint toward Hilla, would redouble his pressure on Najaf from the north. Hodges's battalions would attack from the southeast, south, and southwest, with a sharp increase in firepower. The corps commander two days earlier had been content to bottle up Najaf with the 101st; now, with most of the division committed to the cause, he seemed willing to take the city by force.

After Petraeus finished his report, Wallace stood silently for a minute. Petraeus drummed his fingers on the map. Birds sang in the brush beyond the onion patch. A brilliant fireball rose from downtown Najaf, where a Kiowa had put a Hellfire into a building.

"I think we're going to be seized with this thing for a while, sir," Petraeus said.

"Keep the pressure on," Wallace advised, then rambled back to his helicopter.

As we drove past Checkpoint Charlie to rendezvous with Hodges on the west side of town, Petraeus turned in his seat. "It's looking like a long war again. I'm not even sure 4th ID"— which was just arriving in Kuwait—"is going to be enough. My sense is to pull it back to a tighter cordon, given the long LOCs. The question now is when General Wallace will feel pressure to keep going north."

The forces on hand seemed insufficient to him. "Quantity has a quality of its own," he said. I asked how much more was needed. "I have no clue," Petraeus replied, then added with a grin, "Eight divisions and eight years."

At 3 P.M., after looping around to the city's other flank, we found Hodges on a narrow road a mile from the escarpment, almost within small-arms range of Ali's dome. Brown smoke from American mortar rounds foamed through a palm grove at the base of the escarpment. Artillery tubes barked nearby, and a few seconds later white blossoms of detonating 105mm shells opened along the tree line. Petraeus and Hodges climbed onto a Humvee hood, scanning the city with their field glasses. The direction and timing of the attack had been arranged to fix the afternoon sun in the defenders' eyes.

"They've been forced back into the center of town. As they continue to come out, we're able to kill them, to attrit them," Hodges said. "We are under no time pressure. There's no need to go up there and get stuck."

Two SF gun trucks had parked along the road near Hodges's command post. "Everything we got today, sir, suggests they're pretty much ready to crack," a captain who commanded the team told Petraeus. "The locals wonder why we're not in there already."

Petraeus shrugged. "I just think there's nothing fast about this."

"Sir," another SF soldier said, "the general consensus of the last couple days is that if we commit, and get in and seize some terrain, the population will be with us. The neighborhood near the mosque is a rabbit warren, but we think the locals will help us identify the strongholds." Fedayeen and al-Kuts militia occupied bunkers and trenches along a canal behind the tree line, as well as a white, four-story Baath Party building, easily visible on the lip of the escarpment.

Fifty artillery shells ripped through the trees. "That hurt," Hodges murmured without lowering his glasses. "There are villages in that wood line, so we can't be indiscriminate. But I'm probably pushing it more than I would have two weeks ago."

Several prisoners under guard shuffled down the road, their hands cuffed and their faces so coated with flies as to appear masked. Overhead I heard the muffled growl of U.S. Navy F/A-18s. A GBU-12 bomb detonated with a splash of flame, followed by a rolling boom. Another exploded, and another, until five bombs had smashed the bunker line. Billowing smoke hid the golden dome.

A platoon of Abrams tanks clanked down the road, and soon

the boom of their 120mm main guns echoed against the trees. Through Hodges's borrowed glasses, I could see shells gouge the façade of the four-story white building. The hysterical cackle of .50-caliber machine guns mingled with the *thud-thud* of Mk-19 grenade launchers. Several Humvees scooted across a field into firing positions, and a barrage of TOW missiles erupted with a white *whoosh* before smashing into the building. Kiowas darted along the trees and up over the escarpment, hammering the Iraqi positions with machine guns and hundreds of rockets. Eight hundred men from the 2nd Battalion of the 327th Infantry padded down the road in their infantry waddle and soon vanished into the tree line.

It was all so fierce, so terribly fierce, a symphony of fire. It was combined arms at its most lethal, the relentless orchestration of air, armor, artillery, infantry, and all the other killing modalities. It was combined and, in the Pentagon's vernacular, it was *joint,* with the Army complemented by Navy, Air Force, and Marine aircraft. The U.S. military for sixty years had worked to make this the signature of American firepower, and no other nation could approximate such a synchronized application of violence. Until recently, this synchronization had been the province of senior generals, but now I could see that it was routine for colonels and captains and sergeants on the battlefield to summon the genies of the air and the earth and the sea, and to sic them on the enemy.

Hodges lowered his glasses. "What I haven't been able to figure out," he told Petraeus, "is what happens if they don't fold."

"I think you just keep pounding them," Petraeus said.

"Sir," the SF captain said, "we don't want a war of attrition, but that's where we are."

"We are," Petraeus agreed. "It's a siege."

As we drove back to Shell for the evening, a dozen fires burned across Najaf, and I could only wonder what kind of world existed within the city tonight.

12

NEBUCHADNEZZAR GOES DOWN

Tuesday morning's BUB, on April Fool's Day, revealed an army once again surging forward.

The large map of central Iraq lashed to the tent wall of the Shell command post showed the American advance stretching across a front of more than a hundred miles, from the Marines at Al Kut on the Tigris, in the east, to the 3rd Infantry Division at Karbala, in the west. Actions by the 101st—including 1st Brigade's attack into southern and western Najaf, and 2nd Brigade's feint up the Euphrates—were among a half dozen simultaneous brigade-sized assaults on Monday ordered by V Corps. Troops of the 3rd ID had tightened control of Highway 9 and approaches to the Karbala Gap, and had isolated Hilla, the site of ancient Babylon. In the south, the 82nd Airborne encircled Samawah, finally plucking that thorn from the Army's side. Greg Gass's Apaches also flew armed reconnaissance missions beyond the lakes west of Karbala to cleanse the corps' western flank.

Iraqi defenses, never very coherent, had begun disintegrating. Desertions escalated. Iraqi commanders knew so little about American maneuvers that it often took them twelve to eighteen hours—an eternity in modern combat—to organize a counter-move, and coherent counterattacks rarely exceeded platoon strength. When the Iraqis *did* move, they moved the wrong way at the wrong time. Mistakenly assuming that Wallace intended to fling his main attack up Highway 8 from the south, rather than via the Karbala Gap in the southwest, Republican Guard armored forces had begun exposing themselves by repositioning in daylight to block the attack. U.S. warplanes and long-range artillery were blowing them to pieces.

As the Army and Marines resumed the offensive, their advances were expedited by an air campaign that remained ruthless and unflagging. Of eight thousand precision munitions dropped in the war thus far, three thousand had fallen in the past three days, mostly on the Medina Division and other Republican Guard units south of Baghdad. Iraq would launch almost 1,700 surface-to-air missiles by war's end, but such barrages proved bootless against the 1,800 U.S. and British aircraft pummeling the country. The planes dropped paper as well as steel, including 32 million "give-up" leaflets—enough, by a fatuous set of Air Force calculations, to stretch from Fort Worth to Anchorage, or to make 120,454 rolls of toilet paper.

To be sure, much fighting remained before Baghdad hove into view. Soldiers would still kill, and soldiers would still die. Civilians would die, too, like the ten slaughtered on Monday when a family van barreling down Highway 9 was riddled with 25mm cannon fire by skittish Marne soldiers. Whether Baghdad would be converted into a final, sanguinary redoubt was unclear. Also unclear was whether Iraqi diehards had the fortitude and support needed to wage a protracted guerrilla war.

Petraeus, Fivecoat, Miller, and I returned to Najaf by Humvee at noon on April 1. We found Hodges's command post in a gravel quarry by an abandoned brick factory, close to the spot where we had watched Monday's bombardment. With a map spread as usual across a Humvee hood, Hodges succinctly laid out the developments of the past eighteen hours. In addition to scores of TOW missiles and tank rounds pumped into suspected Fedayeen strongholds, aircraft including F-16s, B-52 and B-1 bombers, and British Tornadoes had dropped a dozen five-hundred-pound bombs and seven one-thousand-pounders. Among the overnight airstrikes, three two-thousand-pound bombs had gutted a reputed Baath Party headquarters and a Fedayeen compound. Hodges's air liaison officer told me, "Each of those has nine hundred pounds of tritonal"—a compound of TNT and aluminum—"and eleven hundred pounds of metal. When the last one hit, it looked like sunrise coming up."

At 6:30 this morning, the 1st Brigade on Hodges's initiative had dispatched seven Abrams tanks from Checkpoint Charlie into Najaf for what the Army called a thunder run, an expedition of reconnaissance and intimidation. With Apaches overhead, the tanks traveled more than a mile, shot up a few Saddam portraits without encountering any resistance, then pulled back out of the city. Petraeus told me that V Corps later in the morning had advised him the maneuver was too risky and ought not be repeated.

"Why would they object to that?" I asked. Petraeus seemed exasperated, even while acknowledging Wallace's reluctance to risk having a small force trapped in the narrow streets.

"Because," he said, "they don't understand the situation on the ground."

Hodges's city map had been divided into a couple dozen sectors. A1, for example, lay north of Ali's tomb; A2 and A6 covered the dense neighborhoods to the south. While Anderson's 2nd Brigade had pivoted to envelop Najaf again from the north, with forces moving on both sides of the Euphrates, 1st Brigade was attacking with Apaches, Kiowas, four artillery batteries, and three infantry battalions. Kiowas had destroyed a trio of technicals in the cemetery, and captured arms caches had yielded 1,500 AK-47 rifles, twenty-five mortars, and thirty-six thousand rounds of mortar and machine-gun ammunition. Many Iraqi defenders evidently had fled or melted into the civilian population, while others continued to launch foolish, doomed forays against vastly superior American firepower.

"Don't go farther than the escarpment," Petraeus cautioned. "The intent is to bring them to us."

"Yes, sir," Hodges replied. "So far we have been able to position ourselves so that when they come at us we're able to engage them either with direct fire, or with artillery and mortars."

"The issue is the sensitivity-to-the-holy-city kind of stuff," Petraeus said.

Wallace joined us at 12:45 after landing in his Blackhawk. He was trailed by an aide carrying a white loose-leaf notebook labeled "Secret ORCON Smart Book." The corps commander leaned against a Humvee side mirror, Olympus field glasses around his neck and a smile softening his craggy face. He seemed imperturbable, despite a *New York Times* article this morning, carrying a V Corps dateline, that asserted antipathy among some Army generals toward Rumsfeld. "By the way," Wallace had repeatedly told General McKiernan over the past few days, "I haven't talked to the press today."

Wallace's alarm at this morning's thunder run had yielded to curiosity; perhaps a similar armored thrust could work in Baghdad. "Don't get stuck in the city," the corps commander often warned, but he and his staff had begun to recognize that Najaf might be a rehearsal for the capital. Armor tacticians for decades had presumed that tanks in cities were too vulnerable to ambush, but even before invading Iraq Wallace and his staff had begun to question that conventional wisdom. Senior officers habitually tried to refine what the Army called TTPs—tactics, techniques, and procedures—and Najaf could yield a new urban warfare TTP: thunder runs supported by attack aviation and close air support; heavy armor forces mingling with light infantry; and humanitarian assistance pouring in even as combat operations continued.

Hodges faced the escarpment and held up his right hand, palm extended upright. "Charlie Company is about three fingers left of that smoke, heading toward the neighborhood south of the mosque." He squinted into the middle distance, then turned to Wallace. "We're going to stop well short of it, sir."

"Any significant contact?"

"Zero, sir. We found sixty-nine mines in two little fields." He pointed to the map. "Here."

"Sixty-nine, not seventy." Wallace smiled again. "There's an old saying: never go any place you've never been before."

"Spoken like an old cav trooper," Petraeus said.

Hodges worked his chewing gum. "There is so much ammunition and so many abandoned weapons in there, it's unbelievable." He cocked an ear toward the radio. The infantry company edging along the escarpment was within a thousand yards of Ali's tomb. We heard the captain again, alluding to the enemy. "They're all gone," he advised.

"Any intel on where they went?" Wallace asked Hodges.

"We had two reports. One said that anybody who was going to escape was going to the north. The other said they were taking this road out." Hodges leaned over the map and pointed at the highway angling northwest to Karbala. Some Fedayeen were also believed to be sheltering in the cemetery or in the Najaf amusement park, while others had retreated eastward into a complex of government buildings.

"The natural tendency is to say, 'We won.' But we're not there yet," Hodges said. "We've hit them very hard the last two days whenever they've fired at us, from homes, from schools. The one place I've absolutely told our troops they cannot fire is into the mosque, even though we put a JDAM"—a satellite-guided bomb—"within about four hundred yards. I believe they were shocked that we would shoot that close and hit that hard. But look, the gold dome is still standing." He grinned like a boy who has pulled off a particularly audacious prank.

Petraeus had seemed somber all day, but he brightened as additional reconnaissance reports confirmed that Iraqi forces had abandoned southwest Najaf. After Wallace left we climbed back into the Humvee. On several occasions Petraeus had estimated that the city could take weeks to fall; he was determined to see for himself that his dire predictions were simply wrong. "I am now bingo on Pop-Tarts," he told Jeremy Miller. "Bingo" was pilot slang for running out of fuel. Miller grinned. "No, sir, you're not." More would soon arrive with the Division Main cavalcade, which finally had made its way from Kuwait.

Hodges led us in convoy through a date plantation and up the escarpment. Soldiers on foot trudged uphill, pulling a Javelin armor-piercing missile on a two-wheeled cart originally designed by hunters to haul game. A few Arabs along the road waved energetically and gestured for us to hurry. "Look at this!" Petraeus exclaimed. He waved back.

We parked near a mechanic's garage on the southern edge of town. Najaf was foul-smelling and very warm. A cubist maze of alleys and flat-roofed ocher buildings stretched north toward Ali's dome. Old men in ankle-length *dishdasha*s stood on the corners, and I could see a half dozen women watching us from a *shanshil,* a screened balcony, next to a rooftop garden. Several pickups with machine guns stood in the street, flying the ostensibly banned American flag. "OGA," Petraeus murmured as he climbed from the Humvee. The team chief, lean and bestubbled, wore a 'Bama baseball cap decorated with an "I Love New York" button and his blood type, A+.

"Get word to the head cleric and tell him that we deeply regret that we've had to fire near some of his holy sites in the city," Petraeus said. "Now we need his help and advice on how to make sure that the city and the shrines are secure. Can we get a cleric to come out and talk to us?"

"We're working on it, General," Mr. OGA said. The most influential Shiite cleric in Najaf was Sayyid Ali Husayni Sistani, who had been born in Iran in 1930, reputedly began learning the Koran at the age of five, and, after eluding a death squad attempt on his life in 1996, had lived under virtual house arrest near the shrine. Sistani was one of thirteen designated grand ayatollahs in the Shiite world, and among four in Najaf considered worthy of the title *marja altaglid,* or source of emulation. His many scholarly treatises included works on usury, marriage to infidels, and "doubtful clothes," of which our OGA friends had an extensive wardrobe.

"Sistani hasn't issued a fatwa," Mr. OGA said. U.S. intelligence hoped for a clerical legal decree welcoming the invasion. "But he's not pro-regime. He's sitting on the fence."

"Again, it needs to be a tone of voice in which we say, 'We need your advice,' " Petraeus cautioned. "We need to make this a cooperative effort."

Mr. OGA nodded, then tapped me on the elbow. "I really liked your last book," he said politely. "I'm looking forward to the next one."

"Thank you," I said. "And you are . . . ?"

"Gary."

"Thanks, Gary. Good luck." Later I was told he was the deputy Baghdad station chief, in waiting.

The crowd had swelled. Boys in baggy trousers capered along the curb, and young men stood next to their bicycles, smoking and watching the Americans watch them. A donkey pulled a cart through the intersection, hooves clip-clopping on the pavement. A green Iraqi flag flapping over one building bore the pious inscription *Allah u akbar* that Saddam had added in 1991 to rally the faithful. More 101st soldiers filled the streets, scanning the shadows for snipers. An SF officer walked up to report that some Baath Party diehards reportedly had changed to civilian clothes and were planning suicide attacks. Several resistance pockets remained, deeper in the city. The crowd had pressed to within twenty yards, and suddenly seemed a bit sinister. I wondered whether there was a residual memory of past conquerors, like the seventh-century Muslim who declared, "I see heads ripe for cutting, and verily I am the man to do it."

"Now we've got to think," Petraeus said. A city he expected to besiege suddenly appeared to be on the edge of capitulating. "What the hell do we do next?" he continued. "We own An Najaf. So what do we do with it? When do we start bringing humanitarian assistance in here?"

"Confusing situation," the SF officer said.

"Sure is."

Petraeus strode back down the street to find Lieutenant Colonel Chris Hughes, whose battalion had seized this corner of the city. "I think we just need to work this for a while. It will be our little science project," Petraeus told him. "I wish I could give you some wonderful guidance here about the perfect way to do this, or how to keep the civilians at bay, or how to keep soldiers from getting blown up."

"We'll be all right, sir," Hughes said. His face was dirty and streaked with sweat. I had not seen him since Camp Pennsylvania. "We're going to do this just like we did it in Haiti."

"There's nothing quick about this," Petraeus added. "There are more civilians on the battlefield than we ever saw in training, by a factor of a thousand."

We drove back down the escarpment, past more smiling pedestrians gesturing with raised thumbs. Petraeus was silent, lost in thought, and I could almost hear the gears shifting as he pondered the abrupt transition from a deliberate urban attack to an occupation.

We stopped at the V Corps command post at Rams on our way back to Shell. While Petraeus met for an hour in a large tent with Wallace, Blount, and other commanders, I chatted with a senior staff officer. The imminent fall of Najaf was "huge, that's one big domino," he said. "The corps' perspective is that Najaf is clearly contained, that the 101st has taken what could have been a very difficult situation and handled it well. There are two more cities ahead, Karbala and Al Hilla"—as with Najaf, the military preferred to add the Arabic article—"and those are the last two before Baghdad. We'll encircle the enemy army and kill it. The regime has limited choices now. It can surrender, it can collapse, or it can die."

At 6:15 P.M., as we left Rams, Freakley called on the radio. "We think we may have broken the back of the enemy in the city," Petraeus told him. Ahead of us, a soldier stood on the road with his arms extended and fists clenched, the signal for a chemical attack. "Gas!" Miller yelled. He slammed on the brakes and we dug into our canvas mask sacks. Unperturbed, Petraeus took a full minute to slip into his M-40, then continued the radio conversation. His voice buzzed in the metallic mouthpiece. There was no gas.

Two leaflet messages fluttered over Najaf on Wednesday, April 2, part of the Air Force's Fort Worth–to–Anchorage papering of Iraq. One read, in English and Arabic: "For your safety stay away from military forces and targets." The other depicted happy children holding hands before Ali's shrine. "We are only here to destroy military targets," it declared, "not the Iraqi people."

Shortly after noon we drove to the 1st Brigade TOC in the elementary school southwest of the city. Squeezing into the rear seat of the Humvee, I was nearly immobilized by the gear wedged around my feet and shoulders: flak vest, helmet, CamelBak, day bag, camera, notebook, gas mask, map board, and the bank of radios. Almost every day I absentmindedly left one or more items behind—in a tent, on the helicopter, atop a vehicle hood—and only the attentive forbearance of Miller and Fivecoat had kept me from scattering half my possessions in a personal debris field across Iraq.

Inside Hodges's dim command post, it took a few moments

for my eyes to adjust from the bright sunlight. A can of Folgers coffee and Field Manual 101-5, "Staff Organization and Operations," occupied a shelf next to the Canon PC941 copier. Another large table map was filled with colored pushpins marking key sites in Najaf, including a distinctive white pin that signified the holy tomb. Three infantry battalions had fanned out through much of the city. Most troops had been greeted by welcoming and even festive crowds chanting, "Die, Saddam, die," although the Grand Ayatollah Sistani had rebuffed American efforts to parley.

Outside I found Lieutenant Joe and quizzed him about the public mood.

"Most of the people here hate the regime," he said. "But they had a hard lesson from '91. Until they see that Saddam Hussein is gone and that the regime is gone, they will be cautious. The imams will wait to see. Are the Americans going to do something good for them or not? We use the words 'liberation' and 'freedom,' and this will be our obligation to them. If we make them feel like human beings, they will support us. Don't think this takes just a couple hours. The regime here has been in charge for thirty-five years."

The usual klatch of SF teams was loitering on the road around a pair of gun trucks when Petraeus emerged from the brigade TOC. On the drive from Shell, we had noticed a proliferation of black banners flying over doorways and farm buildings. "What's it mean, with all these black flags flying?" Petraeus asked a man whose cap, sporting a Samuel Adams beer logo, hinted that he might be OGA or Delta.

"I don't know, sir."

"They like their flags, sir," another OGA type said. "May be just decorations."

Decorations? Impressed as I was by what the American military knew, I was often startled by what it didn't know. Improvisation was part of the military art: an ability to extemporize often distinguished triumph from catastrophe. But ambiguity, misperception, and ignorance also capered across the battlefield like mischievous elves. For example, although analysts had intensely studied the Iraqi terrain for at least a year, the deep dust caught the Army by surprise. A V Corps staff officer had observed that even Wallace sometimes knew little more than a platoon leader. Later, Lieutenant Joe explained that the black flags were Shiite symbols of defiance.

Thumbs hooked into his flak vest, Petraeus stood by the road and contemplated his new suzerainty in Najaf. How, even as fighting continued, could he secure the loyalty of newly won hearts and minds? As Najaf suggested a TTP, a template, for the military conquest of other cities, perhaps it also could be a model for Phase IV, the postwar support and stabilization effort in Iraq. "The desired end state," he told the SF officers, "is that Highway 9 is open, the airfield is open, and humanitarian aid is flowing."

"General, the quicker we can begin that HA, the better," one officer replied.

Another SF officer added, "Today was the Macy's Day parade when we went in there. Tomorrow it will be—" He shrugged to suggest waning Shiite enthusiasm if the Americans failed to improve conditions quickly. "And the next day it will be: What the fuck are you doing for us?"

An SF master sergeant had opened an MRE pouch. "You eat?" Petraeus asked in a perfect deadpan.

"Just once a week, sir."

"It's a sign of weakness."

Two of the men slid into the cab of a white Toyota gun truck. "Lot of white pickups getting shot up around here," Petraeus said.

A man wearing a baseball cap with a Stihl chain-saw logo called through the passenger window, "Sir, these pickups shoot back."

Liberation saturated the air as we drove to Checkpoint Charlie. Iraqis lined the streets, smiling broadly and waving two hands or flashing the thumbs-up sign. Studying their faces for signs of insincerity, I detected only jubilation. Dilip Hiro, a scholar of the Islamic world, had written in 2002, "To imagine that a people who have suffered grievously at the hands of the United States for twelve years, and have grown deep hatred for it, would turn out in thousands to greet American soldiers and their [exiled] Iraqi cohorts as liberators would seem unrealistic."

Yet here they were, belling with delight. I thought of Ernie Pyle's observation that "winning in battle is like winning at poker or catching lots of fish. It's damned pleasant and it sets a man up." We waved back, a benevolent victor's wave, all elbow and wrist.

North of the intersection, we toured the Najaf Agricultural Institute. Captured munitions lay neatly displayed in a street beneath the gum trees: eighty rocket-propelled grenades; twenty-seven 82mm mortar tubes; a machine gun with a sticker that read, in English, "Arm Palac-Sana, Yemen Arab Republic." Jefferson Smith, the first sergeant of Bravo Company, 1st Battalion of the 327th Infantry, nudged a crate of rifle ammunition with his boot. "The weapons were in the schools and in the houses and in buses, all over the compound," he said. "We found an AK-47 behind the bed headboards of every house."

The company command post was in a two-bedroom town house with maroon Oriental rugs, a Leopard refrigerator full of rancid food, and a working shower. Smith speculated that the owner—an agronomist? a professor of Fertile Crescent Studies?—had been forced to flee when Fedayeen occupied the institute. Domestic touches graced each room: pink hair ribbons, artificial roses in a vase, a plastic model of a Boeing 777 painted with Air France colors. Occasional mortar rounds and RPGs still fell on the compound, particularly at dusk, which soldiers now called the witching hour. I asked Smith, a thirty-nine-year-old from Worthington, West Virginia, how he felt about the war so far. "Tax free, get to eat MREs, get to blow up stuff. It's a great life," he said, and I detected no insincerity in *his* face, either.

We drove up Highway 9 to the center of town, past houses with papaya trees sprouting from the courtyards. A large portrait of Saddam in a khaki uniform loomed above the front gate of an abandoned military casern. Chris Hughes's 2nd Battalion had moved into a two-story junior high school. Three little boys peddled packs of Gold Seal and Manhattan cigarettes out front. "Is one dollar," they chirped as we drove through the school gate. "One dollar." The official battalion motto was "No Slack," but I noticed "NFS" written on the doors of several vehicles parked in the courtyard, which, a soldier explained, abbreviated the unofficial motto: "No Fucking Slack."

We found Ben Hodges in the headmaster's office. Damask curtains covered the window, and soldiers occupied a pair of couches and three chairs with striped, threadbare upholstery. A 2001 calendar on the desk depicted a Swiss chalet with geraniums blooming on the balcony; the caption read, "Anyone who has ever struggled with poverty knows how extremely expensive it is to be poor." The battalion intelligence officer had posted a red-lettered sign that read: "Strip maps of the stars' homes available! Baghdad tours available soon!" Hodges looked worn. "I've done a poor job at getting into a battle rhythm," he told me.

Chris Hughes sat in the courtyard shade outside, and I asked him about the attempt to contact Sistani.

"This guy has pope status with these people, as I explain it to my guys. I'm trying to find the right cardinal to talk to him," Hughes said. This morning, the battalion had pressed to within a few blocks of Ali's tomb, where they lingered while various lesser clerics and OGA intermediaries swapped messages.

"We waited about an hour and a half, and the hair on the back of my neck began to stand up. The crowd got bigger and bigger, so we pulled back out. But it was like the liberation of Paris. There must have been two or three thousand people by the time we left," Hughes said. "All these things we're learning in An Najaf are going to be golden when we get to Baghdad. It's been very, very docile since we came in. We're dividing the paramilitaries into the weak, the stupid, and the brave. What we've got to do is find the brave—the ones who let us bypass them, then attack from the rear. We need the civilians to rat them out."

Petraeus had joined us. "We're not trying to generate our own Gestapo here," he cautioned.

"No, sir," Hughes agreed. "By the way, sir, every company has at least one car thief, so we've been able to make use of some of these civilian vehicles we've found."

Petraeus had another rendezvous scheduled with Wallace, and at 4 P.M. we drove through the clapping crowd outside the school to the gravel quarry west of town. The corps commander soon arrived, removing his helmet and sunglasses after bounding off the helicopter. Perspiration beaded on his forehead and deranged his thinning hair.

One brigade of the 3rd Infantry Division had bulled through the narrow Karbala Gap, he told Petraeus, while another brigade had isolated Karbala city on the east to prevent Iraqi reinforcement or retreat. The division's 1st Brigade was within sight of a critical Euphrates River bridge at Objective Peach. Marne troops were about to pour through the outer ring of Baghdad defenses, into the area the Army had dubbed the Red Zone. Soon, very soon, U.S. forces would approach both Objective Saints, the vital intersection of Highways 8 and 1, just south of the capital, and Objective Lions, the international airport.

Wallace wanted Buff Blount's 3rd ID to be deliberate, because the Marines were still at least two days from Baghdad, and V Corps had no additional combat troops to reinforce Blount in the event of a counterattack. Also, U.S. eavesdroppers had intercepted a report that commanders in Baghdad and Basra had been authorized to use "special munitions."

"I'm flabbergasted that he"—Saddam—"hasn't slimed us," Wallace said. "Karbala is going to be another An Najaf. And north of Al Hilla there are two battalions, about a thousand knuckleheads. I've got some concern about the area from Objective Jenkins to Al Hilla."

"In truth," Petraeus said, "I'd rather have them come at me than go at them. They seem to generally accommodate us if we pressure them."

"Umm." Wallace studied the map. "What's the chance of doing a feint up the road toward Al Hilla, then pull back?"

"Sure."

"Can you afford to air-assault infantry?"

"Yes, sir."

"Day? Night?"

"I'd do it in daylight."

Wallace settled into Petraeus's seat in the Humvee and radioed his command post. "I told Eagle Six to do a feint up the road and pull back," he said. He listened for a moment and hung up the handset, giving an extravagant and somewhat enigmatic Bronx cheer before walking back to his helicopter.

"It's a very ambiguous situation," Petraeus said. "There's a threat around every corner."

Before returning to Shell we again drove into Najaf and parked on Highway 9, a mile north of the agricultural institute. Hodges had spotted Fedayeen vehicles camouflaged with palm fronds among the garbage trucks in a municipal parking lot. We watched infantrymen work their way toward the area at 5 P.M., then heard the brisk report of machine-gun and rifle fire. A pair of Kiowas, followed by two Apaches, swooped over the target, guns chattering.

Perhaps a hundred yards to our left, a mortar round detonated in a brown geyser of dirt and smoke. Hodges's artillery answered quickly.

An Iraqi pushing a cart loaded with a battered suitcase and a propane tank hurried past us, fleeing the gunfire. His wife and two small children in dirty robes held hands at his side. Their eyes were wide with fear, and no one looked back, as if afraid of turning into pillars of salt. The man sobbed great, heaving sobs, and all the agony of war was etched in his face. Lieutenant Joe stopped him momentarily, then waved him on.

"He's worried about his kids, that they're going to die," Joe told me.

Watching them recede down the highway, I felt pity at their plight, and debased by the victor's pleasures the day had brought. But most of all I felt gratitude that the man had not been a suicide bomber, intent on sending us all to hell by detonating his propane tank.

Ben Freakley was in good form in the tent that night. With his gift for mimicry, he imitated a commander who, before the attack into Iraq in 1991, had gathered the division's chaplains together and declared, "Now I want every one of you praying for me, goddammit."

I asked Freakley to assess the Najaf operation.

"It's the commanding general's division, no doubt about it. But I'd like to get a little more directly into the fight with the enemy. *The* enemy, not these niggling forces." Was the 101st's being too cautious? I asked. The O arched his eyebrows. "I've thought for a while that we could be more two-fisted in our offensive, get both divisions punching for the corps. We've mostly been punching with one arm."

At 10:30 P.M., the flap parted and Petraeus pushed into the tent to report that two soldiers had been lightly wounded in the late-afternoon firefight off Highway 9. "Every day brings incremental improvement," he said. "Today was better than yesterday, but there are still bad guys in town." After chatting for a few minutes, he turned to go. "How does this end?" he asked again, then slipped out into the night.

Two more days would be needed to fully subdue Najaf, but the weakening resistance could be seen in the dwindling number of Iraqi mortar rounds fired daily since Monday—from twenty-eight, to twenty, to two. By contrast, all sixty of the 101st's artillery tubes and eighteen MLRS launchers had joined the fight, while the Kiowas alone put two hundred rockets and ten thousand .50-caliber rounds into Najaf. Another Apache crashed during a dust landing, but otherwise the division was mostly unscathed. The number of Iraqi fighters killed in Najaf was put at 373—the sort of number known in the Army as a SWAG, a silly wild-ass guess—and another 182 had been captured. No SWAG of civilian casualties was ventured, although Human Rights Watch later charged that cluster munitions used in the March 31 feint at Hilla had killed 38 civilians and wounded 156. A U.S. military spokesman in Qatar declared, inaccurately, that paramilitaries had used Ali's mosque as a firebase.

Meanwhile, the larger war proceeded apace: 3rd Infantry Division troops were approaching Objective Lions, ten miles west of central Baghdad. A battalion from the 101st would travel by truck to provide the Marne with more infantry firepower at the airport. Intelligence analysts now assessed the Medina Division at 38 percent of full strength, a figure that by any military standard was commensurate with annihilation.

Thursday, April 3, was moving day. After a week and a half at Shell, we were leaving the desert paradise forever to join the Division Main, which had arrived from Kuwait, and set up the long-lost TOC Mahal tent above the escarpment, between Najaf and Karbala. Miller helped break down the ACP, and then pressed ahead with our baggage in the Humvee.

Petraeus, Fivecoat, and I flew to Najaf in Warlord 457 at 11:20 A.M. Over the Blackhawk's radio, I heard Hodges report that after 1st Brigade soldiers seized a municipal complex in Najaf that afternoon, 150 "indigenous forces will arrive wearing white armbands, claim credit for the operation, and declare intifada," or uprising, against Saddam loyalists. This clumsy effort to suggest that Shiites were rallying to the American cause unraveled over the next few hours, as the "indigenous forces" dwindled to forty, then thirty, and, in the event, twenty-three. The white armbands notwithstanding, a staff officer told me: "Now we're in the extremely confusing situation of trying to link up with a bunch of guys who look exactly like the guys we're trying to kill."

On the other side of the Blackhawk's bay, Petraeus was trying to sort out his enemies. "I should have thought about this earlier, but the people who have control of these towns, the Baath Party officials, have a bigger stake in this than the Republican Guard," he mused. "The ones who are really fighting are those who have the most to lose, the local power brokers who are losing their cars, their headquarters, their houses, everything. In hindsight, we should have anticipated this. It's the local power brokers we're going to have to root out."

After crossing the escarpment just thirty feet off the ground, Warlord 457 touched down on Highway 9 about five hundred yards from Najaf's northern edge and within scent of a very large chicken coop. We found Joe Anderson, Freakley, and Dwyer leaning against a Humvee. I sliced open MRE No. 4, Country Captain Chicken, and nibbled on a fig bar as Freakley briefed Petraeus on the morning's events. Chris Hughes's battalion had again pressed toward Ali's shrine only to encounter an agitated mob of perhaps two thousand Iraqis who were convinced that the Americans had come to arrest Ayatollah Sistani. A few rocks flew, hitting Hughes in the chest and helmet. An expatriate Iraqi trying to soothe the crowd over a public-address loudspeaker instead inflamed it. "Take a knee and point your weapon to the ground," Hughes had yelled to his men. "Smile, and show no hostility." He sank to one knee and held his rifle upside down in a gesture of passivity, then yanked out the microphone cord and backed the battalion from the neighborhood. Sistani apparently felt vulnerable to Fedayeen renegades, Freakley added, and wanted his protection guaranteed.

"I'll give him what I'm giving everybody else, an infantry platoon," Petraeus said. "This is almost bizarre. In fact, it's beyond 'almost.'"

Anderson removed his helmet to blot his shaved head. He

bore a fair resemblance to a young Yul Brynner. Part of his 2nd Brigade was searching for Iraqi troops along the Euphrates—he likened it to "flushing out the pheasants"—while others had linked up with Hodges's 1st Brigade on Highway 9 to bisect Najaf. V Corps now wanted the brigade to again strike north and seize Hilla.

"We'd been told before we came in here that every school had weapons in it, and every damned one of them in fact did," Anderson said. He pulled out a list of twenty-four schools, labeled "A" through "X" and identified with six-digit grid locations. Each had been converted into an armory, with a particularly big cache discovered in "S."

"What we're seeing is movement up and down the river, where there's cover for them to shoot mortars," said Lieutenant Colonel Henry W. "Bill" Bennett, 2nd Brigade's senior artillery commander. "It's kind of like hunting whitetail deer." Hunting metaphors appeared to be in vogue this morning.

"Have they actually put civilians in front of you?" Petraeus asked.

"They've never interfered," Anderson said.

"Are there any other bridges you want to take down above Al Hilla?"

"No, sir. I'm good."

Moving his soldiers around was still difficult, Anderson complained. "This has already been ten times harder than Desert Storm," he said. The brigade's three infantry battalions had only twenty-seven trucks among them, "and that's horseshit."

"At Al Hilla, what's your task and purpose?" Petraeus asked.

"Task is to destroy the remnants of the Republican Guard," Anderson replied. He did not mention his purpose.

The huge tent of the D-Main rose from the desert like a tell awaiting excavation. After so many days in the cramped ACP, the TOC Mahal with its cathedral ceiling and wide bays seemed cavernous, even if the desert conditions at Camp Eagle Three were hardly less austere than Shell's. I tossed my bags in an enlisted tent and walked two hundred yards around the earthworks girding the TOC to find the entrance. Inside, Petraeus was studying the video screens and eating MRE iced-tea powder straight from the packet. The day's challenge and password— RESTLESS and KIDNEY—appeared above the doorway. Staff officers hunched over their laptops at tables on three tiers of stadium seating. It was good to be reunited with E. J. Sinclair, Tom Schoenbeck, Trey Cate, and others we had last seen at Camp New Jersey, although I quickly discovered that many felt excluded from the war—having spent much of it crawling by convoy across southern Iraq—or else harbored doubts about the role of the 101st.

"Is the CG being *awfully* cautious?" one officer asked me in a low voice. "There's a lot of talk in the division about why the 101st isn't in the fight more."

I was unsure how to answer. Petraeus was doing Wallace's bidding, although I didn't sense that he was hectoring the corps commander for a bigger role. With the Apaches sharply constrained by weather and unexpected resistance, and with dust hampering all helicopter operations, the 101st had been partly neutralized. Unlike the 3rd ID, the division had no tanks or armored personnel carriers—except the borrowed battalion from the 70th Armor—and few trucks. Even a feeble enemy armed with artillery and armor could devastate light infantrymen of the 101st if they were used recklessly.

Late that afternoon, Ben Hodges dispatched tanks and an infantry battalion to an elliptical traffic island on the eastern edge of Najaf. Zinnia beds and dwarf palms lined the ellipse, and a Red Crescent flag flew above a hospital down the street, not fifty yards from a building that had been reduced to powder by an Air Force JDAM missile. On a twenty-foot travertine pedestal in the center of the road stood a bronze equestrian statue of Saddam, upraised sword in hand and hair plaited to resemble the hair of Nebuchadnezzar, whose sixth-century B.C. exploits—particularly in sacking Jerusalem and burning Solomon's temple—the Iraqi leader much admired.

With Freakley watching—"Do you have a countersniper team out?" the O asked—Hodges's engineers placed eight blocks of C-4 plastic explosive, six bangalore torpedoes, various shock tubes, and fifty feet of demolition cord. A sergeant scrambled up a rope ladder to affix extra explosives to the legs of the rearing horse. Hodges fretted that the charges would fail at the critical moment, handing Saddam a propaganda coup, so two M-81 fuse igniters also were rigged for redundancy.

Three SF gun trucks pulled up to the ellipse, carrying a compliant cleric and the "indigenous force" of twenty-three Shiites, who called themselves the Coalition for Iraqi National Unity. In a moment of inspiration, Petraeus had proposed that Iraqis themselves dispatch Saddam's statue; television cameras were positioned so that American agency in the matter was mostly invisible. Everyone moved back a hundred yards, then at 4:50 P.M. a dissident Iraqi colonel murmured a prayer in Arabic and tripped the detonator.

Horse and rider shattered into a thousand pieces with a roar, and Nebuchadnezzar's helmet soared through the air like a punted football. Cheering Iraqis poured onto the site, snapping photos and spitting on the rubble. Hodges shook hands with the Iraqi colonel, whose palm was slick with sweat, than picked up a bronze souvenir for the brigade display case at Fort Campbell. "It was so emotional I almost started crying. I know that sounds goofy, but that's how I felt," he told me later. "It was very satisfying, kind of like the Berlin Wall coming down."

On Friday morning, April 4, we drove to Najaf again, this time entering the city from the north after a half-hour drive from the new camp. Petraeus wanted to be sure the city was indeed pacified before turning to his next task. Plans had changed radically overnight: V Corps had ordered Anderson's 2nd Brigade to attack Karbala on Saturday, rather than Hilla, while the 1st Brigade consolidated in Najaf. There was ample grumbling among the division planners, who had been up all night preparing to seize, as it turned out, the wrong city.

"We're supposed to be looking seventy-two to ninety-six hours ahead, but it's just been impossible since the plan has changed every few hours," a staff officer told me. "I'm sure Joshua Chamberlain went into Hancock's tent at Gettysburg and said, 'Your planning is all fucked up.' But our planners simply can't get on top of this, because the corps planners can't get on top of it themselves. For one thing, they're still at Camp Virginia in Kuwait and they have little direct contact with Wallace, or with the battlefield. The planning paradigm is broken."

I had long observed that staff officers in every command post believe that the headquarters immediately above them is callous and misguided, and that the headquarters two levels above is incompetent. At company, for example, battalion always appears daft, while brigade is hopeless. At division, it was de rigueur to believe that corps was confused, while army, which reputedly had twenty-three CFLCC generals toiling in Doha at echelons above reason, was simply bedlam in desert camouflage.

Greenhouses lined Highway 9, and children waved from the median as we sped past the State Company for the Production of Ready-Made Wear. Life and traffic had returned to Najaf in equal measures. White city buses and taxis with distinctive orange fenders clogged all six lanes, blue exhaust pouring from every tailpipe. A portrait of Saddam in a peaked cap, firing a rifle with one hand, loomed next to an establishment called the Abu Akeel Restaurant and Butterfly Refreshment. "Yes," the inscription urged, "yes, for the Leader."

Petraeus was in a reflective mood, second-guessing whether he had moved the D-Main too far north, whether taking tanks from Hodges and giving them to Anderson made sense, whether Shell should have been closer to the highway. Without prompting from me, he sensed the puzzlement in the division about his caution.

"I am *not* casualty averse," he said emphatically. "I *am* averse to stupid casualties." Freakley was unquestionably loyal and competent, Petraeus said, but he was a mech officer in a light infantry unit. "He's impatient, he wants to be blowing into Baghdad." At times the O could be "diffuse in his energies," and he tended to be hard on the staff.

"There's almost an inherent friction between the CG and the O," Petraeus added, "especially when you're really only able to fight one brigade at a time."

Taxi drivers in slacks and Oxford shirts stood in a queue beside their vehicles at a gas station. Spent brass cartridges littered the gutters.

"I shouldn't talk about it, because it's like talking about pitching a perfect game in the seventh inning. Or maybe the second inning. But I'm pleased with our marksmanship. The enemy seems to be using spray-and-pray techniques, while we're using aimed fire. Knock wood." He rapped his helmet.

Miller swung east, past the shattered pieces of Saddam's Nebuchadnezzar illusion and the An-Najaf Sea Hotel. Which sea, I wondered, could the owners possibly be imagining? The sea of love? A sea of troubles? On the south side of the road, a young girl squatted over a bowl to urinate. Five large Olympic rings fronted a swimming pool with several diving platforms, and I remembered that one of Saddam's sons reputedly tortured Iraqi Olympians who performed poorly. Men in kaffiyehs sat in a café, working their worry beads and sipping tea with their pinkies extended. The fragrance of apple-scented tobacco carried from a nargileh. Petraeus pointed to a sign for the Southern Cement Company. "We could have these guys put down some helipads," he said.

Every few blocks we passed another JDAMed building, sometimes with an Iraqi flag still flying over the rubble. Every few buildings we passed another huge portrait of Saddam, including one in which he knelt on a prayer rug with palms raised in supplication. I was beginning to understand, viscerally, the Stalinist cult of personality in a country where the Leader's face appeared on a million wristwatches.

Approaching the river we drove through a market. Farmers peddled tomatoes and onions in their stalls, and a vendor tended a pushcart festooned with inflated 7UP beachballs. The crowd thickened, pressing around the Humvee on all sides. Petraeus caught my eye and nodded at Miller, who was steering with his left hand while his right gripped the pistol in his holster.

We turned around. Najaf was at peace, at least for today. Back in the middle school where No Slack had its battalion command post, Hodges told Petraeus that he had declared Ali's shrine a demilitarized zone, "so there's no military presence west of Highway 9." He also had issued edicts outlawing revenge killings, but allowing the looting of Baath Party or Fedayeen properties. "You see guys walking down the street with desks, office chairs, lights, curtains," Hodges said, and I wondered whether authorized pilfering was a slippery slope toward anarchy.

Before we we walked back outside, Chris Hughes showed me a terrain model that had been discovered in a bathroom stall in a Baathist headquarters. Built on a sheet of plywood, roughly five feet by three feet, it depicted the Iraqi plan for Najaf's defense. Green toy soldiers, representing the Americans, stood below the escarpment on the southwestern approach to the city. Red toy soldiers, representing the Iraqis, occupied revetments along the perimeter avenues, with fallback positions designated in the city center. The model included little plastic cars, plastic palm trees, even plastic donkeys. Nowhere did I see JDAMs, Apaches, Kiowas, Hellfires, or signs of reality.

In the courtyard outside, two soldiers wounded in the Wednesday-afternoon firefight stood on the back of a Gator all-terrain vehicle, waiting to receive their Purple Hearts. A hundred comrades stood at attention in the scorching sun as the medals were pinned on. Petraeus strode to the front of the ranks. "There is no greater commitment than that which is made by putting the American infantryman on the ground," he said. "We're here to honor two soldiers who are being awarded the most noble of decorations our country has.

"You've really walked point for our nation in this particular battle and this part of the campaign. You've performed brilliantly in countless ambiguous situations." His strong voice rang through the courtyard, and I noticed that his eyes were moist.

The ceremony ended. A sergeant dismissed the troops. "Hoo-ah!" they bayed. "Hoo-ah!"

13

"WAR IS A BITCH"

In central Iraq's flyblown precincts, the small river city of Kufa possessed a historical pedigree of rare nobility. Local tradition held that here Noah had built his ark of Euphrates poplar and launched it into the Deluge. Kufa later served as the first capital of the Abbasids, the caliphs who dominated the Muslim world for five expansive centuries at a time when Europe was mired in its dark age. Famous for woven silk—only a woman's caress was softer than a Kufa scarf—the city also nurtured piety and scholarship, and one of Islam's great legal codes had evolved here.

But this was Mesopotamia, where by one tally at least eighty of ninety-two Abbasid caliphs had been murdered in various intrigues, and inevitably Kufa's heritage also included mayhem, heartbreak, and bloodletting. Here Ali had been butchered in the mosque; the pulpit where he died remained a tourist attraction. Here, too, the great schism cleaved Shiites from Sunnis in the seventh century. Dead Ali's son Hussein had trekked north to Kufa from Mecca with seventy-two companions, intent on confronting a Syrian usurper who controlled the caliphate and professed to be Muhammad's true successor. Continuing on to nearby Karbala in early October 680, Hussein failed to rally the locals to his cause and soon found himself surrounded by four thousand enemy troops. An effort by his stalwart half-brother, Abbas, to fetch water from the Euphrates ended in disaster, with Abbas losing first his right hand in battle, and then his life. On the tenth day of the confrontation, Hussein and his male comrades were slaughtered, their women and children herded into captivity. Hussein died with a sword in one hand and a Koran in the other. His head was shipped to Damascus as a war trophy, and ever since his Shiite devotees and their Sunni adversaries had often been feuding.

To Kufa we drove on Friday afternoon, April 4, for it was in Kufa that Joe Anderson's 2nd Brigade had assembled for its own imminent march on Karbala. Petraeus was in an expansive mood, having bagged one vital city, with another waiting ahead. "Have you ever read *The Ugly American*?" he asked. "It's interesting that he's literally ugly." He extended his hand out the Humvee window so that it dipped and rose in the slipstream. We crossed the Euphrates atop a concrete dam ten miles north of Najaf. The water was cool and surreal, a delirious relief for the eye after so long in the sere desert. Temperatures climbed toward one hundred degrees and Petraeus sensibly had ordered his troops to shed their JLISTs, preferring the possibility of chemical attack to the certainty of heat injuries.

We stopped in an abandoned elementary school where a battalion had set up its TOC in a classroom festooned with paper chains.

"How you doing, men?" Petraeus demanded. He worked the school like a ward heeler, desert boots scuffing the tile. "Gonna get your CIB, aren't you? Shit hot." Among combat decorations, the Combat Infantryman's Badge—created in 1943—was much esteemed. "Heat's not kicking your butt, is it? Baghdad's not far. Okay, heroes, keep up the great work. You'll have CNN with you tomorrow."

"Good," a soldier replied. "That'll mean we're doing something."

Anderson's brigade TOC was in the Al-Kufa Factory for Soft Drink and Healthy Water, just southeast of the great fork in the Euphrates and about twenty miles from Karbala. At the plant entrance someone had scrawled, enigmatically, "Rhode Island Sucks." Inside, empty bottles stood on an assembly line that had abruptly halted in mid-filling, perhaps when an American tank had smashed through the corrugated metal doors. Cases of Kufa cola, orange, lemon-lime, and apple drink filled an adjacent warehouse, and a small laboratory contained cans of Coke, Pepsi, and 7UP, apparently for taste comparisons and reverse engineering. Soldiers throughout the complex were virtually intoxicated on sugary Kufa soda as they washed their filthy uniforms and cleaned their weapons. The division JAG eventually would track down the owner of the factory and pay him $12,600 for the soft drinks consumed.

We found Anderson with his helmet off, studying a map labeled "WGS84 Karbala," copies of which I had seen stacked at Camp New Jersey the night of the alleged fragging at Pennsylvania. The brigade commander planned to air assault three infantry battalions to the southern edge of the city, while pushing twenty-eight tanks and sixteen Bradleys toward Karbala from the east and northeast, swinging the infantry hammer against the armor anvil. Intelligence estimated that five hundred "robust paramilitaries" remained in Karbala, dangerous if much reduced from an original force of perhaps three thousand that had battled the 3rd Infantry Division on the outskirts of the city.

"I would keep the Apaches over the lake. I am very leery of Apaches above the city," Petraeus said. Of seventy-two Apaches in the 101st, ten were no longer combat ready.

"We just can't see, sir," said an Apache pilot who had joined the conversation.

Petraeus gestured at the map. "This is the second holiest city."

"We were in the holiest in An Najaf, now we're going to the second holiest. If we go to Hilla it will be the third holiest,"

Anderson said. He spoke in clipped cadences, leaning forward as if to impart momentum to his words. He started to complain about something, but Petraeus cut him short.

"Stop whining."

"I have to whine about something, sir."

Wallace arrived by helicopter at 4:20 P.M. and took a chair in the plant's conference room. Another large map of Karbala had been divided into thirty sectors, A through DD. Wallace asked how much the division knew about religious leaders and holy sites in Karbala. "We have good intel on all the sites," Anderson replied, although OGA agents had been less active in Karbala than in Najaf. After listening to the battle planning for a few minutes, a reporter traveling with Wallace, Steve Komarow of *USA Today,* motioned for me to join him outside. In a low voice he told me that Michael Kelly, a columnist for *The Washington Post,* had drowned on Thursday night when the Humvee in which he was traveling with the 3rd ID flipped upside down into a canal near Highway 1. A soldier had also drowned, though two others escaped the vehicle. I had never met Kelly, but I knew of him as a gifted writer with great panache; his death seemed senseless and improbable, an absurdly abrupt end to a life of talent and accomplishment.

Wallace and Petraeus emerged from the soda factory. The corps commander ambled back to his helicopter and a few minutes later we drove back toward camp. Barking dogs raced along the rushes as the sun sank over the Euphrates. Shepherds raised their crooks and yelled, "Hel-lo! Hel-lo!" Dung patties, dried for fuel, were stacked in the paddocks. Wheat stood thigh high, and the silver river reflected palms on the far bank truer than any mirror.

"This is probably as beautiful as Iraq gets," I said.

Petraeus was thinking about Karbala. "The old golden rule is to never leave artillery in reserve, and we're not." He radioed the D-Main with a string of questions, and when the answers failed to come quickly enough, he cocked his head back and forth impatiently. "Do you know," he asked as we pulled into camp, "how huge it is to have a combat patch?"

At 11:30 P.M. I had finished my day's story in the public-affairs tent when an e-mail message arrived asking me to call the foreign desk in Washington. Swearing vividly at the intrusion into my sleeping time, I rigged the satellite phone, dialed the number, and was immediately put on hold. Then Leonard Downie, Jr., the *Post*'s executive editor, came on the line. "We didn't know when we'd be able to get hold of you," he said, "but we wanted to tell you that *An Army at Dawn*"—my recent book on the North African campaign during World War II— "has won the Pulitzer Prize for history."

It was thrilling and discombobulating, like a bolt from the heavens, and only the stars kept me company in the sleeping camp. I called my family with the news, then studied the splindly, silhouetted antennas rising from the TOC Mahal for a few minutes before climbing into my sleeping bag.

By 9:15 A.M. on Saturday we were on the road to Karbala. The 2nd Brigade had begun moving toward the city from Kufa, and already Petraeus was fighting his fight mentally. "The way to destroy the enemy is through combined arms. We've also seen the importance of soldiers and leaders who are flexible. It's the regime, stupid. That's what this is about." The regime seemed to be tottering. The 3rd Infantry Division now controlled Bagh-dad's airport. With Marines pressing from the east, U.S. forces had nearly drawn a noose around the capital. Army intelligence put the Medina Division at 18 percent of full strength. The Ham-murabi was at 44 percent, and the Adnan at 65 percent. "These numbers are somewhat in dispute," an intelligence captain had told Petraeus during the morning BUB. "They may actually be lower." Staff lawyers were puzzling over what to feed the grow-ing prisoner-of-war population; international law required that they receive the same rations as American soldiers, which seemed to rule out the humanitarian rations available in plenty, but MREs were in short supply. "Let them eat cake," Petraeus joked, "but no Pop-Tarts."

At 10:35 A.M. we found Joe Anderson on a two-lane blacktop a half mile south of Karbala. A fleet of Blackhawks and Chinooks swooped over the desert behind us, depositing soldiers at Landing Zones Sparrow and Robin. An officer radioed the welcome news that the LZs were "ice"—not under fire—which was much preferable to "cherry." Brigade staff officers tracked the air assault with an alphabetized checklist of cities, just as female names had been used in the Apache deep attack a week earlier. Company by company, the troops blew in: Akron, Albuquerque, Alexandria, Athens, Atlanta, Bloomington, Boise, Boston.

Artillery dumped more than a hundred smoke rounds to screen the infantry moving into Karbala's perimeter. "When you're making an entry into a city, it sure helps if the enemy can't see you," Petraeus said. Kiowas flitting over the rooftops attacked four Iraqi mortars spotted in a large pit. I heard Freakley on the radio: "Mortars destroyed." Six JDAM missiles had already obliterated the Baath Party headquarters and other targets downtown.

"It's a beautiful morning," Anderson told me with a faint smile. "Kiowas, Blackhawks, JDAMs, mortars, smoke." His makeshift command post was located in Karbala's landfill, a site no doubt chosen for its location on the map without a thought for how incommodious it was. Trash stretched for acres on both sides of the road, emitting a stench that ripened as temperatures rose to 102 degrees Fahrenheit—made even hotter by Humvee engines kept running to prevent the radios from draining their batteries.

At 10:45 A.M., the lead infantry platoons reported seizing several blocks in southwest Karbala; a similar report followed from the southeast a few minutes later. "We have a foothold in G, a foothold in I, and we're in Charlie Charlie," Anderson said, pointing to his sector map. The cackle of gunfire intensified as resistance stiffened, and I heard Freakley's voice proposing more CAS—close air support—against Iraqi strongholds.

"Don't do it, Joe," Petraeus advised. "We've hit six targets. That's enough. We've got guys in the city at this point." Several donkey carts clopped through the landfill, chased by a yapping dog. Lieutenant Joe interrogated the drivers, then asserted that "the town is clear."

It was not. Sixty seconds later Kiowas reported attacking a trench line and trucks carrying rocket-propelled grenades. An Iraqi RPG, apparently aimed at a helicopter, burst with a black puff near a water tower in front of us. Behind, a Chinook lifted off in a cauldron of brown dust, spitting out yellow flares to misdirect any heat-seeking missiles.

At 11:35 A.M. a Bradley commander reported firing at an Iraqi armed with an RPG on a rooftop. "They're not long for this world, I suspect," Petraeus said. The rattle of a Kiowa's .50-caliber carried from the city.

Precisely at noon, a radio call quieted the command post. "Three casualties, one critical. We need a medevac. Others are in the middle of a mine field in a firefight."

"What do you need?" Anderson asked. He sat sidesaddle in his Humvee, clutching the radio handset. "Artillery?"

Petraeus leaned over the open door. "What about the Kiowas?"

"Stand by," Anderson advised. "We'll help you."

Black smoke spiraled above the central and eastern portions of the city. To the northeast stood the great shrines of Hussein and Abbas. To avoid hitting American soldiers, an artillery tube deliberately fired a single round six hundred meters beyond the target. A spotter in the city radioed instructions to walk the artillery back in hundred-meter increments.

Petraeus tugged at Anderson's sleeve. Freakley's earlier suggestion of additional air strikes now seemed more appealing. "What we ought to do is put a precision munition on him instead of walking artillery all over the town."

Anderson nodded. "We'll blow the town apart."

Lieutenant Colonel Bill Bennett, the brigade's senior gunner, called to Anderson from his Humvee, which was parked thirty feet away on the south side of the road. "End the mission, sir?"

"End the mission," Anderson ordered. Bennett and his fire-support officer, Major Dave Ell, looked crestfallen.

Anderson radioed the unit with wounded soldiers. "Medevac inbound, twenty-five minutes. Do your best to stabilize." He then turned to his ALO, the air liaison officer. Captain John Stockwell, U.S. Air Force, sat in an armored Humvee with a small X-wing antenna deployed on the hood. Anderson wanted CAS to hit two buildings sheltering Fedayeen fighters; Stockwell relayed the information to the ASOC, the air support operations center at V Corps, which talked directly to the aircraft. High overhead, I spied white contrails from jets heading toward Baghdad.

"ALO, how we coming?" Anderson asked.

"Just waiting on the aircraft, sir," Stockwell replied. "No word on how long."

"All right. Keep me posted." Drivers and other soldiers scooped out cold MREs with their plastic spoons. A staff officer adjusted the four rocks pinning a map to the Humvee hood. Bennett swatted at flies with his handset.

At 12:35 P.M., Stockwell reported that two F/A-18 Hornets had arrived on station. Each carried an AGM-65 Maverick missile with a three-hundred-pound fragmentation warhead that required someone to hold a laser beam on the first target, a Baathist compound. The Maverick, first employed in Vietnam, would then track the reflected laser energy. "Can we get a Kiowa to lase the target?" Stockwell asked. "He needs to hit the west side of the building."

Dave Ell edged up to Anderson. "We also have Copperhead if you want, sir," he said, alluding to a laser-guided artillery round.

"Today's a CAS day," Anderson said. "Don't be jealous."

"What altitude are the helicopters at?" Stockwell asked.

"Very low," Anderson said.

"Fifty feet," another officer advised.

"The fighters will be ready in about a minute," Stockwell said.

Anderson spoke briefly to Saber Six, Lieutenant Colonel Steve Schiller, whom we could see worrying the target in his Kiowa. Lasers worked poorly in clouds and smoke, and I wondered whether Schiller was having difficulty with his laser designator. "They'll be in place in thirty seconds," Anderson said.

"Sir," Stockwell said, "two-minute delay."

"Laser's on the target," Anderson said.

Now Bill Bennett made a sales pitch. "Sir, we can give the Copperhead a try on the other target, the armory."

"Laser on."

"Tell him to keep it on. Thirty seconds." Stockwell pressed the handset to his ear and sang out the code word for a released Maverick. "Rifle!" Then: "Fuck. Wrong building."

"Wonder where *that*'s going to land," Ell muttered. Everyone looked up.

"Where'd that one go?" Anderson asked.

"He turned off the lase and the bomb went stupid," Stockwell said. "Fighter is heading back out."

"The Kiowa is orbiting over a hot target," Anderson said to Stockwell, with some asperity. "He's the one getting shot at, not your guys."

"Once they've started to lase, keep it on," Stockwell said.

I heard Schiller's voice. "Laser's on."

"Laser's on," Anderson said. "Okay, hold it on. Be careful."

"Colonel Anderson," Stockwell said, "the plane's not in position. You can have him break off."

"How much time?"

"Thirty seconds, sir."

Anderson exhaled sharply and shifted in his seat. "He needs more time than that to get in position."

"We're going to go for a three-minute timeline," Stockwell

said, "and he's to lase for the last minute." Two minutes ticked by. "Should be laser on."

"Saber Six, Strike Six. Laser on," Anderson told Schiller. He turned to Stockwell. "You fuck this up this time and I'm going to shoot you."

"Rifle!"

Ell edged up once more. "Sir, we're ready."

"Sir," Stockwell said, and I could hear misery in his voice. "He doesn't think it guided, again."

Everyone looked up, again. The hair on the back of my neck bristled. Abruptly, a sharp explosion shook the desert behind us. Eyes widened, heads swiveled.

Anderson let out an exasperated groan. "Ahhh, fuck."

"We're fucking the dog here, sir," a staff officer observed.

"Okay, we're doing this with old-fashioned 155s," Anderson said. "Not going to mess with Copperhead."

The artillerymen beamed. Stockwell slumped in dejection. I thought of the Shiite-Sunni schism in Islam; it seemed like a fair historical antecedent for the splintering of the U.S. Air Force from the U.S. Army in 1947 to form two rival sects.

Long bursts of machine-gun fire carried from the north. Schiller radioed the location of a large compound where Iraqi gunners with RPGs again lined the rooftops. A six-gun battery roared behind us. "We've put twelve rounds of 155mm into the compound—air burst so it doesn't destroy the buildings, but kills the people," Bennett told me. "Each shell has a radar sensor in it that causes it to detonate seven meters above the ground. We had a ten-digit grid coordinate, which is accurate to within a meter. The bursting radius is fifty meters. That was enough to ring their bell."

Petraeus had stepped away to his Humvee, recognizing that he had to let Anderson command the battle. He wandered back as Kiowas swooped over the city again, looping up in their distinctive parabolic attack attitude before diving on the target with rockets whooshing. Oily smoke corkscrewed above several neighborhoods. At 1:25 P.M., another hundred air bursts lacerated Karbala, this time from 105mm howitzers. Spotters counted thirty-five Iraqi bodies after the barrage. "You've got an infantry battalion on the ground and Kiowas flying above them," Bennett said, "so it's a little bit hairy. Everybody has to have their head in the game so we don't have fratricide."

A voice on the radio called, "Fire for effect."

"Let's keep poundin' the shit out of them," Bennett answered. "The cav"—Schiller's Kiowa battalion—"has them zeroed in."

A radio voice advised that a large statue of Saddam had been discovered in a Karbala city square. "Do you want us to take it down?"

"You might accidentally back over it," another voice answered.

Petraeus intervened. "Let's kill the enemy before we start thinking about statues."

At 2:30 P.M., a Special Forces team rolled up in a white gun truck and a Humvee. "Where have you been?" Petraeus asked.

"We didn't know you were assaulting today," the team leader replied. Petraeus rolled his eyes.

"The guys we're talking to say the Iraqis are tired, hungry, and ready to give up," the SF soldier said. I heard a sharp whistle overhead—*psshewww!*—then another. An SF sniper stretched out on the road with a high-powered scope; for several minutes he scrutinized a small farm six hundred yards to the north, but was unable to spot the shooter. I put my flak vest back on and moved behind a Humvee. Freakley and Dwyer appeared briefly in the O's vehicle. Another bullet whizzed overhead. (The next day Dwyer would ask indignantly, "Did you know that someone was shooting at us out there on that road?")

At 3:30 P.M. we heard radio reports of a Bradley destroyed by "volley fire with RPGs from three directions." Anderson urged his armor force to push through the city from the east. "Get your tanks in the fight," he ordered. "That will help us get this cleared."

After five hours in the landfill, Petraeus decided to return to the D-Main. I suspected that Joe Anderson had no regrets at seeing us leave. For an hour or more we meandered south of town, visiting an air-defense unit and keeping a wary eye out for Iraqi technicals. A dead cow lay in the road and we were startled to see a scavenging dog emerge from a hole in the bloated carcass. Refugees tramped toward the open desert, the women balancing bundles on their heads, the men holding scraps of white cloth as truce flags. Kiowas reported that Iraqi defenders, with an apparently inexhaustible arsenal of RPGs, occupied a stronghold measuring roughly a square kilometer on the city's southwest edge.

We parked in the desert for a few minutes, and Petraeus studied the smoke columns over Karbala as if looking for auguries. "I don't want to JDAM the whole town, but we may have to," he said. "Too bad we didn't have JDAMs on that Maverick run. This is one of those helpless times as a commander. It's a long, long, hot day for the troops."

The long hot day had cost the 101st thirteen battle casualties, including two gunshot victims, five soldiers hurt in a Blackhawk crash, three wounded in a mine detonation, and three others hit with RPG fire. One of those shot, Specialist Larry Brown, a twenty-year-old tanker with the 2nd Battalion of the 70th Armor Regiment, died that night from a machine-gun-bullet wound. Doc Thomas, the division surgeon, also reported at least two serious heat injuries. One battalion alone, the 2nd of the 502nd Infantry, reported killing 150 Iraqi combatants. Julian Barnes, a journalist for *U.S. News & World Report,* observed Fedayeen dispatching children into the streets to retrieve grenade launchers and AK-47s from fallen fighters. An American sergeant skipped a warning shot off the pavement, then fired two aimed rounds. "One child fell to the ground. The other ran away," Barnes reported.

"I keep trying to think of something else," the sergeant told Barnes. "But I can only think of that boy. War is a bitch."

At 4:35 P.M., before heading south, Petraeus radioed Anderson for a final time and asked for a battle update.

"We're going to get the troops watered up, fed, and get a little rest, and go at it tomorrow," Anderson replied. He sounded confident, even buoyant.

Karbala fell on Sunday morning, April 6, first with a bang and then with a whimper. As in Najaf, American firepower—including another four hundred artillery rounds—and the infantry's aptitude for street brawling proved insuperable. At dawn, 2nd Brigade skirmished haphazardly in sectors I, J, K, and G; then Anderson concentrated his combat strength to systematically clean out the most intractable resistance pockets with infantry, artillery, and armor. "They never got organized, and we overwhelmed them," he reported to Petraeus. "I ended up putting six companies in there because we weren't getting anywhere. I think we killed sixty to a hundred, and the rest fled."

Before returning to Karbala, we made a quick visit to Mike Linnington's 3rd Brigade, which had moved from Shell to the Euphrates valley, north of Najaf. In another abrupt change of plans from V Corps, earlier orders to bypass Hilla had been superseded by a decision to attack the city. Petraeus had spent the early morning in the TOC Mahal prodding his staff to adjust to the new orders. He then worked on the assault plan with Linnington before deciding to postpone the attack by a day, until Tuesday, to allow more time for preparation.

By the time we wheeled into Karbala at 3 P.M., the temperature was nudging 106 degrees Fahrenheit. Preferring comfort to fashion, I swapped my trousers for khaki cargo shorts and took ample ribbing about joining the British army. As we rolled down Highway 9, pedestrians and drivers alike hoisted truce flags fashioned from terrycloth, shredded rice bags, even dead chickens looted from a poultry plant; feathers cascaded to earth with each upraised gesture of submission. We waved our victor's waves, and I asked Petraeus about the combat pattern the Army had established in the past week.

"See, 3 ID was around Karbala for quite a while, and look at how many bad guys were still there," he said. "I think we're going to have to go into every town. 3 ID sets conditions by shooting the big pieces, and then the infantry moves in to clean out the diehards and secure the towns. The lesson in Karbala is that you can run around all you want—you can even run tanks through the streets—yet it doesn't clear the city. It has to be methodical."

He seemed in a reflective mood, and I asked whether commanding a division in combat matched his expectations.

"On some days, there's a certain satisfaction. I've always maintained that a commander has the highest of highs and the lowest of lows, and that probably gets more intense the closer you get to the front." When I asked how he had reacted upon hearing that Specialist Brown had died of his wounds the previous night, Petraeus was silent for a moment, as if sorting his emotions. "That's why it's important," he finally said, "to remember that this is important."

We rendezvoused with Anderson at a busy intersection across from an oil company headquarters. A horse plodded past, pulling a cart with four men. "Hi, boys!" the Iraqi driver yelled. At the abandoned military barracks across Highway 9, a large billboard displayed the Maximum Leader in pinstripes, a red hanky peeking from his breast pocket. The Saddam statue in the center of town had been holed with a 25mm cannon round, then toppled by Iraqis—the singing crowd twice snapped the rope in its exhuberance—after Army engineers weakened his ankles with an acytelene torch. Contemptuous Karbalans had whacked the fallen figure with their shoes. "They are crawling over every building that Saddam owns," Anderson observed, "stealing his uniforms, furniture, everything. I said, 'You can have it all.' "

As in Najaf, innumerable weapons caches had been discovered. Clearly an immense effort had been made across Iraq to disperse guns and munitions—the country reputedly had a million tons of conventional weapons. But to what purpose? To delay the U.S. march to Baghdad? Or to arm a future insurrection?

The Iraqi crowd in the intersection had swelled to more than a hundred and was expanding by the minute. Expressions of appreciation alternated with requests for help, or demands that this rival or that neighbor be clapped in irons. "Thank you very much, Mr. Boss," someone shouted. A certain Akmed pulled up his shirt to display scars inflicted, he said, by regime torturers. "We love you, United States," he said. "Saddam donkey." A man named Akbar added, "Very happy. I love you, George Bush." Another man pleaded, "Night and day, no water. Hospital. No electricity, no food, no medicine."

Fivecoat became increasingly agitated as the jostling crowd swarmed around the Humvees. We were vulnerable in ways that mocked the American quest for standoff weaponry. In occupying Iraq, sooner or later the American soldier had to put himself within arm's reach. "I think that street crowd is a microcosm," Fivecoat said as we finally drove off. "It's like many of the peace-keeping operations that we've had since the 1990s. There are a lot of problems, and a long way to go."

At 5:30 P.M. we left Karbala to Joe Anderson's solomonic ministrations and headed back to Camp Eagle Three. Petraeus and Fivecoat, as usual, peppered Miller with driving instructions—Stay left. Turn here. Slow down, Ranger. Watch that bus. No hurry, Ranger—all of which he answered with good humor: "Roger, sir. Got it, sir. I see him, sir. Thank you, sir."

Petraeus smiled and tilted his hand upward, the incline of a fair day. "What was my toughest decision today?" he asked me.

I pondered the question. "Deciding to delay the 3rd Brigade attack at Hilla a day?"

He nodded, then added, "We'll get to Baghdad. And we'll know our jobs better when we get there."

The sinking sun glowed blood red through the dust. Iraqis waved and displayed their truce tokens. I thought of Austen Henry Layard, among the greatest nineteenth-century archaeologists, and a man whose musings on field life and camaraderie in Mesopotamia seemed relevant to those of us traipsing across the same landscape.

"We are both equally careless of comfort and unmindful of danger," Layard had written. "We rode alone. Our arms were our only protection. A valise behind our saddles was our wardrobe, and we tended our own horses.... Thus unembarrassed by needless luxuries, and uninfluenced by the opinions and prejudices of others, we mixed amongst the people."

14

AT THE GATES OF BABYLON

After a fortnight in the wilderness at Shell, 3rd Brigade had decamped for a palmy oasis along the Euphrates, where the Rakkasans staged for their planned assault on Tuesday, April 8, against Hilla, ten miles to the east. During our brief visit with Mike Linnington on Sunday, we had found the brigade commander airing his boots in a grass-floored tent smelling of sweat and hot canvas. "The boys were screaming when they came in here," Linnington told Petraeus. "I thought they were under attack, but they were just excited to see something green."

Even in bare feet, Linnington towered over everyone else in the command post. His dark hair was cropped so close to the skull that the sprinkle of gray looked like glitter on his scalp. He was an Afghan veteran and a West Pointer who had married another West Pointer; he and his wife had a West Pointer son. Linnington's sunglasses perched on his head, and white perspiration stains splotched the back of his uniform shirt beneath a CamelBak. A five-foot map of Hilla hung on one tent wall. Known as a horse blanket for the way it quilted the city into sectors, the map displayed the brigade objectives by code name: Rat, Cow, Squirrel, Hippo, Llama, Wolf, Newt, Jackal, Hyena, Weasel.

"We don't want to go rushing into town to get into a big food fight," Linnington told Petraeus, who sat on a folding chair. The brigade would begin pressing Hilla's outskirts on Tuesday before attacking full force on Wednesday. "The points you made to us on the phone this morning include deliberate versus swift. We don't want to be lured into an ambush in the center of town."

Petraeus scrutinized a computer printout labeled "Key Facilities and C2 Nodes—Al Hilla." Several dozen protected sites were circled on a second map, including the ruins of Babylon, north of town at Objective Sheep. The no-fire list included the biblical Tower of Babel, the Hammurabi Museum, and the ruins of the temple of Marduk, chief deity of Babylon. "I will ask your clearance before firing on Nebuchadnezzar's tomb," Linnington said.

"Be careful with the attack helicopters," Petraeus cautioned. "They're big, slow targets over the city."

Linnington nodded. East of Hilla the terrain was carved into "engagement areas" with sanguinary names—EA Death, EA Kill, EA Destroy, EA Maim, and EA Smash—where Apaches would ambush Iraqi forces escaping Hilla, or reinforcements rushing from Baghdad. Contiguous to the engagement areas, the airspace was splintered into "attack by fire" positions—ABF 60, ABF 50, and so forth. Here the helicopters would lurk in order to shoot into the engagement areas. Northeast of Hilla, for example, near the Emperor Sargon's ancient capital of Kish, an Apache company might loiter over ABF 60 to hit targets in EA Death.

"I don't know how much we'll see them flee," Petraeus said. "The forces we saw in Najaf and Karbala didn't run."

Scant information was available from inside Hilla, a city of a half million people. Iraqi fiber-optic cables remained intact, so commanders there rarely resorted to the radio, depriving American eavesdroppers of intercept and direction-finding intelligence. To keep defenders unsettled, U.S. psychological operations loudspeakers would broadcast the sound of clanking armor outside the town. More than 120,000 psyops leaflets carried the message: "The Medina Division is dead. You're next."

Linnington consulted a green, clothbound notebook. Nine battalions comprising 4,500 soldiers would attack, with armor spearheads leading infantry from both the west and south. The brigade commander had listed his priorities in the notebook, beginning with "Tactical patience."

"Water," Petraeus said. "Water will bring you to your knees. The leaders will have to step up to the plate. If you get into a big fight, you have two options. You can back out and JDAM it, or you can use your own fires without trying to walk artillery all over the city."

"Yes, sir," Linnington said. "Got it." He pulled his boots on. Sweat glistened on his forehead and ran down his neck in little rivulets.

While Linnington gathered his force on Monday, I took my first day off in nearly two months. Within an hour I felt stir-crazy. Camp Eagle Three offered no more diversions than Shell had. The same tired jokes could be heard near the piss tubes—"Keep searching," a comic invariably called to anyone fumbling with his fly, "you'll find it." "Ray's Boom Boom Room," advertised on a brightly painted sign by the chemical company next door, proved to be just another malodorous tent, hot as a convection oven by midmorning. Heat and noise made daytime sleeping a miserable ordeal for soldiers who worked nights; many dragged their mats into the bomb dugouts scattered across the bivouac, which even at midday remained cool as a Kansas root cellar.

The public-affairs tent had a television satellite dish and, with Trey Cate away for the day, a dozen soldiers surreptitiously watched MTV in defiance of his edict banning all non-news shows. Every video seemed deadweighted with irony, from the Foo Fighters' "Times Like These" to Lenny Kravitz singing, "I want to get away, I want to get awaaaay." Nothing I had seen since leaving Fort Campbell was as dissonant as the sight of pretty girls in thick makeup prancing across the screen, or a pouty young man stroking his guitar like a washboard and complaining about being misunderstood. Ten minutes of this surrealism made even Fox TV's hyperventilating war coverage seem preferable, so I borrowed two plastic tubs, filled them with a dozen bottles of Kufa Healthy Water, and tossed in laundry that had last been washed at Camp Doha. Within thirty seconds the tubs were muddier than the Euphrates, and the makeshift clothesline—with paper clips fashioned into clothespins—proved to be a dust magnet. Still, the effort brought a measure of domestic achievement, if not quite domestic tranquillity.

At 6 P.M. I wandered into the D-Main and sat behind Petraeus to listen by radio speaker to a conference call between Wallace and his senior commanders. The war seemed to be going well. The Medina Division had been whittled to 17 percent of full strength, the Hammurabi to 29 percent. Emulating Ben Hodges's modest "thunder run" into Najaf on Tuesday, the 3rd Infantry Division on April 5 had swept up Highway 8 into Baghdad and then veered west to Saddam International—now renamed Baghdad International—with twenty-nine tanks and fourteen Bradleys. The twelve-mile excursion had taken more than two hours, with Iraqis firing from overpasses and side streets. Emotionally spent soldiers wept upon reaching the airport runway.

This morning, 3 ID's 2nd Brigade had conducted a second, bigger run toward Objective Diane—the city's center—and then held fast. Wallace, who several times had found himself restraining the aggressive impulses of Major General Buff Blount, went to bed Sunday night believing the brigade would pull back out of the city; a glance at Blue Force Tracker when he awoke showed otherwise. "I first knew they were going all the way in when I watched the blue icons turn and head downtown," the corps commander said. Marne troops had seized the Republican Palace, official seat of Saddam Hussein's government, and Wallace agreed to let them remain.

Logistics remained precarious; the lead unit reported itself black on ammunition, and the tanks were burning so much fuel—fifty-six gallons an hour for each Abrams—that some engines were shut down to conserve JP-8 until a supply convoy had raced up Highway 8 at fifty miles per hour, the intrepid drivers steering with one hand and firing out the window with the other. Some besieged American soldiers had cut down metal light poles to build an improvised abatis. Iraq's clownish information minister had asserted on Sunday that the Republican Guard was "tightening the noose around the U.S. enemy." In truth, Iraqi conventional resistance had been badly battered despite the regime's plans to convert Baghdad into another Grozny.

Blount's drawl emerged flat and toneless from the speaker box as he ticked off the number of Iraqi tanks, trucks, armored personnel carriers, and antiaircraft guns his division had destroyed during the day. Hundreds of Iraqis had been killed, more than two thousand in the past two days. The Marines were also squeezing Baghdad from the east. Meanwhile, after a two-week standoff, British armor forces had punched into Basra.

Wallace sounded in high feather—"Spectacular performance by your folks today," he told Blount—but his mood abruptly darkened. Earlier that morning, as the thunder run began, three soldiers and two journalists had been killed and seventeen others were wounded when an apparent Iraqi Astro rocket struck a command post of the Marne's 2nd Brigade, south of Baghdad. The blast gouged a crater ten feet wide, demolishing or damaging twenty-two vehicles and igniting thousands of rice bags in an adjacent warehouse. The incinerated remains of one victim had been found seared to the front seat of his Humvee.

"Security of your positions has got to be a major consideration," Wallace said. "This is big-time leader stuff." The corps commander suspected the Iraqis had pinpointed the command post by intercepting Army radio traffic. He was especially angry at lapses in COMSEC—communications security—over Iridium satellite phones, which usually were not secure. The 3rd Infantry Division had forty-three Iridiums, but some users lacked the PIN codes needed to encrypt a call. U.S. security agents had monitored an Iridium call in which the precise grid locations of the 2nd Brigade command post had been given in the clear. Although it was uncertain whether poor security had led to the rocket attack, the usually mild-tempered Wallace worked himself into a molten rage.

"If you don't get the message," he thundered, "I'll come shove it up your ass." Petraeus's head jerked in recoil at the rebuke. Wallace ended his tirade by demanding that each division commander personally acknowledge his message, which they did, meekly, one by one.

Perhaps it was this tongue-lashing, or perhaps it was the heat, but the subsequent 8 P.M. BUB was uncommonly fraught. When a supply officer admitted uncertainty about the stocks of a certain artillery shell, Petraeus stood and faced the staff. "I want to make this point again. We know we're shooting artillery, so why the hell do we wait for them to ask for more rounds? We know we're shooting tank rounds, so why do we wait for them to ask for more? We need to anticipate. That's what a proactive staff does."

Delays in fixing several damaged Apaches also irritated him, but not as much as a plan—displayed in a PowerPoint slide—to sling-load more cargo, only two days after yet another Blackhawk had gone down while moving the ACP. "How many more helicopters do we have to crash before we realize that slingloading out here is not a good idea? What's the deal?" Petraeus demanded. "You just putting that in there to screw with me, or what?" Also, for the first time since leaving Kuwait, every Blackhawk and Chinook battalion in the 159th Aviation Brigade was rated red or amber rather than the preferred green; two weeks in the desert had taken a severe toll.

He paused, and I could see him recapturing his composure by force of will. "You lost my trust and confidence," he said, with the hint of a smile. "Now I'm going to scrutinize everything."

"As if," a staff officer whispered in my ear, "he isn't scrutinizing everything already."

We set off for Hilla at 10:30 A.M. on Tuesday, April 8. The morning was hazy and slightly cooler as we rolled north up Highway 8 and then across Route Aspen, the four-lane road that approached Hilla from the west. Smoke curled from a meat grill beside the road, and a long line of taxis and John Deere tractors snaked toward a single pump at a filling station. A woman draped in a black *abaya* squatted by the curb like a big spider, selling bundles of dried flowers with help from a boy wearing a Dallas Cowboys shirt. Four young men streaked past inside an elegant new Mercedes sedan; privilege was still easy to spot in Saddam's Iraq. A white mare pawed the ground at a watering trough, and an old potter shaped a huge urn on a wheel, his hands gray with wet clay. So many portraits of the Leader stood along the road that it would take weeks to deface them all.

In the river town of Hindiyya, traffic was jammed into a bottleneck at the Euphrates bridge. Vendors along the road peddled prayer rugs and Kit Kat bars and cartons of cigarettes arranged in intricate, architectonic stacks. A shop window displayed a large poster of Mickey Mouse, given distinctive Iraqi features and an Asian cast to his eyes. Pedestrians swarmed around our stalled convoy, and when a man with a scraggly beard leaned into the front passenger window to grab a water bottle, Petraeus shoved him back with a sharp "Stay away!" Tank crewmen in coveralls finally cleared a path for us, past a taxi with Betty Boop painted on the rear window and an orange Volkswagen belonging to the "Iraqi State Organization of Imports," which no doubt was responsible for all those Kit Kat bars.

Across the river, boys capered on a stony soccer field with goals fashioned from plastic tubing. They turned to wave, as did a little girl in braids and a print dress. "This is a hell of an experience, isn't it?" Petraeus said. "We have won over the children of Iraq." I recalled how often through five millennia invaders here had been greeted with the open, toothy smile that surely was a Mesopotamian cultural trait. They had cheered Alexander with his Greeks, and even Cyrus with his conquering Persians. An Akkadian inscription on a clay cylinder described how

> [a]ll the inhabitants of Babylon . . . bowed to [Cyrus] and kissed his feet, and with shining faces happily greeted him as a master through whose help they had come to life from death, and had all been spared damage and disaster.

And usually, in short order, life had soured. Liberator had become occupier, occupier had become oppressor, and oppressor had become someone whose throat needed cutting.

"Visibility is shit today," Linnington said upon greeting us at noon. He stood on the median of Route Aspen, several miles west of Hilla, wearing cotton gloves and a radio headset. Freakley and Dwyer were already there, monitoring a skirmish that had begun twenty minutes earlier, when a Humvee came scorching back down the highway, its whip antenna sheared away by a rocket-propelled grenade. An unknown number of Iraqi defenders had blocked the road five hundred yards ahead before falling back to Objective Hippo. "The locals told our guys, 'You're not fighting Iraqis, you're fighting Syrians,'" Linnington said. "Everything you'd expect: obstacles, berms, mines, RPGs, Syrians."

Kiowas darted east toward the city, and then banked north over a field of sunflowers. A battery of 105s yelped behind us, followed a few seconds later by the kettledrum thud of detonating shells.

"You see the infantry commanders getting comfortable using artillery," Freakley observed. "They're getting hardened."

"This is real walk-and-shoot," Petraeus agreed. "It's not as easy as it looks." He turned to Freakley. The O had appeared at length on television the previous evening during febrile coverage of a suspected chemical-weapons cache. Discovered in a compound on the Euphrates, it soon proved to be a pesticide dump. "You got more air time last night than Larry King," Petraeus said.

Freakley smiled his bashful smile, and changed the subject. "Saddam Hussein has claimed that he's the new Nebuchadnezzar and is establishing a new Babylon. We're going to secure old Babylon and Nebuchadnezzar's tomb, and return them to the Iraqi people." He smiled again. "That's my story, and I'm sticking to it."

JDAMs had already eviscerated a military barracks, a radio station, Baath Party headquarters, and other targets in Hilla. Now the growl of two more high-flying F/A-18s, invisible through the haze, swept across the landscape. "Goddamn," Petraeus said, "they have to hear *that*." Two miles ahead, the heavy footfall of detonating bombs marched from north to south, followed by more artillery explosions and tank fire from the 2nd Battalion of the 70th Armor Regiment.

Freakley studied the map. "It looks like he's trying to block all key road intersections. Analysis would be that he's trying to restrict avenues from the west and south." The 3rd Brigade attack was concentrated on both those approaches.

At 1:15 P.M. Linnington turned to his ALO, Major Greg Gavin, a B-52 electronic warfare officer from Kansas City. "Hey, Greg, do you have any CAS available to go into this intersection up ahead? We're taking RPG fire down there, so anything around that intersection would be good."

"I can ask, sir," Gavin replied.

Linnington called Steve Schiller, the ubiquitous Kiowa commander. "Saber Six, Rak Six. Can you give me an orientation on where the direction of that RPG fire was?" Schiller answered with an eight-digit grid location: 3300 9740.

Gavin pulled out a green pencil and a paper form labeled "Joint Tactical Air Strike Request." He checked various boxes, including "target description" and "munitions effect." For "immediate or preplanned," he circled "immediate." Under "desired results," he checked "neutralize" rather than "destroy." It was like ordering sushi.

Gavin handed the form to an Air Force sergeant. "Double-check it before you call it in," he said.

Freakley sat sidesaddle in his Humvee, eating cold "Western Beans" from an MRE pouch. "I've got my watch on you Air Force guys," he called, pointing to his wrist.

"Roger, sir," Gavin replied. "I've got two F/A-18s with laser-guided Mavericks."

I let out a small groan, recalling the Mavericks in Karbala. Three miles up, a pair of twin-tailed silver fuselages appeared momentarily through the haze.

"I'm not sure that's the best munition for troops in the open," Freakley said.

Artillery roared again, and concussion ghosts rippled across the little command post. A rooster crowed in the laurel shrubs along the road, answered by the distant cackle of heavy machine-gun fire.

"Still good to go?" Gavin asked.

"Yeah," Linnington said.

Gavin listened to his handset for a moment. "He's getting spooked by the artillery," he told Linnington, gesturing overhead. "Can we check fire?"

The brigade commander nodded and gave the order. "Artillery's cut off," Gavin reported.

From the road ahead we heard a ferocious tearing sound, like ripping canvas. I thought it was a Kiowa .50-caliber but someone else insisted it was an F/A-18 on a strafing run. No one seemed certain. I cocked an ear to the radio, straining to hear "Rifle," the signal that a Maverick had been released.

At 1:43 P.M., Linnington, who had been talking to his subordinates over the brigade radio frequency, turned to Gavin and made a slashing motion across his throat. The ground commander ahead was tired of waiting for air support. "He wants to press the attack."

"Abort it," Gavin ordered. "Okay," he called out a moment later, "he's aborted."

Linnington keyed his handset. "You have permission to press the attack." A few minutes later, ten Abrams tanks clanked past us down Route Aspen, followed by a convoy of open trucks packed with infantrymen. Petraeus strolled along the median, allowing Linnington to orchestrate the fight with advice from Freakley.

"You've got to be patient," Freakley told a pair of junior officers standing near his Humvee. "Get your fires in before you maneuver. Use fires to facilitate maneuver. You get in all these reports about this and that, but you have to stop to ask yourself the basic question: What is the enemy doing?"

He studied the canal across the road. "Seeing those bulrushes reminds me of Moses," Freakley said. "Makes me want to go check for babies." It made me want someone to go check for snipers.

Linnington leaned against his Humvee and watched the last truck disappear through the dust. "I could use a beer so bad right now. Wouldn't that go down easy?" he said. "Guys were talking last night about which they'd rather have, sex or beer. You can always get sex."

The whiz of bullets overhead interrupted these pleasant reveries. Linnington jumped in his Humvee and bolted forward, and we followed closely for a quarter mile. Something exploded on our right in an orange flash, and the crackle of gunfire quickly swelled fifty yards ahead. As we spilled from the Humvee, I saw bullets chew the dirt berm ahead and heard the sharp ping of richochets. Several dozen riflemen had taken cover on both sides of the road. The distinctive three-round bursts of M-4 fire grew louder, tentative at first and then quite hysterical, answered by the steadier staccato of AK-47s. An easterly breeze brought the stink of cordite. Bullets sang overhead, and then a burst of Iraqi machine-gun rounds stitched the shoulder of the road along the right side of our Humvee.

Linnington ran forward, studied the terrain with his field glasses for a moment, then ran forward again. Petraeus and I ran with him, before sheltering behind another vehicle. I bent my knees, pulled in my shoulders, and tried to make myself as small as possible. Freakley strode past a truck ahead of us, yelling at soldiers to disperse. "Sir, are you crazy?" someone called. "You don't belong up here." Fivecoat put a hand on his shoulder, urging him to lower his profile.

I now saw what had happened. Iraqi ambushers hidden in a mulberry thicket on the south side of the road had allowed the tanks to pass, then opened fire on the infantry trucks. A Rakkasan had been wounded in the face with a grenade. As soldiers bailed from the truck beds in search of cover, Sergeant Major Savusa had rushed forward from the rear of the column—"like fucking John Wayne," an admiring comrade reported later—pulled the pin from a grenade and hurled it overhand into the brush, killing two Iraqis. An uncertain number of others had retreated several hundred yards into a vast grain-elevator complex, where they now fired on the road. Muzzle flashes winked from at least one of five warehouses on the south side of the compound, and from a cluster of cylindrical silos straight ahead.

"Little too close for CAS," Linnington said. The Army would have to overpower the Iraqis without air strikes.

"I think the Kiowas will take care of it, Mike," Petraeus said. "You have them on your net?"

"Yes, sir." Rakkasans along the berm had recovered their wits and were now pressing forward in small fire-and-maneuver teams. Three Kiowas circled the warehouses.

"We'll get it sorted out," Linnington said. "I'm bringing armor back to clear this complex. We'll spend a couple hours clearing it out."

"Yes," Petraeus agreed. "Yes. That's exactly right."

Rounds continued to whistle overhead. I turned to Petraeus. "It would be really bad if they got a cheap kill on a major general."

"They probably wouldn't even know it," Petraeus said.

"Everybody in the United States would know it."

He smiled. "Reminds me of the former honorary colonel of

the 504th Parachute Infantry Regiment. When he signed his name he would write under it, 'Shoot low.' "

At 2:30 P.M. the Kiowas took station directly over us. Rockets erupted from their pods in a throaty roar, punching black holes in the elevator. Acrid smoke drifted west, and ashes sifted over us like charred snow. The Iraqis answered with more gunfire, and I found myself facedown, embracing the dirt ten feet from the two dead Iraqi soldiers dispatched by Savusa's grenade. One wore green Republican Guard fatigues; the other had the mottled camouflage of the Iraqi regular army. A soldier next to me was hit in the foot, possibly with a richochet or rock fragment, and he rolled over on his back to remove his boot. A CNN camera-man wearing a Rambo rag squinted through his viewfinder and admonished a soldier, "Don't smile. Look serious."

I scrambled over to a truck, which listed heavily to the right. Iridescent green antifreeze pooled on the road. Freakley and Petraeus stood in the lee of the cab. "We've got to regain momentum," Petraeus said.

"What happened to your truck?" Freakley asked the driver.

"Nothing, sir."

"How'd you get a flat?"

"Oh," the soldier said, as if the past half hour had just slipped his mind. "They were shootin' at us, sir."

At 2:45 P.M., a pair of tanks bulled into overwatch positions on the road after being summoned from Hilla's outskirts, two miles to the east. Their coaxial machine guns rattled at length, spraying an administration building next to the silos. Then one tank rushed the main gate, perhaps a hundred yards from us. A tongue of flame spurted from the barrel, and a 120mm round bored a smoking hole in the elevator. I wolfed down a slab of MRE pound cake out of sheer nervousness, and would have eaten ten more had anyone offered them.

"We have to clear that whole complex, sir," Linnington told Petraeus. A psyops sound truck appeared next to us, adding its Arabic broadcast to the din.

"Tell these guys they have to get closer," Petraeus said. "He's talking into the wind."

The sound of AK-47 fire rippled from the elevator, punctuated by the pop of grenades and volleys of tank fire. "Direct fire from that tank is a great way to clear the building," Linnington said. "How many artillery rounds have we fired?"

"One hundred and ninety-eight," his artillery chief answered. "So far."

Just north of the highway, in a grove of date palms, we found the Iraqi camp. Bedrolls and blue blankets were spread around a cold campfire. Flies coated a tray of humus, the lunch that apparently had been interrupted by the American attack. I surveyed the still life: a fire-blackened kettle, an egg carton, a plastic bag of cucumbers and tomatoes, a pair of boots, a 40mm RPG with "Made in Iraq" stamped near the trigger guard.

The owner of the boots had died in his stocking feet among the mulberries on the south side of the road. As the shooting finally ebbed, soldiers wrapped him and his dead comrade in blankets. For reasons unclear, an infantryman logged their personal effects in green ink on the thigh of his own uniform trousers. Another soldier called out the inventory: "Wedding ring. Prayer beads. Skullcap. A bunch of fuckin' money."

Swifts skimmed the canal surface, trawling for insects. At 4:30 P.M., soldiers dumped the dead Iraqis into a hole dug a few feet from where they had died, then shoveled dirt over them with an entrenching tool. Dust to dust.

Petraeus radioed Wallace to report Linnington's progress. "Rak 6 has done a good job of making sure that when we launch the attack tomorrow all berms and obstacles have been removed. They're going to maintain contact with the enemy and take positions in case the crazies come at them tonight."

Freakley strolled among the troops, spent brass crunching beneath his boots. Linnington's brigade counted a dozen Iraqis killed and ten more captured. "A real good combined-arms fight," the O told Petraeus. "When you can produce that level of firepower, word goes back, and the enemy will have to determine how much steel he has for the next day's fight. If the center of Baghdad is to be a violent fight, the 1st Brigade now has An Najaf, the 2nd Brigade has Karbala, the 3rd Brigade has Al Hilla. These boys have the confidence that they can fight, and fight successfully."

Darkness had fully enveloped Camp Eagle Three by the time Miller pulled up to the D-Main at 8 P.M. Petraeus grabbed his map board, shut the Humvee door, and turned to walk inside.

"Embrace the suck," he called to me over his shoulder.

"Yep," I said. "What else are you going to do with it?"

He paused for half a second before continuing to the tent. "I must confess," he said, "I still am wondering how it's going to end."

A brief, fierce storm blew out of the desert on Wednesday morning, April 9, cutting visibility to a hundred feet and filling the Humvee with fine, floating grit as we drove slowly back to Hilla at 7:45 A.M. Dust coated the back of my throat, and the air tasted slightly ashy. Artillery and air strikes had continued in Hilla through the night, and the Rakkasans renewed their attack at 6 A.M. against resistance that disintegrated, as it had in Najaf and Karbala. Apaches shooting up Death, Maim, Smash, and the other aptly named kill zones would claim 228 Iraqi vehicles, 46 artillery pieces, and scores of other targets destroyed. Petraeus radioed Wallace to report that U.S. casualties were very light, although four Kiowas had been hit by gunfire, two seriously. "We may have broken their back in Al Hilla," he told the corps commander. To me he added, "This is sure heartening after those first few days. I'm beginning to think there's an air of inevitability to this."

Handsome, flat-roofed houses lined Route Aspen as we sped past the fatal grain elevator and into the city's western district. Gilded stars and intricate palm silhouettes decorated the wrought-iron gates, and bougainvillea spilled from the walls in bright riots. Linnington and Freakley waited for us at the Hilla water-filtration plant, where the only evidence of earlier combat was a great deal of blood splashed across the vestibule.

"You come in here looking for a fight and you find guys hugging and kissing you," Linnington said. "You hit him hard, don't take any shit from him, and he just melts away."

"What a difference a day makes," Petraeus said. He cautioned against gloating or trophy-taking. "We want to be a benevolent and humble presence."

Dwyer surveyed the festive crowd gathering in the plant driveway. "We're being pelted with love," he said. A distinguished elderly man in a white robe emerged from the throng and identified himself as Abdul-Razzaq Kasbi, a teacher at the Saddam Secondary School. He spoke English with slow formality, enunciating each syllable. Schools in Hilla had closed on March 17, when war became inevitable, Kasbi said, and many had been converted into armories. The water plant had shut down earlier in the week for lack of fuel.

"Mr. General," he said to Petraeus, "we are afraid you will control us, as he has done." There was no need to specify who "he" was.

"No," Petraeus said, "we won't."

Freakley leaned over and told Petraeus in a stage whisper, "He's a show-me guy."

"Any honest Iraqi person," Linnington said, "wants to see a good man control Iraq, not one bad man replaced with another."

"We are still afraid of that," Kasbi said. He kneaded his worry beads.

"We will show you by our actions," Petraeus said. He offered the teacher a brass division coin to seal the bargain, but Kasbi politely refused the token.

"I can't have anything of you unless I am sure you have come for the sake of our people. We want to live in peace. We don't want to substitute one bad person for another bad person."

Petraeus took the rejection gracefully. Another man, sporting a trim goatee, tapped the elbow of a staff officer and offered to help. "Okay," the officer replied, "tell us where all the fuckers are." I edged over to Freakley, who was entangled in a political debate with a French radio reporter. "Would you rather be known as the person who stood for the moral right," Freakley asked, "or would you rather be known as a person who went with popular opinion?"

As we milled about, soldiers pumped five hundred gallons of fuel into a large tank outside the plant. With a ragged cough and a burst of blue smoke, the filtration machinery sputtered and caught. Water gushed from a spigot near the front gate. A man wearing sandals and a stained turban squatted with a bar of soap and began to wash his hands.

"I understand the intellectual aversion to nation-building," Petraeus mused. "On the other hand, I don't see how you avoid it."

We drove into the center of town, past the Alafindee Barber and the Zaid Photo Shop and the State Organization of Buildings. Crowds blew kisses from the sidewalk. "Good! Good!" they chanted, slapping high-fives with the passing soldiers in our convoy. "Wouldn't it be wonderful if this place turns out to be something?" Petraeus said. "There's no reason why it couldn't be. They have lots of money. Unless some other petty despot takes over."

"They have a five-thousand-year tradition of petty despots taking over," I said.

A Saddam statue had been pulled over at the ankles, and the Leader's face lay buried in a hibiscus bed. But a hundred other likenesses loomed on billboards above the streets: Saddam the country-western singer, in sunglasses and string tie; Saddam the pederast, with a little girl on his lap and a small boy giving him a kiss; Saddam the CEO, in a double-breasted suit; Saddam in a fedora; Saddam in Bedouin robes; a bemedaled Saddam in a dress uniform, the apotheosis of a Middle Eastern tyrant. Somewhere,

I speculated, there had to be a State Manufacturing Facility for Reproducing Portraits of the Leader.

"Saddam seems to favor his left side," Petraeus said dryly.

Looters spilled from a military compound, lugging mattresses and ceiling fans and air-conditioning units. A man trotted across the road with a brass coat rack. Another wheeled a bicycle, on which he balanced a six-foot bookcase and two desk chairs.

We stopped briefly to inspirit a double column of infantrymen tramping into town from the south. "How you feelin' here, heroes?" Petraeus sang out. "You have liberated Al Hilla. We just rode through the whole town and they're cheering. It's a great sign when you don't have to fight a second day because you've scared them off the first day. They flat booked." Hoo-ahs, all around.

Other troops guarded a complex of cinder-block warehouses, filled to the eaves with boxes labeled "Oil for Food." As we poked about, I cataloged the emporium. Warehouse No. 4: fifty-kilo sacks of sugar from France and twenty thousand bags of black tea from India. Warehouse No. 10: cooking oil from Malaysia. Warehouse No. 19: detergent powder—the place smelled like a lemon grove—from Algeria and Syria. Warehouse No. 5 was my favorite: bedsheets, Philips flat-screen televisions, men's underwear, throw rugs, lightbulbs, candles, compressors, pencils, erasers, light switches, trash bags, and, not least, a carton of box cutters. Perhaps, I thought, we had found the elusive link to Al-Qaeda.

I had mentioned to Petraeus that during the battle of Kasserine Pass in February 1943, General Eisenhower had taken time to sightsee in the grand Roman ruins at Timgad, near the Algerian-Tunisian border. He took the hint, and we swung north—to Babylon.

"It surpasses in splendour any city of the known world," Herodotus had proclaimed. Even the prophet Jeremiah, no friend of Babylon, called it "a golden cup in the Lord's hand, that made all the earth drunken." Here King Belshazzar had seen God's dire judgment written on the wall during a feast for a thousand of his lords, and here Alexander had died, probably of malaria, in Nebuchadnezzar's palace, at the age of thirty-three. Here was the city of the great god Marduk, of whom it was written, "Four were his eyes, four were his ears. When he moved his lips, fire blazed forth. . . . His members were enormous. He was exceedingly tall." Here was the city of Nimrod, great-grandson of Noah and "a mighty hunter before the Lord," who had founded ancient Babel. Or so claimed Genesis.

Two Abrams tanks stood near the entrance of the archaeological park, their nicknames—"Bad Mo Fo" and "Boomer"—stenciled on their barrels. A tall, grotesque modern statue of Hammurabi was the only sentinel inside, lending the place a "Saddam World" theme-park ambience. A blue canal cut through the complex as an ersatz Euphrates, the original having, over the centuries, shifted fifteen miles west of its antique channel. Water buffalo lumbered along the bank, past picnic tables with concrete sun umbrellas like those found at interstate highway rest stops.

We made for Saddam's palace, a four-story limestone monstrosity on a man-made hill covered with fragrant purple beds of sweet William. Through the massive double doors we strode, like centurions taking possession of an enemy's inner keep. The place was empty, devoid of furniture or other signs that it had ever been inhabited, despite the gold-plated faucets and porcelain sinks and parquet floors. Rosettes with inlaid brass decorated the cavernous reception hall, and delicate carvings of palm fronds covered the teak doors. A stele depicted Saddam's head in profile above a bas-relief Hammurabi, that self-styled "King of the Four Quarters of the World."

We climbed a grand staircase to the roof and there, spread below us, was ancient Babylon. Saddam in the late 1980s had built a replica of Nebuchadnezzar's palace adjacent to the ruins, with crenelated towers and forty-foot walls of yellow brick. But it was the old, partly excavated city that held the eye, though there was little more than meandering, rectilinear ruins to suggest grandeur. Hilla and the dam at the head of the Hindiyya canal had both been built with scavenged Babylonian bricks. Somewhere in that heap the Hanging Gardens had hung and the Tower of Babel had soared seven stories into the heavens. Eight gates, each named for a god, had pierced the double walls—I had often seen the Ishtar Gate in Berlin's Pergamon Museum, with its ceramic lions and winged bulls and horned, fork-tongued walking serpents. Nearly twelve hundred temples had been crammed into Babylon's inner five hundred acres; Herodotus claimed that over three tons of frankincense was offered to the gods annually. Had we arrived in early spring a few thousand years earlier, we could have attended the eleven-day New Year festival, when a priest severed the head of a ram, smeared blood on the temple walls, and threw the carcass into the river so the "scapegoat" could carry away the year's sins. The ruins at Babylon, the historian George Roux once suggested, "offer perhaps the best lesson in modesty that we shall ever receive from history."

Petraeus had drawn his own lessons, and now he turned on his heel. "Okay, guys, let's roll. Let's get back to the war." Clattering down the stairs, we piled into the Humvee and drove off. Looters would find the place within hours.

But war was getting harder to find. As we drove through more cheering throngs—"an absolute victory tour," Petraeus called it— V Corps radioed with new orders. Resistance in Baghdad had collapsed. 3rd ID and Marine units had swept across the capital, seizing all remaining strongpoints. The 101st was to dispatch two infantry brigades immediately to take control of southern Baghdad below the Tigris, a sector of roughly three hundred square kilometers.

Petraeus seemed delighted. "Happy to help," he said to me as we recrossed the Euphrates. "I was getting a little bored, anyway. Couple hours of peace and I'm ready to do something else.

"Okay," he added, "so on to Baghdad."

15

"EVERY THING HAS ITS PLACE"

"There is no beauty in her that arrests the eye," an Arab traveler wrote of Baghdad in the twelfth century, "or summons the busy passerby to forget his business, and gaze." The eight intervening centuries had not enhanced the city's pulchritude. No one came to Baghdad to gaze. The self-proclaimed City of Peace was a vortex of war, fire, pestilence, and now war again. The Mongol invasion in 1258 had left at least 800,000 dead. Poets were slaughtered, and their skulls stacked to form a bony ziggurat; the invaders rolled the ruling Abbasids into carpets and trampled them beneath their horses' hooves. More recent catastrophes included bubonic plague and a flood, in 1831, that swept two-thirds of east Baghdad down the Tigris River.

Yet, another twelfth-century visitor could justly claim, "Nothing equals it in Mesopotamia." Baghdad once had been the world's wealthiest city, not only in the African ivory, Malayan dyes, and Chinese porcelain stocking her souks, but in accomplishment and lyricism. It was the sort of city where a clever cartographer devised the first map of the known world, and where a sonneteer whose verses pleased the caliph earned five thousand gold pieces, ten Greek slave girls, and a fine horse.

In its thirteen-hundred-year history, Baghdad had been conquered thirty-one times, according to an Arab tally. Now the
count was thirty-two. American soldiers had secured most of
the city; Abrams tanks roamed the boulevards at will. From the
southeast on April 9, U.S. Marines stormed the capital and,
shortly before 7 P.M., diverted an M-88 tank recovery vehicle to
help an Iraqi mob pull down a twenty-foot statute of Saddam
Hussein in Firdos Square, east of the Tigris. "There is no god but
God," the crowd had chanted while whacking the fallen figure
with sticks, sledgehammers, and shoes. "Saddam is the enemy of
God."

Our first view of the capital was from the air on Thursday
afternoon, April 10. As we left Camp Eagle Three for the last
time and flew north, the landscape organized itself into a flat
checkerboard of wheat and bean fields, a veritable Iowa with date
palms. The Tigris and Euphrates closed to within twenty miles
of each other in a fecund neck, where gum trees lined the country
roads and cows lowed in their pastures. Beets and tomatoes grew
along the canals, protected from the wind by brushwood screens.
Drying clothes flapped like signal flags on lines behind the farmhouses, and flumes of canal water gushed from pumps into the
crop rows. Less bucolic were the fire trenches, inky ribbons of
oil along Highways 8 and 1; here, at least, the 3rd Infantry Division juggernaut had been too swift for defenders to ignite the
ditches. Every few hundred yards the stigmata of black smudges
signified the fate of Iraqi diehards, the modern equivalent of
being stomped in a rolled carpet.

Warlord 457 sheared to the northeast, and farmland yielded to
flat-roofed villas as we sped across the city's southern districts.
"Well," Petraeus said over the intercom, "there's Objective
Lions." And there it was, the former Saddam International, seven
miles southwest of downtown. I could see the charred cruciform
of an airliner on the taxiway. Scorch marks stained the tarmac like
shadows. We set down near the jetway for Gate D-42. Signage
pinpointed our location—N 33 159' E 44 139'—and informed us

that the ramp could handle aircraft ranging from Boeing 727s to Airbus 300s. No mention was made of U.S. Army Black-hawks.

Wallace had converted the waiting room at Gate 41 into his office, but a staff officer asked Petraeus to wait outside because "the corps commander is meeting with OGA." A Chevy pickup truck with a machine-gun mount was parked on the tarmac, and a mustachioed desperado with a civilian haircut leaned against the cab. Petraeus nudged me. "Pretty inconspicuous, eh?"

A major emerged from the terminal. "Heavy fighting in Kik-ruk," he said solemnly. Sensing that his pronunciation of the city was suspect, the major tried again. "Kikruk?"

"Kirkuk?" Petraeus said.

"Yes, sir. CNN's reporting that. And you heard about An Najaf?"

"It's in my AO," Petraeus said, alluding to his area of oper-ations, "but somebody else was handling the event."

"Successful assassination, sir."

"What's that mean?"

"Sir, apparently the cleric we were trying to turn this over to was assassinated."

Sad, but true. We already had heard a sketchy account of the incident, and additional details only made it uglier. In the unend-ing effort to recruit Ayatollah Sistani to the American cause, OGA agents that morning had transported a cooperative Shiite cleric, Abdul Majid Khoei, to Najaf in hopes that he could con-vince Sistani to issue a fatwa proscribing cooperation with a par-ticular mullah favored by Iran. An outraged mob, perhaps incited by yet another Shiite faction, had confronted Khoei, who had spent years in exile in London. Shots may or may not have been fired, and a grenade may or may not have been thrown. Khoei ended up dead, hacked to ribbons with swords and knives. Trey Cate had been escorting a busload of sixteen journalists into Najaf to witness the anticipated embrace of pro-American Shiites, only to make a hurried retreat through a mob of fifteen hundred riled and baying Iraqis. The murder was a chilling portent of the occupation ahead: confused, violent, and medieval, a labyrinth of factions and seething resentments.

While Petraeus met with Wallace and other V Corps commanders, I explored the empty terminal. The power was out, but fading afternoon light filtered through windows dimpled with bullet holes. Signs pointed to "Hotel Reservations" and "Baggage Arrival" and the duty-free shop, which had been ransacked. I studied a mural of Babylonian kings, gimlet-eyed monarchs with square-cut beards. The TV monitors remained dark, but a flight board still listed a half dozen planes to Jiddah, presumably for the haj in February. Beyond a door labeled "Iraqi Airways Flight Crews" all the wall lockers had been jimmied. "Notice to Pilots," a sign advised, "Change of Flight Pattern, February 2003." A crew chart listed captains—Jibouri, Nassiree, Mansoor, Karmil—and their flights, which were penciled in through January 12. Load-sheet forms included boxes for "Takeoff Weight" and "Last Minute Changes." Pink plastic roses filled a dish and a Bartholomew World Wall Map covered an office wall, next to a photo of a Pratt & Whitney engine. A stench hung in the office, as if something had died in the ductwork. Downstairs, a lounge—for Fedayeen VIPs? for frequently flying Baathists?—was appointed with gold carpeting and a velvet painting of a Bedouin camp. An SF team darted through the crepuscular terminal, padding past a snack bar with a stainless-steel espresso machine before vanishing down a long corridor.

Outside, I found Petraeus ready to go. Soldiers kicked around a Hacky Sack near the baggage carts. Four Iraqi Airways jets stood near the terminal, their doors yawning. A radar dish was frozen in mid-spin. A Bradley Fighting Vehicle raced down the runway, as if building toward takeoff. Warlord 457 lifted into the air at 7:30 P.M. A magenta glow in the western sky reflected off the control-tower windows and ignited the canals, like fire trenches belatedly lit. It was almost lovely.

Until the D-Main could pack and move into southern Baghdad, we would again cohabit Ben Freakley's assault command post, which occupied a former Iraqi air base twenty-five miles south of the capital, at Iskandariyah. Troops found the multisyllabic name vexing and instead called the place El Gonorrhea. There was ample dust, in the tents and even on the hard-surface runway, but for the first time since leaving Fort Campbell our living conditions improved with relocation rather than declined. Fivecoat and Miller moved their cots into a single-story adobe building dubbed the Mexican jail, and Fivecoat could be heard whistling the theme song to a spaghetti western. Soldiers gave each other Bert-and-Ernie haircuts and began catching up on mail and sleep. The end of the war was in sight, and if it was too early to feel jubilant, there was a sense that jubilation might lie in our future. My only regret was that Dwyer had declared victory and gone home, among the growing exodus of reporters. I would miss him.

Just before 9 P.M. Thursday, I walked into the cramped ACP tent to hear Petraeus discuss the move into Baghdad with his senior commanders. Linnington and Anderson stood next to him at the front table, along with Freakley, Greg Gass, E. J. Sinclair, and artilleryman Bill Greer. Hodges remained with 1st Brigade in Najaf. Baghdad had been subdivided into fifty-five zones; the 101st was to clear ten zones in the southern part of the city, including three near the airport—designated 42, 43, and 44—that would allow fixed-wing aircraft to land without fear of snipers. Anderson's 2nd Brigade would take the southwestern sector after air-assaulting into Landing Zones Oriole, Dove, Sparrow, and Dodo, while Linnington's 3rd Brigade seized the southeast. The task at hand had been summarized on butcher paper with a marking pen: "Attack in zone to clear non-compliant forces. Transition to stability forces, or head north. End state: non-compliant forces destroyed, civil unrest minimized, capable of introducing HA"—humanitarian assistance—"and U.S. forces supporting the new Iraqi government." The plan struck me as linear, logical, and unlikely.

Petraeus reiterated the prewar order against displaying American flags. "We're not an occupation army. We're a liberation army. So we're not trying to plant the flag," Petraeus said. Soldiers were to continue wearing helmets and body armor; no do-rags or other sartorial deviations allowed. "We've got to keep our guard up. The corps commander this afternoon said, 'We are closer to the beginning of this thing than we are to the end.' " War trophies, including bayonets and Iraqi army flags, were prohibited for individual soldiers; each battalion was authorized one captured weapon and a dozen smaller items approved by higher authority.

"A tank, sir?" Anderson asked.

"That counts as one weapon," Petraeus said.

The first allied reinforcements would soon arrive, a paltry force consisting of a single Albanian company with seventy-one soldiers and ten Land Rovers. "They're yours," Petraeus told Linnington. "They fire AK-47s, so your very first task will be to figure out how to distinguish them from the Iraqis so we don't shoot them."

Commanders were to document any Iraqi violations of the laws of war, such as feigned white-flag surrenders. "This is a huge deal at the national level," Petraeus said. Troops must respond to lingering pockets of resistance with proportionate force. "There may have been a case of a sniper on the roof and another in the basement, and they JDAMed the whole building," Petraeus said. "I'm not saying we did it, but someone around the table at the corps meeting today acknowledged that." As for looting, he added, "We should discourage it, but we're not going to stand between a crowd and a bunch of mattresses."

Petraeus scanned the faces of his colonels. "Any questions?"

There were no questions.

Freakley was kind enough to again give me shelter in his personal tent, and as we slid into our sleeping bags at midnight he was in a reflective mood. He had just learned that he would soon be promoted to major general and take command of the Army's Infantry School at Fort Benning, Georgia, a fine job for a gifted teacher.

"The division's role in the war was about right," Freakley said. Still, he wondered whether the 101st should have been more aggressive. He again used the metaphor of V Corps "punching with one fist." At times he wondered if the division appeared to be "looking for reasons *not* to do things." Had they used armor as robustly as possible? Were there other occasions when the 101st could have pushed more than one brigade at a time into battle? The helicopter's role in Army operations was certain to be much debated. "If we're going to be fighting enemies who take refuge in cities and who are capable of massing small-arms fire, I'm not sure what those helicopters can do for you." He seemed a bit frustrated, and I recalled Petraeus's observation that the battlefields in this war had been too small for more than one general. I asked about Petraeus's command style.

"He did a good job," Freakley said, propping himself up on an elbow. "General Petraeus is a sponge for information. In order to come to the right decisions that are aggressive and tactically sound, he needs huge amounts of information from his G-2 and G-3. He has the ability to process all that. He is extremely proficient at the staff portions of the job, and at absorbing information."

Petraeus infrequently asked for tactical advice from the O or the S, Freakley added, and he kept his inner circle small. "You're probably closer to him than anyone in the division," he told me.

"Really?" I said. That seemed unlikely.

"He's very competitive, even with E.J. and me, although there is absolutely no question about who commands this division. His competitiveness sometimes pins him to the wall."

Freakley's tone was analytical and pensive, the tone of a professional officer pondering the art of generalship. I knew that he was loyal to Petraeus and admiring of his many talents. But I was reminded again of how personalities played an outsized role in war, and had since the age of Agamemnon and Achilles.

"He did a good job," Freakley repeated, nodding. "You'll come to your own conclusions."

Shortly before noon on Friday, April 11, Miller swung the Humvee around a quartet of abandoned Iraqi T-72 tanks and into the northbound lanes of Highway 8. The terrain was marshy and canal-striped, with white salt flats interspersing the fields. A scarecrow dressed in a head scarf and a black *abaya* guarded the barley. Palm fronds wore a light brown coating, as if the trees had sucked up dust through their roots. As we drew closer to Baghdad, demolished Iraqi vehicles littered the roadbed, including some dismembered into pieces no bigger than a card table. In the suburb of Mahmudiyah, clambering children had converted a charred tank hulk into a jungle gym; an old woman whose face was etched with blue tattoos sold Sumer cigarettes from the fender. Seven T-72 tanks and four armored personnel carriers had been destroyed here in a surprise 3rd ID attack out of the north, from the Iraqi rear. At Objective Curley, the highway interchange where 3rd ID had waged a brisk firefight, we stared at the wreckage of an ambushed U.S. Army supply convoy. A well-aimed RPG round had apparently triggered a chain reaction: fire spreading from an ammunition truck had engulfed four other trucks. It was near here that Sergeant First Class John W. Marshall had died; his body would be found the next morning in a shallow grave by Mike Linnington's soldiers.

The day was gorgeous, a fair replica of California, and we found Freakley and Linnington inside a Pepsi bottling plant on the east side of the highway. The offices had been ransacked, but a photo remained on the wall showing the presumptive plant manager with Saddam's son Uday, whose pompadour and open-necked shirt gave him the greasy look of a lounge-singing extortionist. The floors were littered with bottle caps and Viceroy butts and a crushed box of Al Reem Luxury Dates. Soldiers discovered a litter of puppies who had survived by eating the carcass of their dead mother.

Petraeus sat at a table in the courtyard. So far the air assault and occupation had gone smoothly, although Linnington noted that "these are not the cheering crowds of Al Hilla." The 3rd Brigade would secure two sectors by day's end, and two more on Sunday; 2nd Brigade already occupied four sectors and soon would seize its final pair. As we left, Freakley was negotiating with an Iraqi cabdriver who claimed his taxi had been destroyed by 3rd ID gunfire. "He'd like reparations. Three thousand dollars for his car," Freakley said. "Or forty-seven million dinars, if you have it handy."

A double archway over Highway 8 signaled our entrance into the city, and now the looting began in earnest. Scores, and then hundreds, and finally thousands swarmed through the industrial parks fronting the highway; a few carried truce flags, but most were too intent on pilferage to worry about gunplay. Men, women, and children wheeled, dragged, carried, and drove away booty, converting side streets into shopping aisles. Three men, waving gaily, each rolled a fifty-five-gallon drum past the Humvee. A man in a green skullcap pushed a three-wheeled handcart piled high with copper wire; two little boys helped him negotiate the street curb. Drawing a blue cart piled with boxes of tile, a spavined donkey trudged through the gutter. Four men shouldered a wagon loaded with air-conditioning ducts; a Kawasaki front-end loader rolled past with two water pumps in the bucket; two women pulled a pair of plastic tubs brimming with linens; three men on an ancient John Deere tractor towed a large motor on a wooden sled.

Propane tanks and pipes, school desks and trash dumpsters, lamps and ladders—it all swept past us in a great river of loot.

At the Alalaf Marble and Granite Company, a mob hoisted a generator into a truck bed, while others cavorted through the Al-Aamawhi Dairy and the Economy Bank for Finance and Investment, where the metal window grills had been smashed. A Chevrolet Caprice trundled past with nine new tires, still wrapped in brown paper, lashed to the roof and trunk. Crowds swarmed over bulldozers and a Caterpillar steam shovel in a parking lot, evidently trying to hot-wire the heavy equipment. A young man emerged rolling an enormous truck tire.

"What in the world would you do with that?" Petraeus murmured.

"Lay it on its side," I suggested, "and use it as a coffee table." Just hours after Saddam's statue toppled in Firdos Square, the liberation of Iraq had become the plundering of Baghdad.

Petraeus was scouting sites for the Division Main, and we pulled into the compound of a company that made firefighting equipment and safety helmets. A tank round had punched through the administration building's portico, and smoke boiled from a warehouse. Dozens of red extinguishers lay scattered across the parking lot. Fivecoat flipped off the safety of his M-4, shooed away a few looters, and poked around a smoky office suite before returning to the Humvee. "This looks like it could be too much of a fixer-upper, sir."

"Yeah," Petraeus agreed, "it's a money pit." I wondered whether the same could be said of the entire country. Fivecoat subsequently recorded the ineluctable course of the pilferage: "First, they removed the furniture; then the doors, windows, and light fixtures; then bannisters, light switches, and wires; and then, finally, they would take the building down, brick by brick."

Later in the day Defense Secretary Donald Rumsfeld would deny that looting was widespread. "The images you are seeing on television you are seeing over and over and over, and it's the same picture of some person walking out of some building with a vase." The Pentagon press corps laughed, but Rumsfeld's remark was inane, as was his assertion that "freedom's untidy." The abrupt transition to anarchy was a disaster not only for Iraq but also for the United States. The cultural losses were bad enough: the National Center of Books and Libraries was on fire downtown, although some collections reportedly had been saved; the Religious Endowment Library also burned, with an estimated loss of 6,500 manuscripts, and the Central Library of Baghdad University had been ransacked and torched. Mobs rampaged through eighteen galleries of the National Museum, although they stole many fewer items than at first was feared—by June, officials would reckon that ten thousand pieces were missing, but only thirty or so highly prized treasures remained unaccounted for.

If it was dispiriting to see a nation's heritage despoiled, the stripping of Iraq's industrial, commercial, and bureaucratic infrastructure was simply catastrophic. Clearly, it would take years and many billions of dollars to set things right. How Iraqis would view U.S. authority in the face of such disorder was difficult to imagine. Too little thought had been given, by the Army or anyone else in the Defense Department, to securing Iraq, except for oil fields and the WMD depots, which would prove nonexistent. Detailed studies compiled by the State Department in 2002, known collectively as the Future of Iraq Project, had been mostly ignored by a White House and Pentagon determined to cede the country to a few pet ex-patriots of dubious legitimacy, and get out.

The military had barely enough troops to wage war, much less to simultaneously put a country bigger than Montana into protective custody. Civil stability was ad hoc. Although a V Corps planning cell formed in December had drafted plans for postwar Iraq, few senior officers believed that the only warfighting corps stationed outside the United States would remain in Iraq for more than three to six months. "The intent is not to have a long-term occupation," the senior V Corps lawyer had declared in mid-March. Officers even avoided uttering what they referred to as the O-word.

Moreover, Army planners had anticipated that it could take

weeks to reduce Baghdad through a series of raids launched from five firebases outside the city, allowing more time to bring forward military police, civil affairs, and other units required to keep order. Even with the Baath Party leadership routed, most rank-and-file bureaucrats were expected to remain on the job to safeguard facilities and to keep essential services running. "The security of industry, of power plants, of water plants, was a big issue that we really hadn't dealt with," Wallace later told me. "There was an assumption that all of us made that there would be some fiber of the infrastructure, and some fiber of the federal government remaining when the regime left." Instead, "the whole damned place closed down." Parts of Baghdad already had been bereft of utilities for more than a week.

Miller made a U-turn on Highway 8 and again headed south. "I don't think the speed of the collapse of Baghdad was anticipated," Petraeus said soberly. "This is really enervating. It doesn't have the excitement of bombing An Najaf."

At 3:45 P.M. we pulled into a chicken-processing plant a few hundred yards west of Highway 8. Petraeus eyed the plant as a potential site for the D-Main, until the odor of decaying poultry persuaded him to reconsider. Rubber stamps and ledger books lined the desks in the executive offices on the second floor, where glass cases displayed the company's products—Potato Kuba and Chicken Nuggets seemed particularly successful lines. A Republican Guard uniform was neatly folded in a desk drawer of the corner office, where a coaster on the blotter advertised, "Bates Motel—Universal Studios." Reprieved chickens pecked about the courtyard outside, tentatively enjoying their liberation.

Wallace showed up in a convoy a few minutes later. He had taken up smoking again, and he lit a Marlboro as Petraeus smoothed the map on the Humvee hood. "I talked to the chief of station," the corps commander said. OGA agents were trying to enlist Iraqis to help stabilize central Baghdad, but it was hard to know where to start imposing order on the chaos. Just clearing bodies from the airport would take days. Army engineers had dug more than a hundred graves on the southern edge of Objective Lions, each six feet deep, eight feet long, and facing Mecca.

"Getting water and power and sewage back on in this city is going to be a monumental job," a V Corps major said. "We've been trying to find Iraqi civil authorities who ran the utilities, but without much success." Iraqi troops continued to shed their uniforms and melt into the population. In one memorable encounter, five soldiers had stripped completely before surrendering to a U.S. tank company at a location now known as the "Five Naked Guys Checkpoint."

Yet they were among only seven thousand Iraqi prisoners of war, less than 10 percent of the number captured during the Gulf War. Certainly the Iraqi military was spavined, even compared to the feeble force that fought in 1991. The troops were poorly trained—most had fired little, if any, ammunition in the past year—and their marksmanship had been abysmal, with repeated instances of Iraqi infantry and artillery missing point-blank shots. Poorly prepared, they also were excessively led: an army of a half million included eleven thousand generals and fourteen thousand colonels. (The U.S. Army, roughly the same size, had 307 generals and 3,500 colonels). But all of those soldiers, at all ranks, had gone *somewhere,* and it was impossible to know whether it was to await the flowering of a democratic Iraq, or to join a well-armed insurgency.

Petraeus pointed to a spot on the map near the Tigris. "This one here will be interesting," he said.

Wallace peered through his sunglasses. "That's the power plant?"

"Yes, sir. That's the power plant."

Wallace pursed his lips. He put a gloved finger on the plant site.

"Yesterday they seemed to be taking everything they could carry," the major said. "Today it seems to be mostly vehicles they're stealing."

"Actually," I said, "they're still pretty undiscriminating."

Wallace lit another cigarette.

The weekend in Baghdad was wonderfully weird. On Saturday, April 12, we followed a winding road to a three-story Baathist villa with a balcony overlooking the reedy Tigris. The river was a fabulous aviary of stilt-legged waders and exotic semitropical species, although I wondered how long that would last with Baghdad's power down and dysfunctional sewage-treatment plants dumping millions of gallons of untreated effluent every day.

Empty shipping containers—Ikea, Loyd Trestino, Maersk—stood in the villa's side yard. Below the balcony a masonry bird of prey with a fifteen-foot wingspan perched on a pedestal, a potential souvenir for the Screaming Eagle museum at Fort Campbell. Looters had pillaged the main house, and the floors were strewn with cans of Vitalact baby formula and books, including a volume titled *Law Studies*. The reception hall was large and garish, with a decor derived from Eastern Europe, perhaps the Bucharest of 1971. Round kerosene containers the size of volleyballs, evidently used for illuminating garden parties, lay scattered in the driveway. We could hardly imagine the frolics this place had seen in happier times.

Next on the tour was Clarksville, the division's moniker—after a town near Fort Campbell—for another Baath Party compound where one of Mike Linnington's battalions had bivouacked. As we drove through the gates, a sharp boom carried from a neighboring villa where ordnance teams were blowing the tails off five Iraqi helicopters discovered in a courtyard—including four German models and an old Huey. Miller parked the Humvee near the Clarksville swimming pool. Several peafowl strutted across the deck in advance of a grinning Geraldo Rivera, the television personality; evicted from the theater for allegedly disclosing troop movements near Najaf, Rivera—the troops called him "Grrr-aldo"—had somehow insinuated his way back into the division. As he pursued Petraeus for a stand-up interview by the pool, I wandered inside. The foyer was dominated by a breathtaking piece of kitsch: a laquered wood sculpture, eighteen inches high, of an elephant fighting five lions. Two cats had embedded their claws in the pachyderm's back; another clawed at his knee; a fourth was being stomped to death; and a fifth howled in evident agony at being crushed in the elephant's trunk.

The foyer opened onto a *diwaniyah*, a large, rectangular meeting room with tea tables and divans upholstered in blue fabric. Soldiers had discovered a liquor cabinet and dutifully emptied the bottles down the sink drain: two fifths of Clan MacGregor scotch, a liter of Stolichnaya vodka, and a bottle of arrack, the Iraqi national drink made from fermented palm sap. The kitchen smelled like a distillery. This compound allegedly had links to Ali Hassan al-Majid, a Saddam intimate known as "Chemical Ali" for his prodigal use of mustard gas against the Kurds in the 1980s. U.S. intelligence believed al-Majid had been killed in an air attack, but later he would be captured, very much alive. The compound was said to belong to his brother, or perhaps a cousin. The precise connection was vague but pleasantly menacing.

A Rakkasan driver rifled through several MRE packets stacked on the dashboard of his Humvee. "Hey, Cap'n," he called, "did you eat my pound cake that was sittin' up here?"

The captain answered carefully. "I did have one today."

"Was it vanilla?"

"I didn't know it came in different colors," the captain said.

The driver muttered maledictions under his breath. "I can't believe you ate my damned pound cake."

We drove to south-central Baghdad, where Joe Anderson's soldiers had conquered an amusement park. Sentries stood on the balconies of three onion domes above the park gates. Inside, we walked beneath mimosa trees past a haunted house and a merry-go-round with a Wild West motif. The Karkh Orient Express, once used to haul Iraqi children around the grounds, featured open-sided wagons pulled by a tractor tricked up as a locomotive; a painted happy face beamed above the cowcatcher. Other concessions and kiddy rides featured Pinocchio and

Mickey Mouse, both with vaguely Semitic features. An employee told us that four thousand visitors came to the park each weekend before the war. Now it was an arsenal, and soldiers tallied the mortar rounds and innumerable 7.62mm ammunition crates hidden in the ladies' restroom, in the little cars shaped like swans that revolved around a central pole, and in the gaping mouth of a large, papier-mâché clown originally used for a beanbag toss. It was clear that in Saddam's Iraq, nothing was sacred.

Early on Saturday Petraeus had decided to put the D-Main in the Al Qadisiyah State Establishment, the rambling munitions plant on the west side of Highway 8 near the junction with Highway 1. As we drove south on Saturday afternoon to pack up our kit at El Gonorrhea, traffic slowed to a crawl through Mahmudiyah. Crowds pressed close on both sides of the road, and I felt the the back of my neck prickle. "There's something sinister about this town," I said.

"They're waving," Petraeus said.

"The kids are waving. There are a lot of hard-eyed guys back in the shadows."

Mahmudiyah was forgotten as we settled into our new home on Sunday. Three dozen buildings composed the walled compound at Al Qadisiyah, which covered at least thirty acres. "Think Safety," a placard in a workshop urged, in English. "Every Thing Has Its Place." Hundreds of AK-47s were stacked on workbenches and the floor, along with spare barrels, stocks, sights, and bayonets. Rifle racks lined an adjacent room with a hundred newly refurbished weapons; each carried a tag clipped onto the sight: "Control Card of Assembly and Final Test, Automatic Rifle Takuk M70s, cal. 7.62mm." Blue work shirts hung from pegs, and in an open shed outside stood a long line of lathes, presses, and machine tools: Pittler, Hitachi, Kellenberger, Weisser Heilbronn.

Another warehouse was crammed with RPG-7s, and several hundred wooden crates, labeled "Product 663 Al Qadisiyah State," contained cloth carriers for RPG rounds. I had seen an identical carrier at the grain-elevator ambush site in Hilla. Some doors had been splintered by rampaging 3rd ID soldiers—"I think their blood was up when they went through here," Petraeus said—but a small glass tank still contained a pair of live if undernourished goldfish. Scattered around the plant were blue velvet pistol cases for gift weapons presented to Baath Party worthies. A display case in the seven-story office building known as the Hotel showed off Al Qadisiyah's finest wares, including a silver-plated AK-47, dart guns, and RPG night sights. It was said that an Al Qadisiyah assault rifle could be bought on the street for 150,000 dinars, or $83.

A small soccer field, with the goals still netted, abutted two rifle ranges and a rambling garden abloom with roses, snapdragons, and pansies. A plastic press made pistol grips, and a large repair shop was full of twin-barreled ZU-23-2 antiaircraft guns. Another sign urged: "Think Quality." A Saddam shrine stood outside the Hotel. For sheer artistic pretension, it was my favorite of all those we had seen: a ten-foot, head-and-shoulders portrait of the smiling Leader, favoring his left side as usual, with a lush backdrop of palms and hibiscus, as if painted by Henri Rousseau.

Petraeus turned to me and smiled. With perfect ironic pitch, he said, "And the guns fell silent."

Ben Freakley was right. I *did* come to my own conclusions. Petraeus, I believed, had done his duty very well. He had proved himself worthy of the extraordinary responsibility of commanding a U.S. Army division in combat, doing all that was asked by his superiors while losing only two soldiers in action, with another forty-six wounded. The stress of combat was indeed a revealer of character, and I had watched him grapple with his doubts, then steel himself and soldier on. He had taken care of his troops and executed his mission, the two essentials of command, while asking no more of subordinates than he asked of himself. If others found him hard to love—his intensity, competitiveness, and serrated intellect made adoration difficult—he was nevertheless broadly respected and instantly obeyed. I was certain he would excel in the netherworld between war and peace that no doubt would characterize the occupation of Iraq. His pragmatism and broad peacekeeping experiences in Haiti and Bosnia had prepared him for the thankless work of a proconsul in the American imperium.

The division's soldiers had also done well, demonstrating competence and professionalism. Capably led—the division's brigade commanders and two assistant division commanders were uncommonly excellent—they took hardship in stride and refused to let bloodlust, cynicism, or other despoilers of good armies cheat them of their battle honors. They were better than the cause they served, which would soon be tarnished by revelations that the casus belli—that Iraq posed an imminent, existential danger to America and its allies—was inflated and perhaps fraudulent. If the war's predicate was phony, it cheapened the sacrifices of the dead and living alike. Yet such strategic nuances were beyond the province of soldiering, and I believed it vital not to conflate the warriors with the war.

Over the weekend I had decided to leave. Twenty *Post* reporters now flooded the region, including a half dozen or more in Baghdad, and I was beginning to feel like a supernumerary. The 4th Infantry Division was scheduled to arrive for occupation duty on Monday evening, and Petraeus abruptly received orders to move his division yet again, this time to Mosul, 230 miles north. There the 101st would likely remain for months, perhaps many months, along the Tigris near the ancient Assyrian capital at Nineveh, a sanguinary land of bulls and winged lions and merchants who once were "more numerous than the stars in the heavens." Xenophon had marched through with his ten thousand

Greeks, and now Petraeus would follow in trace with his seventeen thousand Americans.

I packed in the spacious corner office where I would spend my last night in Iraq. The previous occupant had left in a hurry: his reading glasses lay on the desk, along with ledger books and a robe made of fine wool. The red Wonderland phone emitted no dial tone, nor did the Samsung air conditioner blow cold air. Heavy damask drapes with gold tassels covered the windows.

Sunday evening's BUB was held at 7:45 P.M. in a cavernous paint shed, where the D-Main stadium seating and video monitors had been set up. Staff officers droned on in the usual sequence, describing preparations for the move north and plans for welcoming the 4th Division. The routine atmosphere abruptly dissipated when an officer stood to report that at least sixteen soldiers had been wounded in an ambush in Mahmudiyah, the suburban town that had given me the heebie-jeebies on Saturday. Petraeus had ordered a battalion from Anderson's 2nd Brigade to sweep the dense neighborhood along Highway 8; as a platoon assembled in a police station courtyard, the assailants heaved a grenade over the wall and fired automatic weapons from nearby buildings.

Six soldiers were wounded badly enough to require medical evacuation by helicopter, including one with a serious eye injury and another with fragments in the groin. Return fire with rifles, .50-caliber machine guns, and Mk-19 grenade launchers killed two Iraqis and wounded three. A few hours later, a hand grenade accidentally detonated in a division air-defense unit, killing two soldiers and wounding two others. The incidents seemed ominous, dark portents in this land of portents.

For the final time I scribbled down the day's challenge and password—GUILTY and HISTORIC—then shook hands with the officers who had become friends and comrades. Petraeus gave me a Screaming Eagle combat patch and an air assault pin, and wished me Godspeed. I thanked him for his indulgence, and for his service, and I tried with limited success to stifle feelings of guilt at leaving the division behind. I cared about these soldiers a great deal. Although I believed it possible to write about them with the requisite objectivity, and to bear witness with cool detachment, I also knew that every subsequent report of a 101st Airborne Division soldier killed in action or grievously wounded would break my heart.

The next day, Monday, April 14, the Pentagon would declare an end to major operations in Iraq. Early that morning the MPs drove me to Iskandariyah—we drove past the ambush site in Mahmudiyah without incident—and I boarded a Chinook with tail number 665 for the three-hour flight to Kuwait. A forklift hoisted a load of cargo nets into the bay through the rear clam-shell door, and a gunner reset his machine gun into the mount, tapping home the cotter pin with a ball-peen hammer. The ammunition belt snaked from the weapon into a metal box; every fifth round was a tracer, tipped with orange. Five other passengers buckled themselves into the web seats, including two soldiers headed home on emergency leave because of deaths in the family.

The engines caught. "Taking off is always an adventure," said the senior pilot, Warrant Officer Matthew J. Carmichael. Black shadows from the turning rotors flitted across the ground like wraiths fleeing the dawn. Dust smothered the fuselage as the Chinook lifted off the ground, nose down.

Old number 665 raced south at 130 knots, 150 feet above the peeling landscape. Ungainly and ancient, Chinooks could still outfly any helicopter in the fleet. From the open rear bay the gunner dangled his legs, scanning the countryside for enemies of the Republic.

The helicopter bucked through the hot air like a horse galloping across a rolling meadow. Over a farm hamlet we flew, and a dozen gleeful children ran after us, leaping and tumbling as if they had just won the lottery.

AFTERWORD

They were the best of times. The worst, or at least much worse, would come soon enough. By late November 2003, American soldiers in Iraq were under attack, on average, every forty-one minutes. Insurgency bombers also blew up the United Nations and International Committee of the Red Cross offices in Baghdad, as well as an Italian barracks in Nasariyah and police stations hither and yon. As 2004 began, the death toll among U.S. troops climbed toward five hundred, most of them killed *after* the collapse of Saddam Hussein's regime in mid-April. They were shot, mortared, grenaded, rocketed, and bombed. Medical evacuations approached eleven thousand wounded, injured, and sick; of the twenty-eight hundred soldiers wounded in action, many were grievously hurt by RPGs and what the military called IEDs, improvised explosive devices. Walter Reed Army Medical Center alone treated fifty-eight amputees by mid-November.

Among the dead were seventeen soldiers from the 101st Airborne Division killed on November 15 after ground fire caused two Blackhawk helicopters to collide. Two more Screaming Eagles were shot dead in Mosul a week later; a celebratory mob stripped the corpses of their jackets, boots, and wristwatches. Division casualties in Iraq during 2003 included 46 killed in action, plus 17 dead from "non-hostile actions," and 459 wounded. Among the dead was Lieutenant Colonel Kim S. Orlando, commander of the division's military-police battalion, killed in a firefight in Karbala on October 16. He was the highest ranking American officer to die in Iraq. Also among the U.S. dead was Sergeant Paul J. Johnson, who had twice served with General Petraeus, including a stint as his driver in Bosnia. Sergeant Johnson was killed on October 20 in Falluja by a homemade bomb that tore apart his Humvee and burned 80 percent of his body. He was twenty-nine years old.

The Iraq War in the months after the capture of Baghdad was marked by incremental progress, disheartening setbacks, and administration rhetoric that ranged from resolute to hallucinatory. President Bush on May 1 appeared aboard the carrier USS *Abraham Lincoln*, beneath a banner proclaiming "Mission Accomplished," and announced that "in the battle of Iraq, the United States and our allies have prevailed."

A few weeks later, after a mobile chemical laboratory was discovered in an Iraqi trailer, Bush declared, "We've found the weapons of mass destruction. You know, we found biological laboratories." No such thing had in fact been found—the trailer's actual purposes remained ambiguous—and the hunt for nuclear, biological, and chemical weapons throughout Iraq turned up nothing other than evidence that Saddam Hussein, whatever his sinister aspirations, had basically shut down his WMD programs.

By New Year's Day 2004, none of the administration's most incendiary prewar accusations about WMD and Iraqi support for international terrorism had been confirmed. Not the president's October 2002 declaration in Cincinatti that "the Iraqi regime . . . possesses and produces chemical and biological weapons," nor Bush's State of the Union assertion, on January 28, 2003, that "war is forced upon us" because Iraq posed "a grave and gathering danger." Not Deputy Defense Secretary Paul

Wolfowitz's claim in October 2002 that there had been "a decade of senior-level contacts between Iraq and al-Qaeda." Not Secretary of State Colin L. Powell's charge at the United Nations in February 2003 that "Iraq today has a stockpile of between 100 and 500 tons of chemical weapons agent" and possessed "the wherewithal to develop smallpox." And not the CIA's National Intelligence Estimate that Iraq "possesses . . . chemical and biological weapons," and could fashion a nuclear weapon within a year, if it obtained fissionable material.

The central provocations for war proved spurious. As 2003 unspooled, justifications for the Anglo-American invasion shifted, retroactively, to construction of a democratic beachhead in the Middle East, and to the deposition from high office of Saddam Hussein as a general menace. *The Washington Post* described the process as "reinventing the rationale for the war." Still, polls continued to show that many Americans believed weapons of mass destruction had in fact been discovered in Iraq, and that Saddam—whose capture in December provided an exhilarating grace note after a somber autumn—was linked to the atrocities of September 11, 2001.

In early July 2003, noting a rising tide of violence in Iraq, Bush had seemed to solicit further attacks on his own soldiers. "There are some who feel like—that the conditions are such that they can attack us there," he said. "My answer is, bring 'em on." On they came. Attacks through the fall increased in magnitude, sophistication, and frequency, organized mostly by recalcitrant Baathists, criminal mercenaries, and disaffected former soldiers and security agency thugs. (In an unfortunate blunder, the U.S. administrator in Iraq, L. Paul Bremer III, abolished the Iraqi army wholesale, putting 400,000 or more former troops on the street, many of them armed, angry, and broke.)

Hundreds of Iraqis also were murdered, and assassinations of policemen, civil authorities, and ordinary citizens employed by the Americans became commonplace. Bombers in Najaf killed a moderate ayatollah and eighty of his acolytes. For average Iraqis, the postwar months brought both hope—in the toppling of Saddam's tyranny—and despair. Schools, colleges, banks, and health clinics reopened; infrastructure repairs to the power grid and oil production facilities began. The Bush administration agreed to spend more than $160 billion in Iraq during the first two years of the occupation. Yet, in late November, a *New York Times* portrait of Kifl, the Euphrates town where Ezekiel is buried, tallied the persistent miseries: fitful electricity; few jobs; sewage in the streets; primitive medical care, with outbreaks of cholera, typhoid, and meningitis; rampant crime; and soaring prices for cooking oil, gasoline, grain, and other necessities.

In nearby Najaf, Ayatollah Sistani, whom the 101st and CIA operatives had wooed in March and April without conspicuous success, finally issued a fatwa in late June. Sistani declared that he would support only a national constitution written by Iraqis chosen in a general election, rather than by an American-picked council. Bremer found himself outflanked, and eventually agreed to cede sovereignty to Iraqis in June 2004, with constitutional guarantees of free speech, due process, religious freedom, and an independent judiciary to follow later—or at least that was the hope.

While the political tussle continued, the military occupation devolved into a brutal counterinsurgency. U.S. military reprisals intensified through the fall, with a renewed use of JDAM missiles, Apache attack helicopters, and artillery. Thousands of suspected insurgents were summarily imprisoned; hundreds of others were killed. Secretary Rumsfeld in a private memo conceded that the war resembled "a long, hard slog," and Pentagon wits noted that Rumsfeld's extensive collection of aphorisms included this one: "It's easier to get into something than to get out of it." CNN captured the average soldier's perspective with footage of a Marine barking at an angry Iraqi mob: "We're here for your fucking freedom!"

The military success of the spring threatened, by the end of the year, to become a politico-military morass, even if Saddam's apprehension renewed hope for happier times. Pentagon planners in early May had predicted that U.S. troop levels would be down to 30,000 by late summer; instead, at Christmas the figure was 130,000 American soldiers in Iraq, with another 30,000 in Kuwait. Some 28,000 allied troops augmented the occupation, but Washington's call for larger commitments were ignored in part because many governments resented the U.S. refusal to cede greater authority to the United Nations. The White House envisioned reducing the U.S. troop level in Iraq to 105,000 by May 2004, a decline conveniently coincident with the 2004 presidential election campaign. Yet senior Army officers assumed that at least 100,000 troops would be required through early 2006, even if Iraqis regained sovereignty. Although new Iraqi security forces totaled more than 130,000—predominately police and facility guards—most had little training. Many observers, both inside and outside Iraq, feared that a precipitate U.S. withdrawal—a decision not to cut-and-run so much as cut-and-strut—would trigger civil war and aggravate instability in Southwest Asia. As Machiavelli once observed, "Wars begin where you will, but they do not end where you please."

Certainly the U.S. Army was stretched and stressed. Before September 11, 2001, roughly 20 percent of the active-duty Army had been deployed overseas; two years later the figure had climbed to nearly half, with 10,000 soldiers in Afghanistan, 5,000 in the Balkans, 37,000 in South Korea, and troops scattered through more than 110 other countries. "Beware the twelve-division strategy for a ten-division Army," the chief of staff, General Eric Shinseki, had warned at his retirement ceremony in June 2003. No less strained were the National Guard and Reserves. The Pentagon in early November alerted another 43,000 troops from those units for extended service in Iraq or Kuwait, joining 155,000 already on active duty worldwide. A sign frequently seen in reserve bivouacks observed: "One weekend a month, my ass."

In an effort to preserve vital training and schooling programs, the Army tried to keep a normal semblance of individual rotations. Thus, Ben Freakley and E. J. Sinclair left their posts in the 101st as the O and the S, respectively, for new assignments: Freakley took command of the Infantry School at Fort Benning, Georgia, and Sinclair became commander of the U.S. Army Aviation Center at Fort Rucker, Alabama. Jeremy Miller gave up driving for the commanding general to attend helicopter flight school, and Dave Fivecoat, promoted to major, went to Fort Leavenworth, Kansas, to attend the Command and General Staff College.

Also moving to Leavenworth, as commander of the Army's Combined Arms Center, was Lieutenant General Scott Wallace, whose competence in marshaling and leading V Corps was widely acknowledged. Still, when I asked him during a conversation in August 2003 how he felt upon leaving Iraq, Wallace's eyes welled. "I felt like shit. Because a commander is supposed to be the last guy in the chow line and the last one off the LZ. . . . I felt like I was leaving soldiers in combat that I'd trained and led that far, and there was still work to be done. I felt that there were sacrifices they were making that I wasn't being asked to make."

If hope could be found in Iraq, nowhere had it seemed brighter than in the country's northern provinces, where the 101st Airborne Division arrived from Baghdad in late April. Petraeus proved dogged and ingenious as the viceroy of Mosul, a diverse city of two million. The 101st sector extended from the Syrian border in the west to Kurdish lands in the north and east. Most of the division's experienced brigade commanders remained in place during the occupation—including Colonels Hodges, Anderson, Linnington, and Gass—and their collective achievements included organizing quick, credible elections; underwriting reconstruction projects for schools, universities, hospitals, irrigation systems, and other civic endeavors; reopening trade with Iraq's neighbors; training police and civil-defense battalions; attracting investors; stimulating employment; conducting an effective counterinsurgency campaign; and, in July, trapping and killing Saddam Hussein's fugitive sons, Uday and Qusay, who were dispatched with a smoking volley of TOW missiles.

In seven months the division spread around $35 million confiscated from Saddam's regime, and another $155 million in various aid undertakings. Posters in the 101st's barracks asked, "What have you done to win Iraqi hearts and minds today?"

Whether it was enough remained to be seen. After months of relative peace, greater Mosul erupted in a series of bloody guerrilla attacks—six to ten incidents each day, by Petraeus's count—that cost the lives of more than thirty soldiers in October and November. Petraeus remained optimistic and determined, even after the Blackhawk crashes in mid-November.

"Nothing prepares a commander for the loss of seventeen soldiers in one night," he told me in an exchange of e-mails. "I think I've mentioned to you before that division command in combat is a roller-coaster experience, with real highs and real lows."

The 101st countered with up to eight raids a day against suspected insurgents, and Iraqi attacks ebbed significantly in December. The Pentagon planned to bring the division home to Fort Campbell beginning in January 2004, with the redeployment completed by April.

If the future of Nineveh Province remained as shrouded in uncertainty as the rest of Iraq, Petraeus saw hope. "We've got to have determination, perseverance, and patience, as there inevitably will be many more reversals along the way," he wrote me. As for his own coming-of-age as a commander, Petraeus added a postscript in early January: "It's been a long, tough year, and I am older in more ways than just age."

Rick Atkinson
Washington, D.C.
January 14, 2004

AUTHOR'S NOTE

This account is drawn, overwhelmingly, from what I saw, heard, smelled, tasted, and felt, with all the advantages and disadvantages inherent in first-person, picaresque narratives. Nevertheless, I have also benefited from a variety of other sources for insights on topics ranging from Mesopotamian history to what was happening on the battlefield just over the horizon.

For example, my understanding of various actions and decisions was enhanced by access to the V Corps situation reports from January through June 2003; the V Corps "Commander's Comments" from January through May 2003; V Corps "MOAB 7" (Mother of All Briefings); a draft version of *On Point*, the official Army history of the Iraq War; scores of interview transcripts, including many conducted by Col. French MacLean; "The 101st Aviation Brigade in Iraq" by Col. Gregory Gass, and other documents and after-action reports relating to division aviation, air assault, and logistics operations, such as "The Battle at Karbala, 5 April 2003," the "101st Airborne Division Chronology," and notes from the 2nd Battalion of the 187th Infantry regarding the recovery of SFC John W. Marshall's body; "11th AHR Attack on the 2nd Brigade, Medina Division"; various documents and after-action accounts from the 3rd Infantry

Division; "Ruck It Up!: The Post–Cold War Transformation of V Corps, 1990–2001," by Charles E. Kirkpatrick; "Iraq and the Future of Warfare," by Stephen Biddle and others at the U.S. Army War College's Strategic Studies Institute; and the U.S. Air Force summary report, "By the Numbers."

The other 776 embedded reporters accompanying U.S. forces in Southwest Asia wrote many insightful, vivid dispatches about the war, complemented by hundreds of correspondents in the region and in various national capitals. Beyond my talented colleagues at *The Washington Post,* I would single out for particular commendation Jim Dwyer of *The New York Times;* James Kitfield of *National Journal;* and Jon Lee Anderson of *The New Yorker.*

Other exceptionally helpful articles included "Blueprint for a Mess," by David Rieff, in *The New York Times Magazine,* November 2, 2003; "The New War Machine," by Peter J. Boyer, in *The New Yorker,* June 30, 2003; "War After the War," by George Packer, in *The New Yorker,* November 24, 2003; "The Vanishing Case for War," by Thomas Powers, in the *New York Review of Books,* December 4, 2003; "Stumbling into War," by James P. Rubin, in *Foreign Affairs,* September-October 2003; "Iraqi Town Relishes Freedom," by Steven Lee Myers, in *The New York Times,* November 23, 2003; "Wrap These Guys Up," by Christian Caryl and John Barry, in *Newsweek,* December 8, 2003; and an opinion piece by Walter B. Slocombe in *The Washington Post,* November 5, 2003. Also useful were various articles about media coverage of the war, including "War Stories: Reporting in the Time of Conflict," by Harold Evans, and the *Columbia Journalism Review* issue of May-June 2003.

In addition, I drew from *Martyrs' Day,* by Michael Kelly; *The Shi'is of Iraq,* by Yitzhak Nadish; *Iraq: In the Eye of the Storm,* by Dilip Hiro; *Iraq: The Bradt Travel Guide,* by Karen Dabrowska; *Inside Iraq, Ancient Iraq,* by George Roux; *Gods, Graves and Scholars: The Story of Archaeology,* by C. W. Ceram; *A History of the Ancient World,* by Chester G. Starr; *Historical*

Atlas of the Ancient World, by John Haywood; *Great Britain and the War of 1914–1918*, by Llewellyn Woodward; *The Myriad Faces of War: Britain and the Great War, 1914–1918*, by Trevor Wilson; and *The Imperial War Museum Book of the First World War*, by Malcolm Brown.

Several early books on the Iraq War proved meritorious, notably *A Time of Our Choosing*, by Todd Purdum and the staff of *The New York Times*, and *The Iraq War*, by Williamson Murray and Robert H. Scales, Jr.

None of the names in this book have been changed with the sole exception of a CIA operative in Najaf.

In writing this account it is to the 101st Airborne Division that my largest debt is owed, beginning with Generals Petraeus, Freakley, and Sinclair. Soldiers and officers at all ranks and in all units were unstintingly generous in sharing everything from expertise to MREs. My gratitude is matched only by my admiration.

I am also grateful to my friends and colleagues at *The Washington Post*, particularly Donald E. Graham, Bo Jones, Leonard Downie, Jr., Steve Coll, Phil Bennett, David Hoffman, Ed Cody, Fred Hiatt, David Maraniss, Robert G. Kaiser, Tom Ricks, Vernon Loeb, Bradley Graham, Anthony Shadid, Rajiv Chandrasekaran, Peter E. Baker, Susan Glasser, Bill Branigin, David Ignatius, Dana Priest, Steve Vogel, Mary Beth Sheridan, Matthew Vita, Sham Rampersad, and Christopher W. White.

Many others contributed advice, encouragement, and insights. They include Gen. B. B. Bell, Gen. (ret.) Jack Keane, Lt. Gen. Richard Cody, Lt. Gen. William S. Wallace, Gen. (ret.) Gordon R. Sullivan, Lt. Gen. (ret.) Theodore G. Stroup, Jr., Lt. Gen. (ret.) George A. Crocker, Maj. Gen. Larry Gottard, Maj. Gen. (ret.) William A. Stofft, Maj. David G. Fivecoat, Maj. Trey Cate, Col. Richard Hooker, Maj. William R. Abb, Lt. Col. Stephen

Twitty, Lt. Col. (ret.) Roger Cirillo, Tami D. Biddle, and Charles E. Kirkpatrick.

I give particular thanks to the Operation Iraqi Freedom Study Group, which is writing the Army's official history at Fort Leavenworth, Kansas, especially Col. (ret.) Gregory Fontenot, Lt. Col. E. J. Degen, Maj. Travis Rooms, Maj. David Tohn, and Col. James K. Greer.

More than a dozen people generously read all or parts of the manuscript, and offered many valuable suggestions; any errors of fact, judgment, or interpretation, however, are solely my responsibility.

For the fourth time I have had the good fortune to write a book in partnership with the extraordinary John Sterling, president and publisher of Henry Holt and Co., and with Rafe Sagalyn, my agent and friend. I am grateful for the efforts of the entire Holt organization, including Denise Cronin, Flora Esterly, Fritz Metsch, Tom Nau, Lucille Rettino, Richard Rhorer, Maggie Richards, Kenn Russell, Elizabeth Shreve, and, especially, Christine Ball. Many thanks, again, to my copy editor, Jolanta Benal, and to my proofreader, Chuck Thompson. The maps in this book, as in my last, were drawn by master cartographer Gene Thorp. The resourceful Eric Goldstein helped with valuable research.

A final thanks goes to my family—Jane, Rush, and Sarah—who, in war and in peace, are always with me.

GLOSSARY

U.S. military jargon is, alas, freighted with acronyms, abbreviations, nicknames, and technical terms. Among those most commonly used in the 101st Airborne Division:

ACP	assault command post
AHR	attack helicopter regiment
ALO	air liaison officer
APC	armored personnel carrier
ASR	alternate supply route
ATACMS	Army Tactical Missile System
Bastogne	1st Brigade, 101st Airborne Division
BUB	battle update briefing
CAS	close air support
CENTCOM	Central Command
CG	commanding general
CLFCC	Combined Forces Land Component Command
DCU	desert camouflage uniform
D-Main	division main headquarters
Eagle 6	radio call sign, commanding general, 101st Airborne Division
EPW	enemy prisoner of war
FARP	forward air refueling point
G-2	division intelligence officer
G-3	division operations officer

GAC	ground-assault convoy
HA	humanitarian assistance
ID	infantry division
JAG	judge advocate general
JDAM	Joint Direct Attack Munition
JLIST	Joint Service Lightweight Integrated Suit Technology
JSTARS	Joint Surveillance Target Attack Radar System
LBE	load-bearing equipment
LOC	lines of communication (supply and reinforcement lines)
LRSD	long-range surveillance detachment
LZ	landing zone
Marne	3rd Infantry Division nickname, from Rock of the Marne
MEF	Marine Expeditionary Force
MLRS	Multiple Launch Rocket System
MOPP	Mission-Oriented Protective Posture
MP	military police
MRE	meals ready-to-eat
NBC	nuclear, biological, chemical
NCO	noncommissioned officer
O	assistant division commander for operations
OGA	other government agency, i.e., CIA
PX	post exchange
Rakkasans	3rd Brigade, 101st Airborne Division
ROE	rules of engagement
RPG	rocket-propelled grenade
S	assistant division commander for support
SAM	surface-to-air missile
SASO	stablization and support operations
SEAD	suppression of enemy air defenses
SF	Special Forces
TLAM	Tomahawk Land Attack Missile
TOC	tactical operations center
TOW	Tube-launched, Optically tracked, Wire-guided missile
TPFDD	Timed, Phased Force Deployment Data
TTP	tactics, techniques, and procedures
UAV	unmanned aerial vehicle
WMD	weapons of mass destruction

INDEX

Entries in *italics* refer to captions.

ABOUT THE AUTHOR

RICK ATKINSON was a staff writer and senior editor at *The Washington Post* for twenty years. His most recent assignment was covering the 101st Airborne Division in Iraq. He is the best-selling author of *An Army at Dawn, The Long Gray Line,* and *Crusade.* His many awards include Pulitzer Prizes for journalism and history. He lives in Washington, D.C.